Shadow Libraries

D1708955

Shadow Libraries

Shadow Libraries

Access to Knowledge in Global Higher Education

Edited by Joe Karaganis

The MIT Press
Cambridge, Massachusetts
London, England

International Development Research Centre
Ottawa • Cairo • Montevideo •Nairobi •New Delhi

The American Assembly at Columbia University
New York

© 2018 Massachusetts Institute of Technology

This work is licensed under a Creative Commons Attribution-NonCommercial 4.0 (CC BY-NC 4.0) International License.

A copublication with
International Development Research Centre
PO Box 8500
Ottawa, ON K1G 3H9
Canada
www.idrc.ca/ info@idrc.ca
and
The American Assembly at Columbia University
475 Riverside Drive, Suite 456
New York, NY 10115
USA
www.americanassembly.org

The research presented in this publication was carried out with the financial assistance of Canada's International Development Research Centre. The views expressed herein do not necessarily represent those of IDRC or its Board of Governors.

This book was set in ITC Stone Serif Std by Toppan Best-set Premedia Limited. Printed and bound in the United States of America.

Library of Congress Cataloging-in-Publication Data

Names: Karaganis, Joe, editor.
Title: Shadow libraries : access to knowledge in global higher education / edited by Joe
   Karaganis.
Description: Cambridge, MA : The MIT Press ; Ottawa, ON : International Development
   Research Centre, [2018] | Includes bibliographical references and index.
Identifiers: LCCN 2017033629 | ISBN 9780262535014 (pbk. : alk. paper)
Subjects: LCSH: Scholarly publishing--Economic aspects--Developing countries. | Scholarly
   electronic publishing--Developing countries. | Piracy (Copyright)--Developing countries. |
   Intellectual property infringement--Economic aspects--Developing countries. | Copyright--
   Electronic information resources--Developing countries. | Photocopying--Developing
   countries. | Open access publishing--Developing countries. | Communication in learning
   and scholarship--Technological innovations--Developing countries. | Education,
   Higher--Developing countries.
Classification: LCC Z286.S37 S48 2018 | DDC 070.5--dc23 LC record available at https://lccn.loc.
gov/2017033629

10   9   8   7   6   5   4   3   2   1

Contents

Contents

1 Introduction: Access from Above, Access from Below

Joe Karaganis

In 2009, a Russian neuroscience student named Aleksandra Elbakyan started a master's thesis on biometric scanning at Kazakhstan University. Like many students and academics outside U.S. and European universities, Elbakyan had little access to research on her topic: her university didn't subscribe to the international databases that contain most of the world's scientific articles. Like many scholars in similar positions, she relied on material shared by colleagues based at or visiting universities that do provide access. Finding articles under such circumstances was haphazard and slow. For the most part, Elbakyan obtained them through personal contacts or professional networks that tried to match individual requests for articles with copies.

Unauthorized digital copies of books and articles began to be aggregated into online collections in the early 2000s. In most cases, these collections were small—personal collections of scanned materials shared via listservs and social media accounts. In a few cases, these collections grew into larger, curated archives—the Russian-language Library Genesis site (usually called LibGen), the Spanish-language Hansi library, and the social theory archive Aaaaarg (yes, the pirate sound) were early examples. Together, these methods of collecting and sharing enabled a slow osmosis of scholarly literature from more privileged to less privileged students, researchers, and universities. Elbakyan found a way to accelerate the process.

In 2011, Elbakyan launched Sci-Hub, a search and download service for journal articles. Sci-Hub was connected to LibGen, which by then had grown into a mostly academic, mostly unauthorized archive of over half a million books and articles. By most accounts, Elbakyan's innovation was to mobilize university colleagues to share not individual articles, but "virtual private network" credentials for campus intranets in Western universities, which enabled access to the major journal databases.

The core method was simple but ingenious. On Sci-Hub, a search for an article triggered a search of LibGen. If the article wasn't found in LibGen, Sci-Hub searched the major journal databases using the acquired credentials. When the user downloaded a copy, Sci-Hub simultaneously uploaded a copy to LibGen, ensuring that the next request for the document could be met from within the collection. By 2016, Sci-Hub/LibGen had grown to around fifty million articles. Over a six-month period in 2015–2016, it had over 28 million downloads (Bohannon 2016).

Because Sci-Hub circumvented the paywalls on which much of the scientific publishing world was built, the major publishers were eager to shut it down. In late 2015, Elsevier, whose ScienceDirect database was a major source for Sci-Hub, obtained an injunction in a U.S. court targeting the service, LibGen, several other unauthorized book archives, and Elbakyan personally—one of the only publicly identified individuals in this world of shadow libraries. In early 2017, the outcome was still uncertain: Sci-Hub had been forced to switch domains twice and had disabled its direct search capabilities. The LibGen site had been up and down several times in the preceding year. Although the Russian services that hosted Sci-Hub and LibGen remain relatively insulated from U.S. injunctions, the sites depend on other parts of the Internet that are more vulnerable to legal pressure—domain name registrars, search engines, and Internet service providers especially. When these companies comply with injunctions, they can make life difficult, though rarely impossible, for the targeted services.

As everyone from Elbakyan to Elsevier knew, however, Sci-Hub's importance was not its permanence as a service but its status as a proof of concept. Its core archive of fifty million articles was freely available and its basic search and archive features easily replicated. Elbakyan herself estimated that the full archive has been copied many times, moving well beyond the network of Russian academics and hackers who formed the core community behind LibGen and many of the other top-level archives. Although Elbakyan made no significant effort to hide her identity and may face arrest on charges of copyright infringement, the larger network of pirate archivists behind the other services has kept a much lower profile.

The Sci-Hub story made headlines as the authors and researchers involved in this book were wrapping up our study of this rapidly changing knowledge ecosystem. *Shadow Libraries* explores this reorganization of the flow of educational and research materials as they pass from authors to publishers and libraries, to students and researchers, and from comparatively rich universities to poorer ones.

From the top down, *Shadow Libraries* explores the institutions that shape the provision of these materials, from the formal sector of universities and publishers to the broadly informal ones organized by faculty, copy shops, student unions, and students themselves. It looks at the history of policy battles over access to education in the post–World War II era and at the narrower versions that have played out in relation to research and textbooks, from library policies to book subsidies to, more recently, the several "open" publication models that have emerged in the higher education sector.[1]

From the bottom up, *Shadow Libraries* explores how, simply, students get the materials they need. It maps the ubiquitous practice of photocopying and what are—in many cases—the more marginal ones of buying books, visiting libraries, and downloading from unauthorized sources. It looks at the informal networks that emerge in many contexts to share materials, from face-to-face student networks to Facebook groups, and at the processes that lead to the consolidation of some of those efforts into more organized archives that circulate offline and sometimes online—the shadow libraries of our title. If Elbakyan's Sci-Hub is the largest of these efforts to date, the more characteristic part of her story is the prologue: the personal struggle to participate in global scientific and educational communities, and the recourse to a wide array of ad hoc strategies and networks when formal, authorized means are lacking. If Elbakyan's story has struck a chord, it is in part because it brings this contradiction in the academic project into sharp relief—universalist in principle and unequal in practice. *Shadow Libraries* is a study of that tension in the digital era.

Piracy

Shadow Libraries grew out of a book called *Media Piracy in Emerging Economies* (Karaganis 2011), which brought a similar perspective to bear on the question of access to media outside the high-income West. To a large extent, our work on *Shadow Libraries* started where *Media Piracy* ended, with the confirmation that the main factors underlying high rates of piracy in the developing world were the obvious ones: high prices for legal media, low incomes, and the continued diffusion of cheap copying technologies. At the time, we focused on music, movies, and software, for which the CD and DVD were the enabling technologies of large-scale informal exchange. But it seemed very likely that the market for books and articles was shaped by and vulnerable to similar dynamics. We assumed that the copying and downloading that provided access to movies and music for several billion people would soon be reproduced in the publishing sector.

As we explored these issues in 2009 and 2010 for the *Media Piracy* study, however, this was manifestly not the case. The digital transition for print had not yet expanded beyond a narrow, privileged digital reading public. Reading on screens remained an expensive and, in many contexts, poor substitute for reading on paper—indeed this is still a major factor shaping student practices. Large informal markets for "pirated" physical books were well developed in some countries, but the scale of the enterprise was small compared to the massive pirate markets for music and film, and targeted at mass-market titles rather than educational ones. At universities, access was still built around the last technological revolution—the photocopier—rather than the next one, for which the network and device infrastructure was still emerging. Digital editions and the means of distributing and consuming them—via both legal and illegal channels—were unevenly developed in high-income countries, and largely absent from middle- and low-income ones.

Because of the comparative durability of the print market, publishers have had the benefit of time to think through transitional strategies for the digital ecosystem. Having witnessed the speed with which digital culture overtook music, many were—and still are—waiting for their Napster moment, when the loss of control of digital distribution forces a reorganization of the business. For big research publishers like Elsevier and Wiley, the major online pirate libraries—with names like Gigapedia, LibGen, and now Sci-Hub—clearly represent that larger threat. And yet they're still waiting. The sky still hasn't fallen.

It hasn't fallen, in large part, because the educational publishing ecosystem is much more complex than the business monoculture that emerged around the music CD in the 1990s, and it is, in important respects, correspondingly more flexible and adaptable. Access to educational materials is shaped by a wide array of policies, institutions, and forces for change that have already reconfigured large parts of the ecosystem, and will continue to do so regardless (if not entirely independent) of what happens to Sci-Hub and its inevitable sequels. The higher-education ecosystem is composed of different yet overlapping ecosystems governing three major categories of material: textbooks, monographs, and scholarly journals. It is also divided by business models, with licensing to institutions the rule in the journal world and sales to individual students (mediated by faculty choices about what to teach) dominating textbooks and monographs. It is further differentiated by geography, wealth, and political history as countries have developed distinctive systems of support for research and higher education.

It is hard, in short, to tell a story about an ecosystem with so many moving parts. This is why, to the best of our knowledge, there aren't any comprehensive examples. Academic publishing is a subject surrounded by a surprisingly thin scholarly tradition, with comprehensive work largely limited to the Anglo-American world.[2] Student practices are typically the subject of applied and often narrow educational research—complemented in a few countries (such as the United States) by publishing industry surveys (Paxhia and Parsons 2013). Work on the changing relationships between publishers and libraries is scarce, mainly because financial data and other important structural information are usually hidden behind nondisclosure agreements. Libraries have paid little attention to the circulation of documents through other channels within the university—in part because, in an environment shaped by publisher lawsuits, the university has little incentive to uncover widespread infringement.

Shadow Libraries doesn't aim to offer a comprehensive account of these developments, but rather, to provide a framework for understanding the evolution of this ecosystem across a range of very different national contexts, including Brazil, Poland, South Africa, Argentina, Uruguay, India, and the United States. The conditions that produced Sci-Hub are part of this story, but our larger goal is to explore the question of access against the backdrop of the complicated globalization of higher education and the digitization of knowledge.

The Common Thread

To a considerable extent, these different national experiences share an underlying story. We are in the midst of a massive expansion of higher education systems in middle- and low-income countries. We are also in a period of broad retreat of the state from responsibility for funding and managing that expansion. Where public provisioning of instructional materials was often seen as a necessary, if not always realized, part of the postwar expansion of primary and secondary education,[3] the more recent expansion of higher education produced no comparable public mandates. Instead, as the cost of textbooks, journal subscriptions, and monographs rose (pegged to the pricing strategies of the increasingly dominant international publishers), the challenge of providing affordable access to materials was left to strained libraries and, more often in practice, to students and faculty to figure out for themselves. Because these shifts coincided with the spread of cheap copying technologies—photocopiers and later the Internet, computing, and device ecosystem—the weakness of the formal models of access were partly compensated for by the growing strength of the informal ones. By the early 2000s, the principal form of access to materials in most countries, across most fields and types of scholarship, was informal copying and sharing.

Although plans for new forms of public support circulate at the margins of education policy debates, the main efforts to reimagine access in this context have come from two directions. First, from publishers and educational technology companies, which are assimilating many of the roles of libraries in the course of the shift to digital collections and are evolving into platforms for connected teaching, research, and learning services. Second, from faculty, librarians, and research funders advancing various articulations of "open" publishing in which works are made freely accessible.

Open and the more traditional "closed" publisher-led models have been generally viewed as competitive, but the more salient fact is that they have developed at different speeds. The scholarly publishing sector began to rapidly consolidate in the 1990s as scholarship was digitized, leading to the emergence of a handful of dominant research database providers by the mid-2000s. By 2013, five companies—Elsevier, Springer, Wiley-Blackwell, Taylor and Francis, and Sage—published 50 percent of all research papers, rising as high as 70 percent in the social sciences (Larivière, Haustein, and Mongeon 2015). In textbooks, similar processes of consolidation left three publishers—Pearson, McGraw-Hill, and Houghton Mifflin Harcourt—in command of over half the Anglophone market by 2014, and in positions, together with a handful of technology companies, to dominate the emerging fields of digital delivery and learning platforms.

Open publishing initiatives, in contrast, suffered from the coordination and scaling problems associated with an institutionally fragmented field, and from the incentive problems associated with a field already invested in functional—if problematic— models of access. Since the publication of the "Budapest Declaration" in 2002, which gave focus to the Open Access movement, open models have gained traction in some contexts, such as the growth of "prepublication" article archives that operate in parallel to the traditional journal system. The publicly funded SciELO project in Brazil has been an important model for developing-world scholarship, with over 43 percent of Brazilian research publications now available through open access channels (Van Noorden 2013b). More recently, both the United States and the European Union have taken steps to require open access publication for publicly funded research, though neither is a reality yet (Enserink 2016; Van Noorden 2013a). In contrast, "open educational resources"—generally abbreviated to OER—have made only limited progress in the general curriculum and remain a novelty in the world of scholarly books (Crossick 2016; Wolff, Rod, and Schonfeld 2016). The slow, uneven pace of these developments provides a context for impatient projects like Sci-Hub and the "guerilla open access" efforts of activists like Aaron Swartz, who was prosecuted for unauthorized bulk downloading of academic articles from the JSTOR database.[4]

As evolving closed, open, and informal models shape the landscape for research and instructional materials, the borders between them have become complex—crisscrossed by different pricing models, definitions of openness, institutional cultures, varied and often poorly defined flexibilities in copyright law, and a wide array of tolerated, assumed, and asserted uses. The result is a hodgepodge system that routinely fails to meet the demand of the hundreds of millions of students and researchers who need it and—at the same time—provides the best system yet for channeling the expanding wealth of human knowledge to the rapidly growing number of new knowledge seekers.

The Higher Education Boom and State Retreat

While the growth of higher education is often identified with the expansion of the U.S. and European public systems in the postwar period, the real global boom has occurred in the past twenty years in middle- and low-income countries. In 1995, there were 283 million people with postsecondary educations. In 2015, there were 725 million (IIASA 2015). In the past twenty years, India's student population quadrupled.[5] Brazil's tripled. South Africa's population, leaving behind the apartheid legacy, doubled. Poland's, leaving behind communist rule, more than doubled. So did Mexico's. In contrast, by the 1990s, growth in most high-income, low-birthrate countries had slowed: the U.S. university student population has grown at an annual rate of under 2 percent since 1990. German, French, Spanish, and Japanese enrollment fell slightly in the same period (OECD 2012). In middle- and low-income countries, high growth rates are expected to continue, leading to an increase in the overall number of college and university students from 100 million in 2000 to around 150 million in 2025 (Goastellec 2008).

Rising family incomes enable much of this growth, allowing parents to support years of additional education for their children. Changing aspirational horizons also play a large part, as higher educational achievement becomes the officially supported pathway for a rising middle class. Because these aspirational effects outpace the economic ones, growing educational systems often serve poorer and less prepared students than the comparatively elite systems they replace. Although access to higher education has proved achievable across a wide range of societies and political cultures, ensuring that those students can complete a quality education has proven far more challenging—and costly. Educational policy debates that focused for decades on issues of growth and access are evolving into debates about institutional quality and student support. The South African case documented in chapter 6 is telling: the government's post-apartheid commitment to expanding access to universities has been a clear success in terms of numbers enrolled but is severely challenged in other respects, with a nearly 50 percent dropout rate for three-year degrees and a massive student movement mobilized around issues of costs and stipends. A vulnerable student population is a volatile one, reactive to what can seem minor changes in fees or conditions. As we will see, the cost of materials has become a regular flashpoint in these contexts.

The financial underpinnings for educational expansion have also changed in the past several decades. Investment in higher education was a cornerstone of the post–World War II state, tied to a wide array of nation building, scientific, and social agendas. But by the 1990s, public commitment to education as an instrument of those agendas was in broad decline in many countries. As public investment flagged, private investment boomed—in India, private university enrollment increased from 31 percent of all students in 2001 to 59 percent in 2015; in sub-Saharan Africa, private institutions numbered 24 in 2000 and 468 in 2007; in 2011, private universities enrolled over 75 percent of all students in Brazil, supported by a shift in public resources from the support of public institutions to the subsidization of private ones (Almeida 2014). As the private sector played a larger role, students bore more of the financial burden of their educations.

In the United States and many other high-income countries, this transition was buffered by the accumulated strength of the public systems, by the relatively high purchasing power of students and institutions, and by the gradualism—after the 1980s—of both student growth and state retreat.[6] In many other countries, it more closely resembled a series of shocks, in which rapid expansion took place in the wake of economic crises, political revolutions, and compressed adoption curves for new technologies.

Access from Below

The stagnation or decline of public support for public universities sharply constrained thinking about access to materials. Postwar plans for national development often prioritized improving access to books as a vehicle of social progress—perhaps nowhere more so than in India, where S. R. Ranganathan stamped government policy with his vision of a democratic, user-focused library science. Expansion of the public university system was usually accompanied by expansion of the public library system, in some cases complemented by cheap books initiatives designed to increase access to literature, science, and contemporary scholarship (Argentina's remarkable Eudeba publishing initiative is examined in chapter 4). U.S. cultural diplomacy, for its part, was heavily invested in cheap books policies until the late 1970s, and sent millions of books overseas as both instruments of development and weapons in its ideological struggle with the Soviet Union (Arndt 2005).

Few of these commitments survived into the 1990s to meet the explosion of student demand. Instead, university libraries had to cope with the rising costs of materials across multiple fronts, from journal databases to monographs to the international textbooks that increasingly served as standards within their fields. In the United States, textbook and journal database price increases ranged from 5 to 7 percent per year in the 1990s and 2000s, while library budgets remained largely static (Bergstrom et al. 2014; GAO 2013). Nearly all libraries responded by shifting resources from the acquisition of books to the licensing of databases, producing a boom in journal publisher revenues and a corresponding crisis in the university press world, which depended on library purchases of scholarly monographs (Brown and Boulderstone 2008; Crossick 2016; Thompson 2005).

For faculty and students, the emergence of cheaper and more powerful copying technologies provided a way to mitigate some of these problems, beginning with affordable photocopiers in the 1980s, personal computers in the 1990s, and the Internet and device ecosystem in the 2000s. The latter permitted not only copying but also the efficient resale of used books, creating a market in the United States, especially, that cut deeply into the sale of new textbooks. For each of these technologies, periods of rapid decline in prices resulted in very compressed adoption curves in middle- and low-income countries.[7] As new technologies became commonplace, they allowed for better-organized copying and distribution of materials by students and faculty, resulting in a mixed curricular ecosystem that combined the new, the used, and the copied. By the 1990s, cheap photocopying had produced a powerful side-channel that competed with and frequently surpassed the top-down models of provision organized around publishers and libraries. As the broadband and device ecosystem developed in the 2010s, these channels began to move online.

Conflict

As photocopying became common in the 1980s, publishers began to push back against the uncompensated use of materials by students. For a number of reasons, these efforts rarely involved direct confrontation with or legal action against students themselves. In many countries, notably in Europe, students were legally in the clear: copyright law permitted copying and sharing by individuals under personal use provisions. Publishers generally received compensation at other stages of the copying lifecycle—principally via levies on copying equipment and later blank media (Hugenholtz, Guibault, and van Geffen 2003). In other countries, the scope of such rights was poorly defined, but publishers viewed legal action against students as unproductive—more likely to yield public relations disasters than meaningful impact on student practices. Not all publishers reached this conclusion: in Argentina, where copyright infringement was a criminal offense and educational exceptions were narrow, publishers instigated charges against students and faculty on numerous occasions. Argentine judges, however, showed little interest in applying the prescribed jail terms and fines for such offenses and—over several decades—shielded students and faculty behind rationalizations that carved out a de facto space of tolerated use.[8]

By far, the more common targets of enforcement and legal pressure have been the intermediaries in the copying ecosystem: copy shops and universities. As photocopier prices fell in the late 1970s, copy shops became commonplace around universities and enabled the shift of parts of the curriculum to coursepacks and other reproduced materials. In some countries, legal pressure brought copy shop chains into licensing agreements with publishers—in the United States, for example, via a 1989 lawsuit against the Kinkos copy shop chain. In other countries, the copy shops remained primarily in the informal or unregulated sector and became targets of police action. From an enforcement perspective, this had some significant advantages over the targeting of end users: the shops were easy to raid and easy to prosecute given the applicability of criminal penalties to commercially motivated infringement. The shops also generally lacked major institutional allies to advocate for them or shield them from legal action.

The copy shop raid became the iconic form of conflict between publishers and students in middle- and low-income countries. There is no evidence, however (and indeed no claims that we're aware of), that such efforts had lasting effects on student copying. Copy shops proved to be relatively resilient: easily shut down but also easily reestablished. Police raids generated headlines but also controversy. Raids within campuses, especially, tended to consolidate student and university support for stronger protections for copying, with occasionally important results. In Brazil, raids on copy shops in and around several universities in Sao Paulo in 2004–2005 and again in 2010 prompted a number of schools to declare their own educational exceptions to copyright—including the reproductions of chapters, substantial excepts, and whole works when out of print. In Uruguay, a series of raids during finals in 2011 produced a student-led copyright reform movement that led to a significant (though currently stalled) process of copyright reform. In India, the "Delhi University photocopying case" pitted Oxford University Press, Cambridge University Press, and other large academic publishers against a university-based photocopying center—triggering wider efforts to legalize the zone of informal copying practices that shape much of Indian student life. By late 2017, the university had prevailed on some points but the case was ongoing.

Universities

Universities play complicated roles in these conflicts, shaped by the fact that few make adequate provision of materials to their students. Regardless of copyright law, administrative preferences, or official positions, this reality usually dictates policies of toleration or accommodation of student practices—in some cases turning a blind eye to the copying ecosystem and in other cases moving to formally or semiformally incorporate it. This tolerance also reflects the proliferation of copying and communication technologies throughout the student and faculty population, which makes the copyright management function traditionally centralized in libraries largely obsolete. Few universities have been willing to take on the expanded electronic surveillance of students and faculty necessary to monitor the flow of material across the range of digital platforms and services in classroom use.[9] Official campus systems for classroom support—the various "learning management systems" or LMSs that have recently become common in middle- and low-income countries—have not been adapted to this purpose and in any event host only part of this activity. In most countries, campus LMSs play catch-up with the array of other social media and collaborative tools in widespread classroom use. All of the major social media platforms host student communities, and therefore ad hoc shadow libraries.

Universities also face uncertainty about the scope of educational limitations and exceptions to copyright, especially in regard to the making of digital copies and compilations or coursepacks. As Nobre (2014) documents in the case of the European Union, there is a great deal of variation in national law on these issues, "silence" with respect to many common activities, and very little clarifying jurisprudence. Universities have tended to be risk averse as a matter of formal policy but also accommodating of the evolving communicative and scholarly practices of students, faculty, and staff. In some cases, universities have decided that some regulation is better than none, and opted to incorporate these copying practices. This remains a sharply disputed subject within copyright law and has prompted publisher lawsuits in a number of countries. Although the situations and legal contexts of these cases vary, they generally share the purpose of trying to pull universities back from interpretations of the law that might sanction informal copy culture. These are the stakes of the Delhi photocopying case (chapter 7), which involves a campus-licensed copy service; of conflict over copying at the University of Buenos Aires (chapter 4); of the Brazilian university declaration of educational exceptions (chapter 8), and of the recently concluded Georgia State University case in the United States, which involved the copying of material by library staff for e-reserves.[10]

At one level, these skirmishes testify to the conservatism of universities. Few have followed the Brazilian example of cutting through the knot of narrow or obsolete copyright exceptions. Few have accepted publisher proposals to adopt more extensive surveillance and control of students and faculty—and, to the best of our knowledge, none to any significant effect. Few have moved decisively toward open models for the range of academic and teaching publications in use—though some schools, systems, and national research funders have begun to do so for research articles. In practice, the informal copying ecosystem operates as a safety valve for these conversations, denying publishers the more complete markets they want but also forestalling a sharper crisis of access that might lead to a break with existing publishing and policy paradigms. The copying ecosystem compensates, imperfectly but also cheaply, for the weaknesses of the commercial and library models of provision. Where this ecosystem is not internalized by the university, it is externalized by the students.

Change

Such arrangements can probably continue for some time in most countries, sustained by the inertia of public investment, university conservatism, and policy gridlock. But stresses on the system are growing. The main forms of pushback against unauthorized student copying have been efforts to internalize the cost of materials within the university, shifting the burden from student wallets to less visible and nondiscretionary mechanisms like library budgets and student fees. This is the model for journal database subscriptions (typically paid for by libraries, sometimes in combination with larger consortia or public funding) and for the various collective licensing agreements that cover photocopying in some university systems (typically paid through student fees). The ability to license to institutions rather than sell to students, in turn, allows for complex forms of differential pricing, as publishers set prices based on university ability to pay. Differential pricing, in turn, has provided a framework for the expansion of database access into middle- and low-income countries, especially in the past decade: Harvard University pays much more, for example, than the University of Cape Town for its Elsevier journals (and also more than poorer schools in the United States).[11] But these practices also produce a system that operates at the edge of affordability for all players, creating incentives to defect. As publishers raise prices, the system grows more fragile. Libraries cannibalize other operations to pay for journal databases, notably budgets for the purchase of monographs—the bread and butter of the university publishers. Open access moves a step closer, as institutional and funder mandates slowly spread, but so far without a larger answer to the long-term funding question that would make it a viable replacement for the commercial ecosystem. Copy shops and shadow libraries, meanwhile, operate as stopgaps at the low end, deferring the need for universities to make harder economic and policy choices.

Similar dynamics play out in the textbook market, where price increases have consistently outpaced inflation over the past three decades and where major publishers have relied on differential pricing to serve global markets. Here, the primary threat to publisher interests has not been piracy but the emergence of organized used textbook markets in the United States and—more slowly—in other countries, which have eroded year-to-year demand for new books by an estimated one-third. The used book market, in turn, has fueled a cycle of endless and often trivial revised editions designed primarily to make the books already in circulation obsolete. Here the window of time for conventional "piracy" appears to be quite limited as textbooks are combined with (and eventually become) software services that integrate with other systems for classroom support. Several of the major textbook publishers are already moving in this direction, evolving into platforms for learning services capable of supporting many different types of content—including "open" materials.

This evolution is likely to be accelerated by the 2013 U.S. Supreme Court decision in *Kirtsaeng v. John Wiley & Sons, Inc.*, which broke the U.S. ban on the parallel importation of copyrighted works that structured differential pricing in the international market. Supap Kirtsaeng, in the eponymous case, was an American medical student who built a small business importing cheaper international editions of major textbooks from Thailand. Wiley & Sons argued that Kirtsaeng's actions violated its right as the copyright holder to enforce territorial licenses, which set prices in different countries. The Supreme Court ruled that because the books had been legally purchased, Kirtsaeng was free to do with them what he wished (giving precedence to the "first-sale doctrine" in copyright law). The short-term fallout of the case was the withdrawal of cheaper U.S. editions from global markets and a corresponding rise in prices. The medium-term fallout is the opportunity for local publishers and open educational resource initiatives to expand their shares of domestic educational markets as import prices rise. The longer-term fallout is likely to be the reestablishment of differential pricing arrangements through contract rather than copyright law, as textbooks and other materials evolve into more easily policeable software services.

Policy

The advent of large-scale copying by students and faculty has prompted three types of policy response. We have discussed two:

• Efforts to reinforce the boundary between "pirate" and legal markets through copyright enforcement actions against students, copy shops, and more recently the higher-profile shadow libraries.
• Efforts to shift the cost of materials from students and faculty toward institutions via open publishing models, database licensing, and collective licensing agreements, thereby rendering unauthorized copying marginal or irrelevant.

The third policy response is the effort by librarians and educational activists to broaden limitations and exceptions to copyright law in ways that legalize more of the informal copying ecosystem. Such proposals generally seek to expand the scope of permissible copying for educational use so that, for example, faculty do not need permission to put together coursepacks with articles or chapters from copyrighted works, and libraries are freer to distribute materials digitally without arbitrary restrictions, such as measures that limit simultaneous digital access to some number of equivalent paper copies.[12]

Nearly all such efforts have bumped up against the Berne Convention—the 1886 international copyright agreement to which nearly all countries are subscribed. Berne subjects limitations on copyright to the well-known (among copyright scholars, at least) *three-step test*, of which the main requirement is that a limitation or exception not "conflict with a normal exploitation of the work." Because the commercial sale of educational materials is relatively easy to characterize as normal exploitation, Berne poses challenges to expanding educational access. Tensions between developing countries and wealthy countries on this issue are longstanding and led, in the mid-1960s, to a developing country-led proposal for shorter copyright terms and compulsory licensing of works under certain circumstances, such as educational use. British publishers strongly opposed the proposal, and the resulting controversy nearly broke the convention (Wirten 2010).[13]

Few countries, in the end, have made broad accommodations for educational copying in their laws,[14] though the issue continues to percolate through national case law and has become conflated with advocacy on behalf of a broader application of the "right to education" embedded in many post–World War II constitutions (including, in this study, India, Brazil, and South Africa). A number of groups have kept library and educational exceptions on the policy agendas of major international organizations working in this field, including the World Intellectual Property Organization (WIPO), which has appeared ready to take up the question at several points in the past decade.[15] Whether or not expansions of exceptions would materially impact the market for such works—and certainly that is possible—they would also in many cases simply ratify the status quo, ending a situation that leaves much of the educational and research enterprise on the wrong side of the law or, at best, under a cloud of legal uncertainty.

Because states have generally been unwilling to seriously challenge either the rights of publishers or the copying practices of students, the main lines in this debate have tended to shift toward easier bases for consensus, such as figuring out how to get the state to pay more of the cost of materials. Struggles to increase or capture state support for educational materials figure prominently in several of the following chapters, as students and—in some cases—large student movements react to the growing financial burdens of higher education. Such support is widely viewed, moreover, as critical to the success of open access versions of the traditional journal system—especially so-called gold open access, in which the editorial and production process remains the same as for traditional journals, but the results are made freely available online. These efforts may well be able to reduce topline costs vis à vis the large commercial publishers, whose net revenues are commonly estimated at around 35 percent (compared to around 20 percent for journals run by nonprofits such as PLOS [Holcombe 2015]). But they cannot escape editorial costs altogether, which represent the largest share in both journal and monograph publishing (Maron et al. 2016; Van Noorden 2013b). And they cannot escape the increasing scale of the scientific publishing enterprise, as more students lead to more researchers, more published research, and greater expectations of comprehensive access (Larsen and von Ins 2010).

The Country Studies

There are many signs of stress and reinvention in the educational and scholarly publishing ecosystem, which is pushed and pulled in different ways by publishers, libraries, and students—and increasingly by major research funders. But outside the area of publicly funded research, there is little evidence that states are rethinking the underlying dilemmas of access and affordability produced by decades of educational expansion, funding retrenchment, and cheap copying technologies. Instead, as global higher education has grown, informal systems fill the vacuum at many institutions and provide a path for students and faculty into wider-knowledge communities. The nine chapters in this study trace some of the history and politics of these struggles for access around the world.

Chapter 2, by Balázs Bodó, explores the deeply Russian history of the major international shadow libraries, which began with clandestine "samizdat" publishing and archiving under Soviet rule and eventuated in large-scale efforts like LibGen and Sci-Hub. Bodó traces a nearly straight line from the underground photocopying and smuggling networks that resisted Soviet censorship, to the efforts of Russian academics in the 1990s to digitize and distribute Russian academic literature in the face of economic crisis and institutional collapse, to the emergence of more ambitious efforts to aggregate and organize those collections in the 2000s under a vision that was both elitist and universalist—a communism of knowledge rather than production. Bodó's chapter also introduces a recurring thread in this volume: the connection of contemporary practices of copying and shadow library building to histories of censorship and repression. The commercial stakes of many of today's battles over copyright and copying obscure a more important lineage in which resistance to oppression was largely synonymous with the illicit copying and distribution of books and articles.

Chapter 3, also by Balázs Bodó, is a short quantitative account of the expansion of two of the major shadow libraries in the late 2000s, based on traffic data, as they assimilated the majority of Russian scholarly material and began to incorporate large English and other language collections. This period, roughly between 2006 and 2008, marked the emergence of the global shadow library and its unique role in supporting developing-world academics. This geography of knowledge is clearly visible in the top ten countries downloading from these sites: Russia, Indonesia, the United States, India, Iran, Egypt, China, Germany, the UK, and Ukraine.

Chapter 4, by Evelin Heidel, is the first of several chapters to trace the postwar history of efforts to ensure the affordable provision of books and educational materials, followed by the retreat of the major institutional actors and the shifting of the burden of access to students. In Argentina, this story has three main components: (1) the emergence of publishing strategies to increase access to materials during the post–World War II "golden age" of the university system, exemplified by the creation of the university press, Eudeba, in 1958; (2) the often violent attacks on these institutions by the dictatorships of the 1960s and 1970s, and the subsequent failures of both the postdictatorship state and the publishing industry to formulate alternatives under the pressure of the economic crises of the 1980s, 1990s, and 2000s; and (3) in this institutional vacuum, the growth of student-organized efforts to copy and circulate course materials. The chapter provides a brief history of the Spanish-language shadow library, surveying student and faculty efforts across Latin America in the mid-2000s and ending with the still-contested history of BiblioFyL—an online archive built by students at the University of Buenos Aires.

Chapter 5, by Eve Gray and Laura Czerniewicz, is a deep dive into the transformation of South African higher education after apartheid and the transition to democratic rule. The chapter provides this volume's main account of the international dynamics of the Anglophone publishing industry, structured by both domestic and international consolidation over the past two decades; by continuous tensions between domestic and imported supply (mapped to debates over cost and the need for localized content); and by the effort to make affordable, flexible, and digital materials available to the new (and often poor and ill-prepared) students entering the system. The chapter explores the role of education policy in these changes, as the South African government worked to make higher education available to millions of black South Africans and to undo the institutionalized racism of the apartheid era. Finally, chapter 5 examines the daily practices of students whose educational success is shaped by the choices they make about which class materials to buy and which to do without. These are not obscure issues in South Africa: for the past three years, student demonstrations against the cost of higher education have closed major university campuses, in some cases for weeks.

Chapter 6, by Mirosław Filiciak and Alek Tarkowski, looks at access to materials in the context of the roughly contemporaneous boom and restructuring of Polish higher education after the collapse of Communist Party rule in 1989. Widely viewed as a success story in educational modernization and expansion, the Polish situation also epitomizes the dilemma of a "small language"-based educational system operating in an increasingly globalized English-based academic culture—a condition common to most of the countries in Europe and one that promotes forms of parallelism in publishing and digital access. One aspect of this history is the emergence a large, effectively national, shadow library—the file-locker site Chomikuj ("Hamster")—which services the wide array of communities seeking Polish language media, from movies to books. The chapter also explores policy and institutional struggles around open access and copyright exceptions, beginning with debates over requirements for publicly funded research (which, as in most European countries, covers nearly all Polish research publication). Lastly, it looks at the student ecosystem in which the prominence of Chomikuj displaces some of the locally organized sharing and copying practices visible in other countries, and in which a sizeable percentage of students opt to acquire no materials at all.

Chapter 7, by Lawrence Liang, explores the history of Indian struggles for access to books—first through the lens of library policy and later through the myriad channels of student photocopying, sharing, and downloading that accompany the current boom in Indian higher education. The chapter is framed by reflection on the larger aspirational structures that have always shaped library building: at one level, the age-old desire to unify human knowledge visible in the mythologies of Babel, Alexandria, and Google; and at another, the much more personal conceptions of libraries as pathways for self-realization. The Indian versions of this story pass, as all of our studies do, through the contemporary surge in access to higher education and the comparatively slow parallel expansion of legal access to materials. It passes through the experience of arbitrary exclusion from the global culture of knowledge and ideas that shapes the lives of many Indian students and researchers, and that puts strategies for overcoming those obstacles at the center of many Indian intellectual biographies. In this context, the chapter traces some of the specific struggles that shape the Indian politics of access to knowledge, including the Delhi photocopying case and other debates about the scope of educational exceptions to Indian copyright law. As in South Africa, these debates are part of broader efforts to articulate and expand the constitutional right to education.

Chapter 8, by Pedro Mizukami and Jhessica Reia, examines practices of access and sharing among university students in Brazil against a complex backdrop of institutional and political factors, including the restricted legal scope for educational copying, the inability of publishers to set up a functional licensing regime for photocopying, increasingly aggressive enforcement actions targeted at universities and copy shops, and diverse open publishing initiatives. As the Brazilian student population continues to expand—especially, since the 1990s, in the private sector—and as access to digital technologies continues to improve, informal copying is ubiquitous but in a state of transition. Photocopying is still central to Brazilian university life, but newer practices of digital sharing are emerging. Large-scale archives of materials rivaling the scale and efficiency of LibGen have not emerged for Portuguese-language materials, but a close look at student and professor practices reveals a multitude of more precarious, community-based, ad hoc shadow libraries, distributed across millions of flash drives, cyberlockers, social media services, and cloud storage accounts.

Our short coda (chapter 9, by Jorge Gemetto and Mariana Fossatti) offers a brief account of the copy shop raids, publisher politics, and student-led copyright reform effort in Uruguay, underway since 2013.

Most of the studies in this volume use mixed methods, from interviews to student focus groups to surveys and legal research. Broadly, this reflects a decision to give each contributing group of researchers the opportunity to tell the best story they could about educational change and student practices in their respective countries. All of the larger country studies have a survey component based on a common template, conducted at one or more universities and ranging from several hundred respondents to nearly two thousand in the case of Brazil. These surveys were designed to elicit accounts of how students acquire and use materials—a topic that is too often a black box in discussions of educational, curricular, and copyright reform. With the exception of Brazil, none of these surveys are statistically representative of the student body—nationally, or even within their universities. In Brazil, student participation was self-selected and limited to a few disciplines: medicine, media and communications studies, and law—the latter two selected because they were the home disciplines of most of the contributing researchers.[16] Although we report quantitative results from this work, we take pains to situate them within accounts that build on a wider array of evidence—making survey data illustrative of phenomena and practices identified from multiple angles.[17]

We're also mindful of the rapid evolution of the ecosystems we have described, which have changed significantly even within the four-year span of these studies. Our results clearly suggest that we have not yet seen a "native" digital generation. Devices remain poor substitutes for books in many situations and print is heavily favored over screen reading across all of the student groups (to the point where students routinely print out materials they have downloaded). This marks our study as a transitional one, catching the moment of widespread digitization of materials and related infrastructure but not yet the digitization of the wider teaching, learning, and research ecosystem, and not the stabilization of legal models and frameworks that can keep pace with the growth of higher education and the global scale of emerging knowledge communities.

The studies identify no simple path through these challenges, but they do shed uncommon light on the nature of the problem. The democratization of access to higher education is a stunning if also complicated and still-evolving achievement. The democratization of access to the written products of that achievement is incomplete and passes, in middle- and low-income countries, through mostly informal channels.

As we said in our *Media Piracy* study in 2011, this informal copy culture is shaped by high prices, low incomes, and cheap technology—and only in very limited ways by copyright enforcement. As long as the Internet remains "open" in the sense of affording privacy and anonymity, shadow libraries, large and small, will remain powerful facts of educational life. As in the case of music and movies, we think the language of crisis serves this discussion poorly. This is an era of radical abundance of scholarship, instructional materials, and educational opportunity. The rest is politics.

Notes

1. The two most common are open access (OA) and open educational resources (OER)—though the concepts overlap and distinctions between the two are not always precise. OA typically refers to the movement in research communities to archive prepublication versions of journal articles in openly accessible archives, with the expectation that definitive versions will be published through the more traditional journal system. This is often described as "green" open access. When the destination journal publishes under a Creative Commons or other open license (making the finished product freely available immediately), the model is called "gold" open access. OER typically refers to instructional materials such as textbooks published under a Creative Commons or other license that ensures free use. The terms have distinct founding documents in the Budapest Open Access Initiative (2002) and the UNESCO-sponsored Paris OER Declaration (UNESCO 2012). For brevity's sake, the introduction generally combines the two under the rubric of "open" publishing models.

2. See, for example, Thompson 2005. General and especially national histories of publishing are more widely available, including Feather 2006 on British publishing, Lorimer 2012 on Canadian publishing, Hallewell 1982 on Brazilian and Portuguese-language publishing, and Fernández 1977 for Hispano-America.

3. Public provisioning sometimes meant a direct state role in publishing—this was the model articulated, in different ways, in the Soviet Union, India, Brazil, Nigeria, and many other develop-

ing countries. In the United States and Western European countries, it has meant public financing for textbooks purchased from commercial publishers. See Heyneman 2006 on the growth and very uneven success of public provisioning models.

4. Swartz was prosecuted not for copyright infringement (JSTOR did not press charges), but for violations of the Computer Fraud and Abuse Act, including unauthorized access to the MIT computer network through which he downloaded the articles. Facing trial and the possibility of a lengthy prison sentence, Swartz committed suicide in 2013. See Swartz's "Guerrilla Open Access Manifesto" (Swartz 2008) for the most influential, highly political version of this agenda.

5. China's student population also quadrupled and continues to grow rapidly. The very different dynamics of Chinese higher education fall outside the scope of this work.

6. We won't dwell on the well-documented and paradigmatic U.S. case, in which state support for public universities declined by some 37 percent since 2000 (Pew Charitable Trusts 2015) and median tuition increased by over 50 percent (54 percent between 2003 and 2012 according to the GAO (2010). Growing Federal support has moderated some of the apparent decline, but has occurred almost entirely in the areas of research grants and student loans.

7. For photocopiers, this process was driven by the emergence of Ricoh, Minolta, and other Japanese competitors to Xerox in the mid to late 1970s.

8. Among the more prominent current cases is that of the student Diego Gomez in Colombia—which like much of Latin America has had weak copyright exceptions for personal and educational use. Gomez was accused of criminal copyright infringement for posting an academic thesis to the online service Scribd (Stokstad 2014). In this case, prosecutors brought the charges independent of publisher involvement, but the case is widely viewed as an act of adherence to the U.S.-Colombia bilateral trade agreement that entered into effect in 2012, which enjoyed strong publisher support for narrowed fair use and other exceptions. Gomez was pronounced not guilty in March 2017, but the prosecutor has appealed the verdict.

9. Canada's recent "Access Copyright" collective licensing agreements fell apart in 2012 in part over obligations to monitor faculty communication for unauthorized distribution of materials (Amani 2013).

10. The Georgia State ruling was widely viewed as a win for educational fair use: of seventy-five initial claims of infringement brought by the publishers (here, Cambridge University Press, Oxford University Press, and Sage Publications), the court found in favor of only four—in each case representing the copying of multiple full chapters. While the ruling appears to give universities more scope for digitization and compilation of materials for classroom use, the decision was a complicated one that established no clear boundaries or tests (Butler 2016).

11. Price discrimination is also maintained through the secrecy surrounding publisher-university deals, enforced through contracts. In the United States, Bergstrom and Courant have done the most to reconstruct this terrain through Freedom of Information Requests to public institutions. See Bergstrom et al. 2014.

12. Such measures are often combined with a longer list of exceptions and limitations sought by libraries and archives, which have focused in recent years on building digital collections for works that are out of print, "orphaned" (i.e., without an identifiable copyright holder), or otherwise unavailable.

13. In 1971, a compromise "Berne Appendix" was passed that introduced a number of remedies for developing countries, including limited compulsory licensing solutions. In practice, however, these proved very cumbersome to implement and use, and only a handful of countries have done so (Cerda Silva 2012; Chon 2011).

14. The most expansive slate of educational limitations and exceptions currently belongs to Estonia, which permits almost any reproduction or other use of materials for teaching and research purposes (Nobre 2016). Numerous countries vie for the title of most limited educational exceptions, with France and Spain arguably leading the pack due to a lack of provisions for faculty-compiled compilations. For a broad international account, see Crews 2014.

15. Educational limitations and exceptions were split off from library and archival proposals by advocates in a tactical effort to break the WIPO conversation into manageable portions. The first step in this process was the negotiation of a treaty covering expanded limitations and exceptions for the visually impaired. It was passed in 2015. Libraries and archives are generally perceived as next on the agenda, although this is unsettled and not without controversy. For the most developed libraries proposal, see the International Federation of Library Association's "Treaty Proposal on Limitations and Exceptions for Libraries and Archives" (IFLA 2013).

16. The disciplinary differences proved illustrative of the some of the larger dynamics we explore in the studies. Media and communications, for example, showed significantly higher levels of all copying and sharing practices than law or medicine. The most likely explanation is the greater dependence of these fields on international research articles and expensive monographs—both categories that lend themselves to large-scale digital archiving. Legal education, in comparison, relies heavily on locally developed, locally relevant, and up-to-date textbooks and case law. Medical education, in turn, relies on international standard textbooks and reference books, but also on high-production-value imagery that unauthorized channels have been slow to reproduce. These differences in practice also track differences in student resources, with medical students matriculating from wealthier families than law students. Media and communications students trailed well behind both fields in family wealth, making them better representatives of the high-price, low-income dynamics that define the pirate ecosystem around the books and other media.

17. Because not all universities were eager to be named in studies of unauthorized copying, we have anonymized all but a few of the locations and all of the respondent identities.

References

Almeida, W. M. de. 2014. *ProUni e o ensino superior privado lucrativo em São Paulo: Uma análise sociológica*. São Paulo: Musa.

Amani, B. 2013. "Access Copyright and the Proposed Model Copyright License Agreement: A Shakespearean Tragedy."

Arndt, R. 2005. *The First Resort of Kings: American Cultural Diplomacy in the Twentieth Century.* Dulles, VA: Potomac Books.

Bergstrom, T. C., P. N. Courant, R. P. McAfee, and M. A. Williams. 2014. "Evaluating Big Deal Journal Bundles." *Proceedings of the National Academy of Sciences of the United States of America* 111 (26): 9425–9430. doi:10.1073/pnas.1403006111.

Bohannon, J. 2016. "Who's Downloading Pirated Papers? Everyone." *Science.* doi:10.1126/science.aaf5664.

Brown, D. J., and R. Boulderstone. 2008. *The Impact of Electronic Publishing: The Future for Publishers and Librarians.* Berlin: Walter de Gruyter.

Budapest Open Access Initiative. 2002. http://www.budapestopenaccessinitiative.org/read.

Butler, B. 2016. "Transformative Teaching and Educational Fair Use after Georgia State." SSRN Scholarly Paper No. ID 2723611. Rochester, NY: Social Science Research Network. https://papers.ssrn.com/abstract=2723611.

Cerda Silva, A. 2012. "Beyond the Unrealistic Solution for Development Provided by the Appendix of the Berne Convention on Copyright." PIJIP Research Paper no. 2012-08. http://digitalcommons.wcl.american.edu/research/30/.

Chon, M. 2011. "Copyright and Capability for Education: An Approach 'From Below.'" In *Intellectual Property and Human Development: Current Trends and Future Scenarios,* ed. Tzen Wong and Graham Dutfield, 218–249. Cambridge: Cambridge University Press.

Crews, Kenneth. 2014. *Study on Copyright Limitations and Exceptions for Libraries and Archives.* SCCR/29/3. Geneva: OMPI.

Crossick, G. 2016. "Monographs and Open Access." *Insights* 29 (1): 14–19.

Enserink, M. 2016. "In Dramatic Statement, European Leaders Call for 'Immediate' Open Access to All Scientific Papers by 2020." *Science.* doi:10.1126/science.aag0577.

Feather, J. 2006. *A History of British Publishing.* 2nd ed. London; New York: Routledge.

Fernández, Stella Maris. 1977. *La Imprenta en Hispanoamérica.* Madrid; Asociación Nacional de Bibliotecarios, Archiveros y Arqueólogos.

GAO. 2010. *Intellectual Property: Observations on Efforts to Quantify the Economic Effects of Counterfeit and Pirated Goods.* Report to Congressional Committees, United States Government Accountability Office, Washington, DC. http://www.gao.gov/new.items/d10423.pdf.

GAO. 2013. *College Textbooks: Students Have Greater Access to Textbook Information.* Report to Congressional Committees, United States Government Accountability Office, Washington, DC. http://www.gao.gov/assets/660/655066.pdf.

Goastellec, G. 2008. "Changes in Access to Higher Education: From Worldwide Constraints to Common Patterns of Reform?" In *The Worldwide Transformation of Higher Education*, vol. 9, ed. David P. Baker and Alexander W. Wiseman, 1–26. Emerald Group Publishing.

Hallewell, L. 1982. *Books in Brazil: A History of the Publishing Trade*. Lanham, MD: Scarecrow Press.

Heyneman, S. 2006. "The Role of Textbooks in a Modern System of Education: Towards High-Quality Education for All." *International Journal of Educational Development* 23 (3): 315–337.

Holcombe, A. 2015. "Scholarly Publisher Profit Update." May 21. https://alexholcombe .wordpress.com/2015/05/21/scholarly-publisher-profit-update/.

Hugenholtz, P. B., L. Guibault, and S. van Geffen. 2003. *The Future of Levies in a Digital Environment*. Amsterdam: Institute for Information Law.

IFLA. 2013. *Treaty Proposal on Limitations and Exceptions for Libraries and Archives* (V4.4). The International Federation of Library Associations and Institutions.

IIASA. 2015. Global Projection—Medium SSP2. Wittgenstein Centre for Demography and Global Human Capital. International Institute for Applied Systems Analysis.

Karaganis, J., ed. 2011. *Media Piracy in Emerging Economies*. SSRC. http://piracy.americanassembly .org/wp-content/uploads/2011/06/MPEE-PDF-1.0.4.pdf.

Larivière, V., S. Haustein, and P. Mongeon. 2015. "The Oligopoly of Academic Publishers in the Digital Era." *PLoS One* 10 (6): e0127502.

Larsen, P. O., and M. von Ins. 2010. "The Rate of Growth in Scientific Publication and the Decline in Coverage Provided by Science Citation Index." *Scientometrics* 84 (3): 575–603. doi:10.1007/ s11192-010-0202-z.

Lorimer, R. 2012. *Ultra Libris: Policy, Technology, and the Creative Economy of Book Publishing in Canada*. Toronto: ECW Press.

Maron, N., K. Schmelzinger, C. Mulhern, and D. Rossman. 2016. "The Costs of Publishing Monographs: Toward a Transparent Methodology." *Journal of Electronic Publishing* 19 (1). http:// quod.lib.umich.edu/cgi/t/text/idx/j/jep/3336451.0019.103/--costs-of-publishing-monographs -toward-a-transparent/.

Nobre, T. 2014. Mapping Copyright Exceptions and Limitations in Europe. Creative Commons Project Open Educational Resources Policy in Europe.

Nobre, T. 2016. Best Case Scenarios for Copyright: Education in Estonia. Communia.

OECD. 2012. *Education at a Glance: OECD Indicators*. Paris: Organisation for Economic Co-operation and Development.

Paxhia, S., and J. Parsons. 2013. *Student Attitudes toward Content in Higher Education (No. 1 of 2)*. New York: Book Industry Study Group.

The Pew Charitable Trusts. 2015. *Federal and State Funding of Higher Education: A Changing Landscape*. Philadelphia: Fiscal Federalism Initiative.

Stokstad, E. 2014. "Colombian Grad Student Faces Jail for Sharing a Thesis Online." *Science*. July 31. http://www.sciencemag.org/news/2014/07/colombian-grad-student-faces-jail-sharing-thesis-online/ (accessed June 9, 2016).

Swartz, A. 2008. "Guerilla Open Access Manifesto." July. https://archive.org/stream/Guerilla OpenAccessManifesto/Goamjuly2008_djvu.txt.

Thompson, J. B. 2005. *Books in the Digital Age: The Transformation of Academic and Higher Education Publishing in Britain and the United States*. 1st ed. Cambridge, UK; Malden, MA: Polity.

UNESCO. 2012. 2012 Paris OER Declaration. http://www.unesco.org/new/fileadmin/MULTI MEDIA/HQ/CI/CI/pdf/Events/English_Paris_OER_Declaration.pdf.

Van Noorden. 2013a. "White House Announces New US Open-Access Policy." News Blog. *Nature*. February 22. http://blogs.nature.com/news/2013/02/us-white-house-announces-open-access-policy .html.

Van Noorden, R. 2013b. "Brazil Fêtes Open-Access Site." *Nature* 502 (7472): 418. doi:10.1038/ 502418a.

Van Noorden, R. 2013c. "Open Access: The True Cost of Science Publishing." *Nature* 495 (7442): 426–429. doi:10.1038/495426a.

Wirten, E. H. 2010. "Colonial Copyright, Postcolonial Publics: The Berne Convention and the 1967 Stockholm Diplomatic Conference Revisited." *SCRIPTed* 7 (3): 532–550.

Wolff, C., A. Rod, and R. Schonfeld. 2016. *Ithaka S+R US Faculty Survey 2015*. New York: Ithaka S+R.

2 The Genesis of Library Genesis: The Birth of a Global Scholarly Shadow Library

Balázs Bodó

Here's what I see as a consequence of free educational book distribution: within decades, generations of people everywhere in the world will grow up with access to the best scientific texts of all time. [...] [T]he quality and accessibility of education to the poor will grow dramatically too. Frankly, I see this as the only way to naturally improve mankind: we need to make all the information available to them at any time.

—Anonymous administrator of the Russian shadow library site Library Genesis (LG), explaining its raison d'être

(Pirate) Libraries on the Internet

Digital librarianship—the digitization, collection, and cataloguing of texts—was one of the earliest uses of networked computers. By most accounts, the first digital library was Project Gutenberg, which began making public domain works available in 1971 via the Arpanet, the predecessor of the Internet. As computing and network technologies improved in the 1980s and 1990s, the technical obstacles and cost of building digital libraries declined rapidly. The dream of a universal library (Battles 2004; Borges 1998; Bush 1945; Rieusset-Lemarié 1997) began to seem very real. Legal obstacles were another matter. As projects became larger and more visible, they became more vulnerable to copyright challenges in the poorly charted areas around digitization, archiving, and fair use. Some projects responded by moving texts into closed, "dark" collections, maintained offline.[1] Others worked to assert and clarify rights to digitization and online distribution, prompting a flurry of lawsuits from publishers and authors' groups.

Major lines of conflict passed through lawsuits against big players like Google Books and the Hathi Trust, which represented a coalition of universities. Provisionally and only under U.S. law, these cases settled important questions about fair use in digitization projects and the handling of "orphan" works, for which the copyright holder could not be identified. Other conflicts emerged around the scope of permissible use of copyrighted materials in educational contexts—particularly in lawsuits against university libraries and copy centers. Still others involved enforcement against projects that saw free digital libraries as ideological projects—as fundamental social goods.

The latter projects were generally small in scale, volunteer based, clandestine, and sometimes accidental in their origins—personal archives that grew into shared collections. The development of organizational and bibliographical infrastructure was a major challenge for such projects and a signal of larger ambitions. Some remained simple collections of texts bundled and exchanged via DVDs, torrents, or IRC channels online. Others acquired many of the attributes of libraries, including the crucial one: the catalog.

The catalog distinguishes an unstructured heap of computer files from a collectively managed and maintained collection of texts. For users, it has obvious utility for searching and browsing the collection. But it is also the organizing framework for the community of "librarians" who preserve and nourish the collection. The significant academic shadow libraries of the past decade—Textz.org, a*.org, monoskop, Gigapedia (later known as Library.nu), and more recently LibGen and Sci-Hub—took shape and gained traction through cataloguing efforts. Most maintained a bifurcated structure, in which the catalog serves as a platform for searching, organizing, and community engagement, while the actual texts are hosted elsewhere. This was partly a matter of convenience but also safety, as the legal system struggled to draw distinctions between searching, indexing, hosting, and other online functions.

As with the major music file sharing services in the early 2000s, public catalogs made shadow libraries easier targets of law enforcement. All of these services have faced takedown threats and, in several cases, injunctions that targeted the catalog, the text repository, or both. Of these libraries, Gigapedia/Library.nu—was the largest at the turn of the 2010s. At its peak, it was several orders of magnitude bigger than any of its peers, offering access to nearly a million English-language documents. It was not just size that made Gigapedia unique. Unlike most sites, which specialized in literary works, Gigapedia had large collections drawn from a wide range of academic disciplines, especially the sciences. Compared to its peers, it also had a highly developed central database, which contained bibliographic details on the collection and also, significantly, on gaps in the collection, which informed a process of soliciting contributions from users. With scanner and copiers now ubiquitous, users responded to requests and fueled the rapid growth of the collection.

In general, the major academic publishers were wary of following the music and film industries into a game of enforcement "whack-a-mole" against file sharing sites, pouring resources into lawsuits against services that that would be reconstituted quickly under new identities and in other jurisdictions. But such reticence was not universal. By 2010, the apparent size of the Gigapedia had convinced several publishers that it was too big a target to ignore. Led by John Wiley & Sons, a group of seventeen publishers was granted an injunction against the site (called by then Library.nu) and against iFile.it—the hosting site that stored most of Library.nu's content. Under the injunction, the Library.nu administrators closed the site. From the outside, it seemed that the collection had disappeared and the community around it dispersed (Liang 2012). But provisions for the next Library.nu were in place well before the shutdown, circulating primarily through networks of Russian academics and shadow librarians. For reasons that we will explore in this chapter, much of the history of the big digital shadow libraries passes through Russia and the story of Library Genesis.

Library Genesis

Library Genesis[2] (also known as LG or LibGen) is a shadow library started by Russian scientists around 2008 to consolidate the mostly Russian-language text collections circulating on the Russian-language Internet. In 2011, LibGen swallowed the much larger and broader Library.nu collection.[3] For the LibGen community, Library.nu was just another free-floating text archive, ready to be harvested and integrated into the rest of the collection. But with the closure of Library.nu, LibGen inherited the responsibility of serving a larger academic community beyond the boundaries of Russian-speaking academia. The whacking of the Gigapedia mole gave rise to a mole with a large family and a more sophisticated and resilient approach to collecting and sharing books.

As a shadow library and piratical content distribution service, LibGen has a unique modus operandi. Most such websites tend to exercise strict control over the content they make accessible and the infrastructure they build. LibGen's mission, in contrast, is to provide open access to the collection by making *itself* radically open. It collects free-floating scientific texts and other collections from the Internet and consolidates them (both content and metadata) into a single, open database. Although ordinary users can search the catalog and retrieve the texts, LibGen's main focus is the distribution of its own library infrastructure, including its source code, catalog, and terabyte-sized collection to anyone who wants to start his or her own library. In practical terms this means that anyone can freely take a copy of LibGen and start distributing text under his or her own terms. This openness has led to the creation of a lively ecosystem of shadow libraries around the core LibGen collection. The ability to mirror LibGen without restrictions enables these sites to target different audiences by combining the LibGen catalog with books coming from other sources,[4] providing extra services,[5] or experimenting with different financing models.[6]

This two-layered structure enables LibGen to focus its limited resources on maintaining a high-quality scientific collection, while the mirror sites compete to best serve users, carry the costs of distribution, and act as lightning rods for lawsuits. The mirror sites deliver the LibGen collection to the public, and at the same time, increase the likelihood of its long-term survival.

The main mission of the LibGen community is the development of the collection. Its democratic approach to access is matched by an elitist approach to content. As characterized by one of its administrators (admins), these goals are to

• collect valuable science/technology/math/medical/humanities academic literature. That is, collect humanity's valuable knowledge in digital form. Avoid junky books. Ignore "bestsellers."
• build a community of people who share knowledge, improve quality of books, find good and valuable books, and correct errors.
• share the files freely, spreading the knowledge altruistically, not trying to make money, not charging money for knowledge.

LibGen's agenda is marked by deep aversion to a narrowly academic understanding of research and education, especially with regard to elite institutions that provide gated access to knowledge for their communities. Instead, LibGen's statement takes the autodidacticism necessary to education in many parts of the world and reimagines it as a liberatory agenda—a future of self-learning communities based on universal access to knowledge. The LibGen admin further describes site priorities:

The overwhelming arrogance of university staff will gradually be suppressed for a larger flow of exceptionally educated people without special degrees acquired (I am proudly the case, that's why I'm saying this, it's not a fantasy). [...]

The target groups for LibGen are poors: Africa, India, Pakistan, Iran, Iraq, China, Russia and post-USSR etc., and on a separate note, people who do not belong to academia. If you are not at a university, you can't access anything or at least your access will be so much troubled that you won't be able to progress at all.

It is easy to see parallels between LibGen and the agenda of someone like Aaron Swartz in the United States, whose Guerilla Open Access Manifesto touched on many of the same themes in 2008. (Swartz committed suicide in 2013 while under investigation for the unauthorized downloading of large parts of the JSTOR catalog of academic articles). As the technologically possible library surpasses the modest reality and uneven distribution of actual libraries, this sense of relative deprivation can readily become a politics. As Swartz puts it:

Those with access to these resources—students, librarians, scientists—you have been given a privilege. You get to feed at this banquet of knowledge while the rest of the world is locked out. But you need not—indeed, morally, you cannot—keep this privilege for yourselves. You have a duty to share it with the world. And you have: trading passwords with colleagues, filling download requests for friends.

Meanwhile, those who have been locked out are not standing idly by. You have been sneaking through holes and climbing over fences, liberating the information locked up by the publishers and sharing them with your friends.

But all of this action goes on in the dark, hidden underground. It's called stealing or piracy, as if sharing a wealth of knowledge were the moral equivalent of plundering a ship and murdering its crew. But sharing isn't immoral—it's a moral imperative.

The LibGen and Swartz manifestos are remarkably similar documents. There are, however, enormous differences in the contexts in which these texts were born, put into practice, and took effect (Bodó 2016). The limited Russian "success" in building large online shadow libraries where Swartz and many other shadow libraries documented in this study failed is not accidental. The dissonance that Swartz charismatically embodied in the United States within a community of hackers and activists was, to a degree, a societal experience in Russia, passing through clandestine publication practices under Soviet rule, the economic ruin of the intelligentsia in the post-communist period, and the weak legal infrastructure for copyright (and other law) that allowed a pirate Internet to flourish.

The Communist Ideal of the Reading Nation

[T]he library of the Big Lubyanka was unique. In all probability it had been assembled out of confiscated private libraries. The bibliophiles who had collected those books had already rendered up their souls to God. But the main thing was that while State Security had been busy censoring and emasculating all the libraries of the nation for decades, it forgot to dig in its own bosom. Here, in its very den, one could read Zamyatin, Pilnyak, Panteleimon Romanov, and any volume at all of the complete works of Merezhkovsky. (Some people wisecracked that they allowed us to read forbidden books because they already regarded us as dead. But I myself think that the Lubyanka librarians hadn't the faintest concept of what they were giving us—they were simply lazy and ignorant.)
—Aleksandr Solzhenitsyn, The Gulag Archipelago *1918–1956* (1974)

Russian culture has a deep reverence for the printed word and, in many respects, the Soviet state only amplified it. The Leninist program of education created a mass readership for the first time in Russia, but at the same time closed off many of the conventional outlets for it. As Stelmakh (1993) observed: "Reading almost transplanted religion as a sacred activity: in the secularized socialist state, where the churches were closed, the free press stifled and schools and universities politicized, literature became the unique source of moral truth for the population. Writers were considered teachers and prophets."

The Soviet Union was a reading culture until the end. In the last days of the USSR, a quarter of the adult population were considered active readers, and almost everyone else qualified as an occasional reader (Stelmakh 1993). Book prices were low and alternative forms of entertainment were scarce and relatively expensive, making reading one of the most attractive leisure activities.

The communist approach toward intellectual property protection reflected the ideal of the reading nation. The Soviet Union inherited a lax and isolationist copyright system from the tsarist Russia. Neither the tsarist state nor the Soviet state adhered to international copyright treaties, nor did they enter into bilateral treaties. Tsarist Russia's refusal to grant protection to foreign authors and translations had an economic rationale: Russian publishers would pay no royalties for foreign work. The Soviet regime added a strong ideological claim: granting exclusive ownership to authors hindered "the cultural development of the masses," and only served the private interests of authors and heirs. As Elst (2005, 658) states: "If copyright had an economic function, that was only as a right of remuneration for his contribution to the extension of the socialist art heritage. If copyright had a social role, this was not to protect the author from the economically stronger exploiter, but was one of the instruments to get the author involved in the great communist educational project."

The Soviet copyright system, even in its postrevolutionary phase, maintained two features that served as important vehicles for new publication. First was the "freedom of translation," which meant that translations could be published without rights holder authorization. This measure dismantled a significant barrier to access in a multicultural and multilingual empire. By the same token, the denial of protection to foreign authors and rights holders eased the import of foreign texts (after, of course the appropriate censorship review). According to Newcity (1980, 6), due to these instruments: "[S]oon after its founding, the Soviet Union became as well the world's leading literary pirate, not only publishing in translation the creations of its own citizens but also publishing large numbers of copies of the works of Western authors both in translation and in the original language."

Looking simply at the aggregate numbers of published books, the USSR had an impressive publishing industry on a scale appropriate to a reading nation. Between 1946 and 1970, more than one billion copies of over twenty-six thousand different works were published, all by foreign authors (Newcity 1978). This production accelerated rapidly in the 1970s. In 1976 alone, more than 1.7 billion copies of 84,304 titles were printed[7] (Friedberg, Watanabe, and Nakamoto 1984, fn 4).

Censorship

Of course, these impressive numbers did not reflect a healthy public sphere or a well-functioning print ecosystem. The book-based public sphere was both heavily censored and plagued by the growing dysfunctions of the Soviet, and later the post-Soviet, economy.

The totalitarian Soviet state had many instruments to control the circulation of literary and scientific works.[8] Some texts never entered official circulation at all. As Stelmakh (2001, 145) notes: "A particularly harsh prepublication censorship [affected] foreign literature, primarily in the humanities and socioeconomic disciplines. Books on politics, international relations, sociology, philosophy, cybernetics, semiotics, linguistics, and so on were hardly ever published."

Many "problematic" texts were put into limited circulation for the trustworthy few. As the resolution of the Central Committee of the Communist Party of June 4, 1959, stated: "Writings by bourgeois authors in the fields of philosophy, history, economics, diplomacy, and law [...] are to be published in limited quantities after the excision from them of passages of no scholarly or practical interest. They are to be supplied with extensive introductions and detailed annotations" (quoted in Friedberg, Watanabe, and Nakamoto 1984).

The truncation and mutilation of texts were also frequent. Literary works and texts from humanities and social sciences were obvious subjects of censorship, but natural sciences and technical fields did not escape. Dewhirst and Farrell (1973, 127) reported: "In our film studios we received an American technical journal, something like *Cinema, Radio and Television*. I saw it on the chief engineer's desk and noticed that it had been reprinted in Moscow. Everything undesirable, including advertisements, had been removed, and only those technical articles with which the engineer could be trusted were retained. Everything else, even whole pages, was missing. This was done by a photo copying process, but the finished product appeared to be printed."

Mass cultural genres were also subject to censorship and control. Women's fiction, melodrama, comics, detective stories, and science fiction were completely missing or heavily underrepresented in the mass market. Instead, "a small group of officially approved authors [...] were published in massive editions every year, [and] blocked readers' access to other literature. [...] Soviet literature did not fit the formula of mass culture and was simply bad literature, but it was issued in huge print-runs" (Stelmakh 2001, 150).

Libraries were also important instruments of censorship. When not destroyed altogether, censored works ended up in the *spetskhrans,* limited access special collections established for censored works. Besides obvious candidates such as anti-Soviet works and Western "bourgeois" publications, many scientific works ended up in these closed collections (Ryzhak 2005). Access to the *spetskhrans* was limited to those with special permits: "Only university educated readers were enrolled and only those holding positions of at least junior scientific workers were allowed to read the publications kept by the spetskhran" (Ryzhak 2005). In the last years of the USSR, the *spetskhran* of the Russian State Library—the largest of them, with more than one million items in the collection—had forty-three seats for its roughly forty-five hundred authorized readers. Yearly circulation was around two hundred thousand items, a figure that included "the history and literature of other countries, international relations, science of law, technical sciences and others" (Ryzhak 2005).

Librarians thus played a central role in the censorship machinery. They did more than guard the contents of limited-access collections and purge the freely accessible stocks according to the latest Communist Party directives. As the intermediaries between the readers and the closed stacks, their task was to carefully guide readers' interests and report on suspicious reading habits (Stelmakh 2001).

Access to works was limited by economic factors as well. Due to the lack of signals for demand and the bureaucratic limitations of the planned economy, shortages of even censor-approved texts were common, both on the market and in libraries. Access to foreign works was further limited when the USSR joined the UNESCO-backed Universal Copyright Convention (UCC) in 1973. Under the UCC, the USSR finally granted protection to foreign authors and put an end to the "freedom of translation" clause—the exemption in Soviet author rights law that permitted the translation of works without the authorization of the rights holder. Soviet officials feared that granting protection to foreign authors would result in an outflow of royalty payments to Western rights holders. As data shows, these fears proved valid. By 1976, the annual USSR trade deficit in publishing reached a million rubles (around $5.5 million in current USD) (Levin 1983, 157). This imbalance also raised the price of translated works to double that of Russian-authored books (158).

The Soviet and Post-Soviet Literary and Scientific Underground

Various practices and informal institutions evolved to address the problems of access. Black markets for books flourished: "In the 1970s and 1980s the black market was an active part of society. Buying books directly from other people was how 35 percent of Soviet adults acquired books for their own homes, and 68 percent of families living in major cities bought books only on the black market" (Stelmakh 2001, 146). Book copying and hoarding also became widespread strategies for dealing with the short-ages. One administrator of the LibGen shadow library has vivid, firsthand memories of these times:

People hoarded books: complete works of Pushkin, Tolstoy or Chekhov. You could not buy such things. So you had the idea that it is very important to hoard books. High-quality literary fiction, high-quality science textbooks and monographs, even biographies of famous people (writers, scientists, composers, etc.) were difficult to buy. You could not, as far as I remember, just go to a bookstore and buy complete works of Chekhov. It was published once and sold out and that's it. Dostoyevsky used to be prohibited in the USSR, so that was even rarer. Lots of writers were pro-hibited, like Nabokov. Eventually Dostoyevsky was printed, but in very small numbers.

And also there were scientists who wanted scientific books and also could not get them. Math-ematics books, physics—very few books were published every year, you can't compare this with the market in the U.S. Russian translations of classical monographs in mathematics were difficult to find.

So, in the USSR, everyone who had a good education shared the idea that hoarding books was very, very important, and did just that. If someone had free access to a Xerox machine, they were [x]eroxing everything in sight. A friend of mine had an entire room full of [x]eroxed books.

From the 1960s onward, the ever-growing clandestine samizdat networks chal-lenged the censors and provided access to both classics and information on the current state of Soviet society. Reaching a readership of around two hundred thousand, these networks operated in a networked, bottom-up manner. Each node in a chain of distri-bution copied the texts it received, and distributed the copies. These nodes also carried information backward, toward the authors of the samizdat publications.

In the immediate post-Soviet turmoil, access to print culture did not get any easier. Censorship officially ended, but so too did much of the state funding for the publish-ing sector. Mass unemployment, falling wages, and the resulting loss of discretionary income further undercut the shift toward market-based publishing models. The fund-ing of libraries also dwindled, limiting new acquisitions (Elst 2005, 299–300). Economic constraints, in short, took the place of political ones. But in the absence of political repression, self-organizing efforts to address these constraints acquired greater scope of action. Slowly, the informal sphere began to deliver alternative modes of access to otherwise hard-to-get literary and scientific works.

Russian pirate libraries emerged from these enmeshed contexts: communist ideolo-gies of the reading nation and mass education; the censorship of texts; the abused library system; economic hardships and dysfunctional markets; and, most importantly, the informal practices that ensured the survival of scholarship and literary traditions under hostile political and economic conditions. The prominent place of Russian pirate libraries in the larger informal media economy—and of Russian piracy of music, film, and other copyrighted work more generally—cannot be understood outside this history.

The Emergence of Do-It-Yourself Digital Libraries in RuNet

The copying of censored and uncensored works (by hand, typewriters, photocopiers or—later—computers), the hoarding of copied texts, the buying and selling of books on the black market, and the informal, peer-to-peer distribution of samizdat material were part of the everyday experience of educated Soviet and post-Soviet readers. The building and maintenance of individual collections and participation in the informal networks of exchange offered a sense of political, economic, and cultural agency— especially as the public institutions that supported the core professions of the intelligentsia fell into sustained economic crisis.

Digital technologies were integrated into these practices as soon as they appeared. As one shadow library administrator remembers:

From late 1970s, when first computers became used in the USSR and printers became available, people started to print forbidden books, or just books that were difficult to find, not necessarily forbidden. I have seen myself a print-out on a mainframe computer of a science fiction novel, printed in all caps! Samizdat was printed on typewriters, xeroxed, printed abroad and xeroxed, or printed on computers. Only paper circulated. Files could not circulate until people started to have PCs at home. As late as 1992 most people did not have a PC at home. So the only reason to type a long text into a computer was to print it on paper.

People who worked in academic and research institutions were well positioned to support these informal practices: they had access to computers, and many had access to the materials locked up in the *spetskhrans*. Many also had the time and professional motivations to collect and share otherwise inaccessible texts. The core of current digital collections was created in this late-Soviet/early post-Soviet period by such professionals. Their home academic and scientific institutions continued to play an important role in the development of digital text collections well into the era of home computing and the Internet.

Digitized texts first circulated in printouts and later on optical/magnetic storage media and the early Internet. The first platform for digital text sharing was the Russian Fidonet, a network of bulletin board systems similar to Usenet, which enabled the mass distribution of plain text files. These bulletin board systems (BBSs) connected fans around emerging collections of shared texts, such as the Holy Spirit BBS's "SU.SF & F.FANDOM" group, whose main focus was Soviet-Russian science fiction and fantasy literature. As one of the shadow librarians described their experience in the early 1990s:

Fidonet collected a large number of plaintext files in literature / fiction, mostly in Russian, of course. Fidonet was almost all typed in by hand. [...] Maybe several thousand of the most important books, novels that "everyone must read" and such stuff. People typed in poetry, smaller prose pieces. I have myself read a sci-fi novel on a mainframe, which was obviously typed in. This novel was by Strugatski brothers. It was not prohibited or dissident literature, but just impossible to buy in the stores. These were culturally important, cult novels, so people typed them in. [...] At this point it became clear that there was a lot of value in having a plain-text file, and the most popular novels were first digitized in this way.

The next stage in text digitization started around 1994. By that time, growing numbers of people had access to computers, scanning peripherals, and OCR (text recognizing) software. Household Internet and PC penetration, while extremely low overall in the 1990s, (0.1 percent of the population had Internet access in 1994, growing to 8.3 percent by 2003), began to make inroads in educational and scientific institutions and among Moscow and St. Petersburg elites, who were often the critical players in these networks. As access to technologies increased, a much wider array of people began to digitize their favorite texts. These collections began to circulate, first via CD-ROMs and later on the Internet.

Maxim Moshkov and lib.ru

One such collection belonged to Maxim Moshkov, who published his library under the name lib.ru in 1994. Moshkov was a graduate of the Moscow State University Department of Mechanics and Mathematics, which (as we'll see later) played a large role in the digitization of scientific works. After graduation, he worked for the Scientific Research Institute of System Development—a computer science institute associated with the Russian Academy of Sciences. He describes the early days of his collection as follows:

I began to collect electronic texts in 1990, on a desktop computer. When I got on the Internet in 1994, I found lots of sites with texts. It was like a dream came true: there they were, all the books I desired. But these collections were in a dreadful state! Incompatible formats, different encodings, missing content. I had to spend hours scouring the different sites and directories to find something.

As a result, I decided to convert all the different file-formats into a single one, index the titles of the books and put them in thematic directories. I organized the files on my work computer. I was the main user of my collection. I perfected its structure, made a simple, fast and convenient search interface and developed many other useful functions and put it all on the Internet. Soon, people got into the habit of visiting the site. [...]

For about two years I scoured the [I]nternet. I sought out and pulled texts from the network, which were lying there freely accessible. Slowly the library grew, and the audience increased with it. People started to send books to me, because they were easier to read in my collection. And the time came when I stopped surfing the [I]nternet for books: regular readers now send me books. Day after day I get about 100 emails, and 10–30 of them contain books. So many books came in that I did not have time to process them. Authors, translators, and publishers also started to send texts. They all needed the library. (Moshkov 1999)

In the second half of the 1990s, the Russian Internet—RuNet—was awash in book digitization projects. With the advent of scanners, OCR technology, and the Internet, the work of digitization had eased considerably. Texts migrated from print to digital and sometimes back to print again. They circulated through different collections, which, in turn, merged, fell apart, and reformed. Digital libraries with the mission to collect and consolidate these free-floating texts sprung up by the dozens.

Such digital librarianship was the antithesis of official Soviet book culture: it was free, bottom-up, democratic, and uncensored. It also offered a partial remedy to problems created by the post-Soviet collapse of the economy: the impoverishment of libraries, readers, and publishers. In this context, book digitization and collecting also offered a sense of political, economic, and cultural agency, with parallels to the copying and distribution of texts in Soviet times. The capacity to scale up these practices coincided with the moment when anti-totalitarian social sentiments were the strongest, and economic needs most dire.

This unprecedented bloom of digital librarianship was the result of the superimposition of multiple waves of technological, political, economic, and social transformation. "Maksim Moshkov's Library" was ground zero for this convergence and soon became a central point of exchange for the community engaged in text digitization and collection: One shadow librarian recalled this period as follows: "[At the outset] there were just a couple of people who started scanning books in large quantities. Literally hundreds of books. Others started proofreading, etc. There was a huge hole in the market for books. Science fiction, adventure, crime fiction—all of this was hugely in demand. Lib.ru was a large part of the response, and was filled with the books that people most desired and valued."

For years, lib.ru integrated as much as it could of the different digital libraries that flourished in the RuNet—preserving, in the process, many of the smaller, short-lived libraries.

This process of collection slowed in the early 2000s. By that time, lib.ru had all of the classics, resulting in a decrease in the inflow of new material. By the same token, the Russian book market was finally starting to offer works aimed at the mainstream, resulting in an abundance of romances, astrology, crime fiction, and other popular genres. These works started to appear in, and would soon flood, lib.ru. Many contributors, including Moshkov, were concerned that such ephemera would dilute the

original library. And so they began to disaggregate the collection. Self-published literature, "user-generated content," and fan fiction were separated into the aptly named
samizdat section of lib.ru (http://samlib.ru/), which housed original texts submitted
by readers. Popular fiction—"low-brow literature"—was split off. Sites specializing in
those genres quickly formed their own ecosystem. Librusec, the first of its kind, now
charges a monthly fee to provide access to the collection. The Flibusta community
split off from Librusec the same way that Librusec split off from lib.ru, to provide free
and unrestricted access to a similar collection. Finally, some in the community felt the
need to focus their efforts on a separate collection of scientific works. This became the
Kolkhoz collection.

Toward a Million-Book Scientific Library

A *kolkhoz* (Russian: колхо́з) was a type of collective farm that emerged in the early Soviet
period. In those early days, it was a self-governing, community-owned collaborative
enterprise, with many of the features of a commons. For the Russian digital librarians,
these historical resonances were intentional. As the LibGen administrator described:

The [K]olkhoz group was initially a community that scanned and processed scientific materials:
books and, occasionally, articles. The ethos was free sharing. Academic institutes in Russia were
in dire need of scientific texts; they xeroxed and scanned whatever they could. Usually, the files
were then stored on the institute's FTP site and could be downloaded freely. There were at least
three major research institutes that did this back in early 2000s, unconnected to each other in any
way, located in various faraway parts of Russia. Most of these scans were appropriated by the [K]
olkhoz group and processed into DJVU.[9]

The sources of files for [K]olkhoz were, initially, several collections from academic institutes,
downloaded whenever the FTP servers were open for anonymous access. In one case, this included one of the institutes of the Chinese Academy of Sciences, but mostly they came from
Russian academic institutes. At that time [around 2002], there were also several commercialized
collections of scanned books on sale in Russia. Mostly, these were college-level textbooks on math
and physics. These files were also all copied to [K]olkhoz and processed into DJVU. The focus was
on collecting the most important science textbooks and monographs of all time, in all fields of
natural science.

There was never any commercial support. The [K]olkhoz group never had a web site with a
database, unlike most projects today. They had an FTP server with files, and the access to FTP was
given by PM [one of the administrators] in a forum. This server was privately supported by one of
the members—an academic researcher, like most [K]olkhoz members. The files were distributed
directly by burning files on writable DVDs and giving them away. Later, FTP access was closed to
the public and only a temporary file-swapping FTP server remained. Today the [K]olkhoz DVD
releases are mostly spread via torrents.

The Kolkhoz collection amassed around fifty thousand documents. The *mexmat* collection of the Moscow State University Department of Mechanics and Mathematics (Moshkov's alma mater) was around the same size. The "world of books" (*mirknig*) collection had around thirty thousand files, and there were roughly a dozen other smaller archives with approximately ten thousand files in their respective collections.

The Kolkhoz group dominated the science-minded e-book community in Russia well into the late 2000s. Kolkhoz, however, suffered from the same problems as the early Fidonet-based text collections. Since it was distributed on DVDs, via FTP servers and later on torrents, it was hard to search, it lacked a proper catalog, and it was prone to fragmentation. Parallel solutions soon emerged. Around 2006–2007, the early Gigapedia copied the English books from Kolkhoz, set up a catalog, and soon became the most influential pirate library in the English-speaking Internet.

Similar cataloguing efforts soon emerged elsewhere. In 2007, someone on rutracker .ru, a Russian file sharing site, posted torrent links to ninety-one DVDs containing science and technology titles aggregated from various Russian sources, including Kolkhoz. This massive collection had no categorization or particular order. But it soon attracted a librarian: a user of the forum started the laborious task of organizing the texts into a usable, searchable format—first filtering duplicates and organizing existing metadata into an Excel spreadsheet, and later moving to a more open, web-based database. And thus Library Genesis was born.

LibGen inherited more than just books from Kolkhoz and Moshkov's lib.ru. It inherited their elitism with regard to canonical texts, and their understanding of librarianship as a community effort. Like the earlier sites, LibGen's collections are expanded by user submissions. Like the other sites, the number of submissions grew rapidly as the site's visibility, reputation, and trustworthiness were established, and like the others, this growth trailed off as the collection of canonical literature grew more complete. As the LibGen administrator explained:

The number of mankind's useful books is roughly what we already have. So growth is defined by newly scanned or issued books. Also, the quality of the collection is represented not by the number of books but by the amount of knowledge it contains. LibGen does not need to grow further and I am not the only one among us who thinks so. [...]

We have absolutely no idea who sends books in. It is practically impossible to know, because there are a million books. We gather huge collections which eliminate any traces of the original uploaders.

My expectation is that new arrivals will dry up. Not completely, as I described above. Some books will always be scanned or rescanned (it nowadays happens quite surprisingly often) and the overall process of digitization cannot and should not be stopped. It is also hard to say when the slowdown will occur: I expected it about a year ago, but then Library.nu got shut down and things changed dramatically in many respects. Now we are "in charge" (we had been the largest anyways, just now everyone thinks we are in charge) and there has been a temporary rise in the book inflow. At the moment, relatively small or previously unseen collections are being integrated into LibGen. Perhaps in a year it will saturate.

However, intuition is not a good guide. There are dynamic processes responsible for [e-book] availability. If publishers massively digitize old books, they'll obviously be harvested and that will change the whole picture."

The ambitions of LibGen's administrators to create a universal library are limited, at least in terms of scope. It is not intended to contain everything. Its boundaries are created in dialogue with the community, measured by the act of actively digitizing and sharing books. Yet the size of this community is carefully limited. The administrators identified Gigapedia's visibility as the main contributor to its downfall and they wish to avoid that trap. On the one hand, as one admin stated: "Our policy, which I control as strictly as I can, is to avoid fame. Gigapedia's policy was to gain as much fame as possible. Books should be available to you, if you need them. But let the rest of the world stay in its equilibrium. We are taking great care to hide ourselves and it pays off."

On the other hand, LibGen's administrators understand that hiding limits the likelihood that scholars in need can find them. Their solution to this dilemma is to open source their collection and thereby allow others to create better publicized services that interface with the public. They let others run the risk of getting famous.

Copyright and "Copynorms" in Russian Pirate Librarianship

Library Genesis serves as a source archive for around a half-dozen freely accessible pirate libraries on the Internet. The catalog database is downloadable, the content is downloadable, even the server code is downloadable. No passwords are required to download and there are no gatekeepers. There are no obstacles to setting up a similar library with a wider catalog, an improved user interface and better services, a different audience or, in fact, a different business model.

This arrangement creates a two-layered community. The core group of LibGen admins maintains the current service, while a loose and ever-changing network of mirror sites build on the LibGen infrastructure. As the admins explained:

The unspoken agreement is that the mirrors support our ideas. Otherwise we simply do not interact with them. If the mirrors support this, they appear in the discussions, on the Web etc. in a positive context. This is again about building a reputation: if they are reliable, we help with what we can, otherwise they should prove [to] the World they are good on their own. We do not request anything from them. They are free to do anything they like. But if they do what we do not agree with, it'll be taken into account in future relations. If you think for a while, there is no other democratic way of regulation: everyone expresses his own views and if they conform with ours, we support them. If the ideology does not match, it breaks down.

Forum posts asking for donations suggest that funding for LibGen comes from their own personal resources as well as occasional donations when there is a need to buy or rent equipment or services: "[W]e've been asking and getting support for this purpose for years. [...] I asked the community for donations three or four times, for a specific purpose only and with all of the budget spoken for. And after getting the requested amount of money we shut down the donations."

Mirror sites, however, do not need to be noncommercial to enjoy the support of the core LibGen community, they just have to provide free access to users (Bodó 2013; Schultz 2006). This means that ad-supported mirrors are endorsed, but the reselling of texts is frowned upon. The ethical stance of LibGen on this issue is best illustrated via the reconstruction of the conflict with another site, E,[10] which used the LibGen stock to seed its own library and then adopted a "collaborative piracy" business approach.

E is another hugely popular online shadow library, offering access to a million plus titles. It is based on a simple idea: If a user cannot find a book in its collection, the administrators offer to purchase a digital or print copy, rip it, and sell it to the user for a fraction of the original price—typically under $1. Access to E is by invitation only. Payments are made in anonymous Amazon gift cards, which make the purchases easy and protect the identity of the users. E recoups its investment, in principle, through the multiple sales of the same low-priced ripped copy. While clearly illegal, the logic is not that different from that of private subscription libraries, which purchase a resource and distribute the costs and benefits among club members.

Although from the rights holders' perspective there is little difference between the ad-supported and the collaborative piracy approaches, many participants in the pirate librarian community draw a sharp line between the two, viewing the sales model as a violation of community norms. An internal forum post tried to clarify the relationship of LibGen to other services as follows:

E is a scam. They were banned in our forum. Yes, most of the books in E came from LibGen, because LibGen is open, but we have nothing to do with them. [...] If you wish to buy a book, do it from legal sources. Otherwise it must be free. [...]

Here's what E wants:

• make money on downloads of e-books, no matter what kind.
• get books from all the easy sources, spend as little effort as possible on books, maximize profit.
• no need to build a community, no need to improve quality, no need to correct any errors. Just put all files in a big pile and maximize profit.
• keep files in secret, never give them away, and keep no listing of files so there is no information about what books are really available on E or what is being done.

There are very few similarities in common between E and LibGen, and these similarities are too superficial to serve as a common ground for communication. [...]

They [E administrators] run an illegal business, making a profit.

Library Genesis administrators describe a set of values that differentiates possible site models. They prioritize the curatorial mission and the provision of long-term free access to the collection with all the costs such a position implies, such as open sourcing the collection, ignoring takedown requests, keeping a low profile, refraining from commercial activities, and as a result, operating on a minimal budget. E prioritizes the expansion of its catalog on demand, but this implies a commercial operation with a larger budget and the associated higher legal risk. Many of the other sites that mirror LibGen's catalog prioritize public visibility, carry ads to cover costs, but also respond to takedown requests to avoid as much trouble as possible. From the perspective of expanding access, these are not easy or straightforward trade-offs. In LibGen's case, the commitment to the mission of providing free access comes with significant sacrifices, the most important of which is relinquishing control over the shadow library's most valuable asset: its collection of 1.2 million scientific books. But the LibGen admins believe that these costs are justified by the larger goal of making free access independent of the fate of LibGen.

Library Genesis is not the only file sharing community that relies on internal discipline and restraint to ensure the long-term survival of the collection and the community (see, e.g., Bodó 2013). It is unique, however in its radical open source approach. This approach is rooted in the way it regards the legal status of its subject matter—scholarly publications. While openness in the field of scientific research is hardly new, grounded in the understanding that we see further if "standing on the shoulders of giants," LibGen's copynorms are equally shaped by the specificities of the Soviet and post-Soviet era, in which the experiences of repression, scarcity, and expulsion from the first world of scientific knowledge production were paramount.

The Co-development of Copynorms and Copyright Laws in the Post-Soviet Era

The copynorms of the LibGen community were shaped by and reacted to the development of local (Russian) and international laws on the digitization and online distribution of protected works. Russian digital libraries emerged in a period of double transformation: the post-Soviet copyright system had to adopt global norms, while these global norms struggled to adapt to the emergence of digital copying.

The first post-Soviet authors rights law was enacted in 1993. Its major goal was to update the local regulatory framework to conform to at least some international standards, and to the expectations of Western rights holders, for whom such laws were a precondition for entering the newly opened Russian markets. The first two post-Soviet decades saw significant efforts to harmonize Russian law, at least on paper, with the existing WIPO and World Trade Organization (WTO) frameworks. Yet, significant gaps and uncertainties remained in terms of scope, the legal clarity, or the enforceability of the freshly implemented regulations (Sezneva and Karaganis 2011). This was especially true for rules regarding the digital world. "Internet rights" were introduced only in a 2006 amendment to the authors' rights law (Budylin and Osipova 2007; Elst 2005, 425).

During most of the 1990s, user-driven digitization and archiving took place in a regulatory void where such activities were barely addressed. Under such conditions, informally negotiated norms filled the gap. Authors and publishers who saw their works appear in digital form had to rely on these informal norms to establish control over their texts vis-à-vis enthusiastic collectors and for-profit entrepreneurs. Such regulation via norms did not always work, and it was widely ignored when the subject was foreign work, but for some authors, limited control of a work could be exercised through the copynorms in some of the better-organized Russian file-sharing communities.

The roots of the Russian digital copynorms can be traced back to 1997, when HAR-RYFAN, an early Russian digital text collection, was first published on CDs. The CD contained around ten thousand texts, consisting mostly of Russian science fiction. It was originally compiled by Igor Zagumenov, a book enthusiast, from works that appeared on the Holy Spirit BBS. The CD was a nonprofit project, which Zagumenov planned to print and sell in a single run of around one thousand copies. Zagumenov contacted some of the authors and publishers, and received permission from some of them to distribute their texts. But the CD also included many other works that were uploaded to the BBS without authorization. In an effort to legitimize the collection, Zagumenov included the following notice alongside his name and contact information and that of the authors who had granted permission: "Texts on this CD are distributed in electronic format with the consent of the copyright holders or their literary agent. The disk is aimed at authors, editors, translators and fans of science fiction and fantasy as a compact reference and information library. Copying or reproduction of this disc is not allowed. For the commercial use of texts please refer directly to the copyright owners at the following addresses."

As the CD circulated, some authors began to notice that their work was used without their authorization. Some complained about the material damage the collection may have caused them, but most focused on moral rather than strictly economic rights: many took issue with the lack of permission, the mutilation of some of the works, the lack of attribution, and the removal of original copyright and contact notices. Some authors had no problem appearing in the collection per se, but objected to the fact that the CDs were sold (and printed in greater numbers than originally agreed upon in spite of Zagumenov's intentions).

The debate that took place in the book-related fora of Fidonet and drew in a number of the affected authors was useful in revealing and refining community norms. Many participants drew a distinction between the free access provided first by Fidonet and later by lib.ru, which integrated some parts of the Fidonet collection, and what was perceived as Zagumenov's for-profit enterprise—despite the fact that the price of the CD only covered printing costs. The debate also forced authors and publishers to consider the effects of the digital book communities' actions on their business and reputation. Some authors did not want to appear online at all; others wanted only their published works to be circulated, but in any case, the consensus that emerged seemed to agree that online, bottom-up librarianship was beneficial as long as it respected the wishes of the authors.

Moshkov also integrated parts of the HARRYFAN CD into lib.ru. Moshkov's policy toward authors' rights was to ask for permission if the author or publisher could be contacted. He also honored takedown requests. In 1999, he addressed the copyright issues associated with lib.ru:

The author's interests must be protected on the Internet, including the opportunity to link back to the authorized source, assert the right of attribution, and protect the work from distortion. Anyone who wants to protect his/her rights should be ready to address these problems, ranging from the ability to identify the offending party, to the possibility of proving infringement. [...]

Meanwhile, the question how to protect authors-netizens' rights regarding their work published on the Internet has become important. It is known that there are a number of periodicals that reprint material from the Internet without the permission of the author, without payment of a fee, without prior arrangement. Such offenders need to be shamed via public outreach. The "Wall of shame" website is one of the positive examples of effective instruments established by the networked public to protect their rights. It manages to do the job without bringing legal action—relying on polite warnings, indications of potential trouble, and shaming of the infringer.

Do we need any laws for digital libraries? Probably we do, but until then we have to do without. Yes, of course, it would be nice to have their status established as "cultural objects" and have the same rights as a "real library" to collect information, but that might be in the distant future. It would also be nice to have e-library "legal deposits" of publications in electronic form, but when even Leninka [the Russian State Library] cannot always afford that, what we really need are enthusiastic networkers. [...]

The policy of Lib.ru is to take everything users give, otherwise they cease to send books. It is also to listen to the authors and strictly comply with their requirements. And it is to grow and prosper. [...] I simply want the books to find their readers because I am afraid to live in a world where no one reads books. This is already the case in America, and it is speeding up with us. I don't just want to derail this process, I would like to turn it around.

Moshkov didn't have answers to all the problems facing authors, but he worked to chart an alternative to both the lack of legal protection and the public cost of a lockdown of digital rights. He played a crucial role in consolidating norms around these practices in Russian digital publishing—a role that was later recognized in various prizes from the International Union for Internet Professionals in Russia.[11] Ultimately, Moshkov's framework rested on the following principles:

• The digitization of books and the practice of online distribution was to be understood to be part of the history and tradition of "the library."
• As is the case with libraries, such practices had to be nonprofit in nature.
• Digital text collections were expected to respect the wishes of the rights holders even if they were not legally obligated to do so.
• Digital librarians were expected to maintain active communication with the different stakeholders in the community, including authors and readers.
• Digital text collections were understood to respond to a clear gap in affordable, legal access.
• Digital texts were not regarded as substitutes for printed books.

Many digital libraries subscribed to Moshkov's principles. But for multiple reasons, by the mid-2000s this consensus was under substantial stress. The latitude that Moshkov had enjoyed was shrinking. Internet and computer access had become mainstream. The legal environment was about to change. But most important, the commercialization of pirate archives had become a viable option and thus a prominent issue for both the community and rights holders.

Formalization of the IP Regime in the 2000s

Russia formally joined the World Trade Organization in 2012. As a condition of membership, Russia had to bring its intellectual property regulation in line with international standards. The road that led to full harmonization started with the first copyright law reform in 1993. Over the next two decades, the United States put unrelenting pressure on the Russian government for further reforms. Throughout the period—and indeed to the present day—U.S. Trade Representative Special 301 reports (which provide a means for U.S. companies to complain about foreign intellectual property [IP] enforcement) described a litany of Russian failures to protect copyright, from inadequate penalties to weak policing to ill-informed judges. Partly in response to these reports, Russia amended its copyright law in 1998 to the extend the legal framework to encompass digital rights. According to the new rules, digital services had to have a license to distribute digital content on the Internet. The licenses were issued by collecting societies, but the rules did not require that these societies have permission from rights holders, provided that the societies paid royalties to them. The result was a proliferation of collective rights management organizations, competing to license content to digital services (Sezneva and Karaganis 2011). Most of these were regarded as illegal by Western rights holders, who had no contractual relationships with the Russian collecting societies.

The resulting confusion led to many high-profile legal disputes. The best known involved Allofmp3.com, a site that sold music from Western record labels at prices far below those of iTunes or other officially licensed vendors. AllofMP3.com claimed that it was licensed by ROMS, the Russian Society for Multimedia and Internet (Российское общество по мультимедиа и цифровым сетям [НП РОМС]), but ROMS, in turn, was disavowed by Western labels and rights holders. A long legal and diplomatic struggle ensued, leading to a failed criminal prosecution of the site owner and the eventual closure of the site in 2007.

The legal status of online text collections was subject to the same uncertainties and faced similar international pressure. Book piracy was regularly mentioned in Special 301 reports in the 2000s—though the reported losses were small in comparison to the claims of the music, film, and software industries.[12] The regulatory changes implemented in response to the music industry, in any event, affected the digital libraries as well. In most cases, lib.ru relied on direct agreements with authors to make digital texts accessible. However, it also had a license from ROMS to cover works without direct authorization. The outcome of the AllofMP3.com controversy thus had direct consequences on the legality of lib.ru, and for any other digital library that contemplated legalizing its activities through the 1998 licensing scheme.

With a much lower profile and a focus on Russian literary classics, lib.ru avoided the attention of foreign rights holders. It even benefited from state support during the period, receiving a $30,000 grant from the Federal Agency for Press and Mass Communications to digitize the most important works from the 1930s. But the chaotic licensing environment came back to bite Moshkov. In 2005, Moshkov and lib.ru were targeted in a lawsuit brought by an e-book merchant (KM Online), which was trying to establish its own commercial service.[13] The lawsuit was a sign of a slow but significant transformation in the Russian print ecosystem. The first change was economic. The idea of a viable market for electronic books had begun to find a foothold. Electronic versions of texts began to be regarded as potential substitutes for the printed versions, not advertisements for them or supplements to them. Commercial services emerged that regarded the well-entrenched free digital libraries as competitors, not collabora-tors. The second change was regulatory. As Russia continued to bring its laws into closer conformance with WTO requirements ahead of its admission, the legal system of protecting authors' rights became more sophisticated and more effective. Russian rights holders could increasingly rely on local laws to enforce their rights. As with KM Online, the same laws enabled many organizations to claim markets and force out competitors—sometimes in ways that amounted to state-backed racketeering (Sezneva and Karaganis 2011). Western rights holders also gained enough power to demand enforcement against RuNet pirate sites. The copynorms negotiated in absence of the law came into conflict with the varying, often contested, and sometimes violent proc-esses of applying the new legal order.

Closure of the Legal Regime

The legal, economic, and cultural conditions under which LibGen and its mirror sites operate today are very different from those of two decades ago. The major legal loop-holes are now closed, though according to one shadow librarian, Russian authorities have shown little inclination to pursue LibGen so far:

I can't say whether it's Russian or Western copyright enforcement that's most dangerous for LibGen; I'd say that Russian enforcement is still likely to tolerate most of the things that Western publishers won't allow. For example, lib.ru and Librusec and other unofficial Russian e-libraries are tolerated even though far from compliant with the law. These kinds of e-libraries could not survive at all in [W]estern countries.

Western publishers have been slow to join record, film, and software companies in their aggressive online enforcement campaigns, and academic publishers even more so. But such efforts are slowly increasing, as the market for digital texts grows and as publishers benefit from the enforcement precedents set or won by the more aggres-sive rights holder groups. In 2015, LibGen was named as a defendant in an injunction served against pirate book services in a New York court (Bodó 2016). The domain name of one of the LibGen mirror sites, was seized, apparently due to the legal action taken by a U.S. rights holder. Several of the sites now act on DMCA take down notices, remov-ing links to books reported to be infringing (despite the lack of jurisdiction of U.S. law). LibGen has responded to this pressure by receding further into the background, as one anonymous LibGen administrator noted:

We want books to be available, but only for those who need them. We do not want LibGen to be visible. If one knows where to get books, there are here for him or her. In this way we stay rela-tively invisible (in search engines, e.g.), but all the relevant communities in the academy know about us. Actually, if you question people at universities, the percentage of them is quite low. But what's important is that the news about LibGen is spread mostly by face-to-face communication, where most of the unnecessary people do not know about it. (Unnecessary are those who aim [to] profit).

The policy of invisibility is starkly opposed to Moshkov's policy of maximum visibility. LibGen administrators hope that they can survive in the shadows where LibGen can be protected by the Russian academic community:

In Russian academia, LibGen is tacitly or actively supported. There are people that do not want to be included in the archive, but it is hard to say who they are in most cases unless there are DMCA complaints. But in our experience the complainers are only from the non-scientific fellows. [...] I haven't seen a single complaint from the authors who should constitute our major problem: professors etc. No, they don't complain. The other complainers are the ever-hungry publishers.

But the protection the academic community has to offer may not be enough to fend off publishers' enforcement actions. LibGen and other shadow libraries responded to the increased legal pressure in a variety of ways (Bodó 2016). They moved the core service further into the darknets. They dropped the domain names under injunction in favor of new ones. They tightened security protocols in their communities. Yet this may not be enough: LibGen and other services face a critical loss of volunteers who are willing to donate time and money and take substantial legal risks to maintain its radically open service. Some of the shadow librarians have already stepped back, having reached the limits of their tolerance for risk. But the larger expectation of the shadow librarians we talked to is that, even if LibGen disintegrates, there will be someone else to carry on: "[I]f people are physically served court orders, they will have to close the site. The idea, however, is that the entire collection has been copied throughout the world many times over. The database is open, the code for the site is open, so other people can continue."

As the other chapters in this volume document, there are innumerable small digitization projects, archiving communities, sharing networks, and distribution channels operating below the enforcement radar, contributing to a constant diffusion of texts and knowledge across geographical, educational, and income boundaries. The Russian shadow libraries are an experiment in whether such efforts can survive at scale. This is clearly no longer a technical question but rather a social and political one, shaped by the balance of forces between publishers, educators, and states. It seems unlikely, at this point, that the big shadow libraries will prompt the creation of new law. Publishers are well behind the other copyright stakeholders in pushing for stronger enforcement, though they are beginning to make more aggressive use of the available tools. By the same token, there is little prospect of a legal accommodation of large-scale unauthorized distribution of the kind enabled by Library Genesis and its mirrors. But the growth and survival of these sites have a powerful influence on the practices that shape the larger ecosystem, as publishers face pressure on issues of cost and access and as the example of actually existing near-universal libraries pushes academic culture toward open models. The survival of the Russian shadow libraries is an open question, but they can still lose the battle while winning the war.

Notes

1. Michael Hart, the founder of the Gutenberg Project (GP), recalled in his history of the project: "The Bible accounted for all of our successful work in the 1980s except for the preliminary editions of *Alice in Wonderland*. We were working on a *Complete Shakespeare*, but the copyright laws had been changed with so little publicity that we didn't find out about it for years, and thus a huge amount of labor was lost" (Hart 2006).

2. The story of Library Genesis was reconstructed via semistructured interviews with key members of the community, and close reading of the discussions on the closed online forum of the community. Both access to the site and to community members was given under a strict condition of anonymity.

At one point, I shared an early draft of this chapter with interested members and asked for their feedback. Beyond access and feedback, community members helped with the writing of this article by providing translations of some Russian-language source documents, and by reviewing my translations. In return, I provided a small financial contribution to the community, in the value of USD$100.

I reproduced forum entries without any edits to the language, and I edited interviews conducted via instant messaging (IM) services to reflect basic writing standards.

3. See a quantitative analysis in chapter 3.

4. Such sources include collections of fiction, literary works or comics, not collected by LibGen.

5. Such services include automatically providing the same text in different file formats, suited for different e-readers.

6. LibGen is predominantly donation based, while its mirror sites may serve ads or sell documents individually.

7. In comparison, in the United States in 1975 approximately 39,000 new titles were printed (Greco 2005).

8. We share Helen Freshwater's (Freshwater 2003) view that censorship is a more complex phenomenon than the state just blocking the circulation of certain texts. Rather, its modus operandi, institutions, extent, focus, reach, and effectiveness showed extreme variations over time. This short chapter cannot go into this rich history (Alekseeva, Pearce, and Glad 1985; Dewhirst and

Farrell 1973; Ermolaev 1997; Komaromi 2004; Post 1998; Skilling 1989). For our purposes, the key point is that Soviet censorship not only affected literary works, but also extended deeply into scholarly publishing, including natural science disciplines.

9. DJVU is a file format similar to PDF that simplified online book distribution. For books that contain graphs, images, and mathematical formulae, scanning is the only digitization option. However, the large number of resulting image files is difficult to handle. The DJVU file format allows for the images of scanned book pages to be stored in the smallest possible file size, which makes it the perfect medium for the distribution of scanned e-books.

10. Abbreviated to maintain the anonymity of the service.

11. ROTOR, the International Union of Internet Professionals in Russia, voted lib.ru as the "literary site of the year" in 1999, 2001, and 2003; "electronic library of the year" in 2004, 2006, 2008, 2009, and 2010; Moshkov was elected "programmer of the year" in 1999; and "man of the year" in 2004 and 2005.

12. The Special 301 reports cited USD$40 million losses per year to publishers throughout this period, though such estimates were at best a rough guess and by all appearances, a low priority for the USTR. The details, alleged losses, and analysis in these reports changed little from year to year.

13. KMO was an online vendor that sold digital texts for a small fee. Although the KMO collection—like every other collection—had been assembled from a wide range of sources on the Internet, KMO claimed to pay a 20 percent royalty on its income to authors. In 2004, KMO requested that lib.ru take down works by several authors with whom KMO claimed to be in exclusive contract. KMO's claims turned out to be only partly true. KMO had arranged contracts with a number of the heirs to classics of the Soviet period, who hoped to benefit from an obscure provision in the 1993 Russian copyright law that granted copyrights to the heirs of politically persecuted Soviet-era authors. Moshkov, in turn, claimed that he had written or oral agreements with many of the same authors and heirs, in addition to his agreement with ROMS. The lawsuit turned into a major public event, generating thousands of news items both online and in the mainstream press. Authors, members of the publishing industry, legal professionals, librarians, and Internet professionals publicly supported Moshkov, while KMO was generally presented as a rogue operator trying to make easy money on freely available digital resources. Eventually, the court ruled that KMO indeed had one exclusive contract with Eduard Gevorgyan, and that the publication of his texts by Moshkov infringed the moral (but not the economic) rights of the author. Moshkov was ordered to pay 3,000 Rubles (approximately $100) in compensation.

References

Alekseeva, L., C. Pearce, and J. Glad. 1985. *Soviet Dissent: Contemporary Movements for National, Religious, and Human Rights*. Middletown, CT: Wesleyan University Press.

Battles, M. 2004. *Library: An Unquiet History*. New York: W. W. Norton.

Bodó, B. 2013. "Set the Fox to Watch the Geese: Voluntary IP Regimes in Piratical File-sharing Communities." In *Piracy: Leakages from Modernity*, ed. M. Fredriksson and J. Arvanitakis, 241–264. Sacramento, CA: Litwin Books.

Bodó, B. 2016. "Pirates in the Library—An Inquiry into the Guerilla Open Access Movement." Paper prepared for the 8th Annual Workshop of the International Society for the History and Theory of Intellectual Property, CREATe, University of Glasgow, UK, July 6–8, 2016. https://ssrn.com/abstract=2816925 (accessed August 17, 2017).

Borges, J. L. 1998. "The Library of Babel." In *Collected Fictions*, 112–118. New York: Penguin.

Budylin, S., and Y. Osipova. 2007. "Is AllOfMP3 Legal? Non-Contractual Licensing under Russian Copyright Law." *Journal of High Technology Law* 7 (1): 1–18.

Bush, V. 1945. "As We May Think." *Atlantic Monthly* 7:112–124.

Dewhirst, M., and R. Farrell, eds. 1973. *The Soviet Censorship*. Metuchen, NJ: The Scarecrow Press.

Elst, M. 2005. *Copyright, Freedom of Speech, and Cultural Policy in the Russian Federation*. Leiden; Boston: Martinus Nijhoff.

Ermolaev, H. 1997. *Censorship in Soviet Literature: 1917–1991*. Oxford, UK: Rowman & Littlefield.

Freshwater, H. 2003. "Towards a Redefinition of Censorship." *Critical Studies* 22:225–245.

Friedberg, M., M. Watanabe, and N. Nakamoto. 1984. "The Soviet Book Market: Supply and Demand." *Acta Slavica Iaponica* 2:177–192. https://eprints.lib.hokudai.ac.jp/dspace/bitstream/2115/7941/1/KJ00000034083.pdf (accessed August 17, 2017).

Greco, A. N. 2005. *The Book Publishing Industry*. Mahwah, NJ: Lawrence Erlbaum Associates.

Hart, M. S. 2006. "A Brief History of Project Gutenberg." *Michael Hart's Online Writings*. http://hart.pglaf.org/history.06.txt (accessed August 17, 2017).

Komaromi, A. 2004. "The Material Existence of Soviet Samizdat." *Slavic Review* 63 (3): 597–618. doi:10.2307/1520346.

Lessig, L. 2013. "Aaron's Laws—Law and Justice in a Digital Age." Lecture presented at Harvard Law School, Cambridge, MA. http://www.youtube.com/watch?v=9HAw1i4gOU4 (accessed August 17, 2017).

Levin, M. B. 1983. "Soviet International Copyright: Dream or Nightmare." *Journal of the Copyright Society of the U.S.A.* 31:127–162.

Liang, L. 2012. "Shadow Libraries." *e-flux*. http://www.e-flux.com/journal/shadow-libraries/ (accessed August 17, 2017).

Moshkov, M. 1999. "Chto vy vse o kopirayte. Luchshe by *kizhakku* pochitali (Biblioteke *copyright* ne vrag)." *Kompyuter* (300).

Newcity, M. A. 1978. *Copyright Law in the Soviet Union*. New York; London: Praeger.

Newcity, M. A. 1980. "Universal Copyright Convention as an Instrument of Repression: The Soviet Experiment." *Journal of International Law and Economics* 9 (2): 285–324.

Post, R. 1998. *Censorship and Silencing: Practices of Cultural Regulation.* Los Angeles, CA: Getty Research Institute for the History of Art and the Humanities.

Rieusset-Lemarié, I. 1997. "P. Otlet's Mundaneum and the International Perspective in the History of Documentation and Information Science. *Journal of the American Society for Information Science* 48 (4): 301–309.

Ryzhak, N. 2005. "Censorship in the USSR and the Russian State Library." Paper prepared for the IFLA/FAIFE Satellite Meeting: Documenting Censorship—Libraries Linking Past and Present, and Preparing for the Future, The Nobel Institute, Oslo, Norway, August 11–12, 2005. https://www.bibalex.org/wsisalex/8.Censorship%20in%20the%20USSR%20and%20the%20Russian%20State%20Library.doc (accessed August 17, 2017).

Schultz, M. F. 2006. "Copynorms: Copyright and Social Norms." In *Intellectual Property and Information Wealth: Issues and Practices in the Digital Age*, ed. P. K. Yu, 201–236. Westport: Praeger Publishers.

Sezneva, O., and J. Karaganis. 2011. "Russia." In *Media Piracy in Emerging Economies*, ed. J. Karaganis, 149–218. New York: Social Science Research Council.

Skilling, H. G. 1989. *Samizdat and an Independent Society in Central and Eastern Europe.* London: Palgrave Macmillan.

Solzhenitsyn, A. I. 1974. *The Gulag Archipelago 1918–1956: An Experiment in Literary Investigation, Parts I–II.* New York: Harper & Row.

Stelmakh, V. D. 1993. "Reading in Russia: Findings of the Sociology of Reading and Librarianship Section of the Russian State Library." *International Information & Library Review* 25 (4): 273–79.

Stelmakh, V. D. 2001. "Reading in the Context of Censorship in the Soviet Union." *Libraries & Culture* 36 (1): 143–151. doi:10.2307/25548897.

3 Library Genesis in Numbers: Mapping the Underground Flow of Knowledge

Balázs Bodó

Chapter 2 documented the largely Russian social history of pirate book sites. This chapter explores the question of the growth and impact of the Library Genesis (or LibGen) network, via a close look at its collections and traffic. This quantitative analysis clarifies how these services operate, what publics they serve, and ultimately what harms to publishers and authors can be reasonably attributed to them. LibGen and its mirror sites infringe the copyrights on hundreds of thousands of works, potentially undercutting the market for those works. But they also respond to clear (and sometimes not so clear) market failures where work is unavailable or unaffordable, and they play a role in expanding global access to scientific and scholarly work. On what basis can we evaluate these trade-offs? To date, there has been no substantive account of the shape, reach, or impact of these archives. This chapter takes some steps in that direction.

The first section reconstructs the growth of the LibGen collection through an examination of changes in its catalog over time—mapping it by language and subject matter, and evaluating how much of it is accessible through legal alternatives. The second section discusses the demand for books on these sites, based on download data acquired from one of the LibGen mirror sites. Here we look at what is being downloaded and by whom. The third section connects the supply and demand discussions to reflections on the wider impact of these pirate archives on libraries, higher education institutions, and authors.[1]

The Supply of Documents in Library Genesis

Between 2008 (the start of LibGen), and April 2014 (the end of our analysis), the size of the LibGen catalog grew from nearly 34,000 items to almost 1.2 million records.[2] Figure 3.1 shows the number of documents added to the collection each month between January 2008 and April 2014.

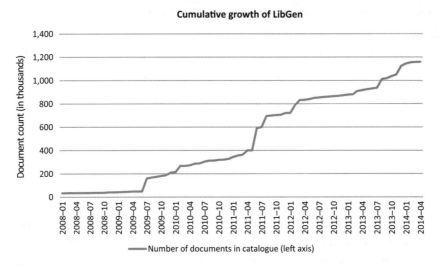

Figure 3.1
The cumulative growth of Library Genesis between January 2008 and April 2014 (full catalog).

Most shadow libraries are thought to be "peer-produced commons" in the sense that they are built from the contributions of many individual users. One example of such peer production is the Gigapedia/library.nu collection, which contained one-half million documents assembled from contributions by thirty major contributors (together responsible for adding a little more than 50 percent of all books), and nearly nine thousand small contributors, who usually uploaded only one or two contributions each. In contrast, LibGen's growth (82 percent of all the records) came from huge, single-day additions of tens of thousands of documents each. These occasions most likely mark the integration of large, preexisting collections into the LibGen collection. Although there are a variety of methods in use in the file sharing community to encourage users to contribute (Bodó 2014), such as social or financial rewards for uploaders, LibGen unlike Gigapedia uses none of these. Individuals can submit documents to the collection, but LibGen does not encourage and definitely does not reward such submissions. Typically, individual submissions add only a few thousand documents each month, accounting for a total of around 18 percent of the collection.

Preexisting Collections

Because the LibGen community is very conscious of its history as an aggregator of collections, data on the provenance of source collections is usually maintained within the database. This allows for a relatively clear picture of the expansion of the collection.

Prior to 2011, Library Genesis was one of several large, predominantly Russian-language archives. It grew through aggressively integrating other, primarily Russian corpuses developed in academic networks in the early and mid-2000s, such as the Kolkhoz collection described in chapter 2. Altogether, LibGen added 330,000 documents in those years. By 2011, however, the preexisting Russian sources were largely exhausted. The corpus of valuable Russian scientific and classic literature was increasingly complete. Then the game changed. Gigapedia/Library.nu began by copying and cataloging English-language texts from the LibGen collection, which it built into a much larger English-language catalog. As publisher-led enforcement pressure on Library.nu grew in 2011, LibGen returned the favor. Between mid-2011 and mid-2012, LibGen integrated nearly half a million new books—by all appearances nearly all from the Gigapedia archive prior to its shutdown. A third wave of growth in 2013 is attributable to the integration of publisher-produced electronic text repositories.

Linguistic and Thematic Expansion of Library Genesis

The integration of the Gigapedia material transformed LibGen from a predominantly Russian, natural sciences-focused collection into a predominantly English-language multidisciplinary shadow library. Since the LibGen records contain document metadata, such as the document language, subject matter, and the date of addition to the archive, it is relatively easy to map how the focus of the collection shifted over time.

Figure 3.2 suggests that the majority of Russian-language documents were added in 2008–2010, whereas around 80 percent of the English language documents arrived in 2011 and after, beginning with the Gigapedia/Library.nu collection in 2011.

The linguistic composition of the database continues to change. German, the third most common language in the collection, representing 8.5 percent of the full catalog, emerged only in 2013, fueled by large, single-day additions of documents from the same publisher. The German additions very likely represent the start of a new trend. As large, peer-produced free-floating text archives are slowly exhausted, and as publisher-developed digital archives grow and become more widely accessible, the major opportunities for expansion will come from the latter. In most cases, such expansion represents a process of leakage, in small and large quantities, from universities and other institutions with legal access to publisher catalogs—a process we see repeatedly in the history of developing-country shadow libraries. Over time, such downloaded collections find their way to LibGen.

Other major languages, such as French, Spanish, and Mandarin are strikingly underrepresented in the collection. Forum discussions on LibGen offer various explanations for the omission of Chinese documents, which on balance appears to be based on

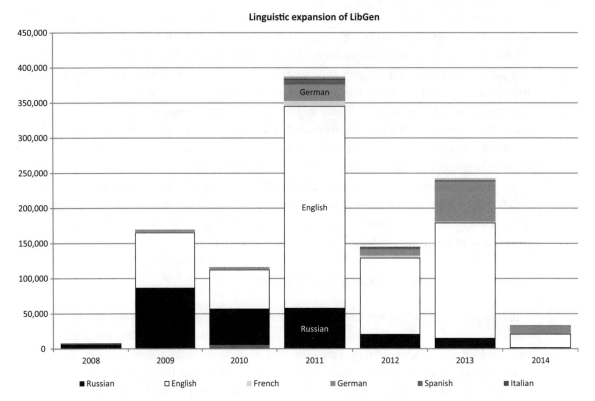

Figure 3.2
Language of documents added to the Library Genesis collection each year (full catalog, document/language > 1,000).

a decision by the LibGen administrators to avoid content that they have no capacity to manage. To date, LibGen has not integrated any of the large Chinese-language shadow libraries available on the web. The lack of scholarship in other major European languages is more puzzling and likely reflects a combination of factors. There appear to be few large, persistent shadow libraries in French or Spanish, and—to the best of our knowledge—fewer for other languages. Where digital collections are available, the social and curatorial networks that underpin the creation of large, online English and German collections do not appear to have developed. To date, LibGen has not become a repository for archive communities in other languages, nor have LibGen administrators sought to significantly expand their linguistic coverage. Such expansion remains opportunistic.

As figure 3.3 suggests, the majority of works in the natural sciences, mathematics, and computer science were added in 2009–2010. The 2011 integration of Gigapedia also substantially changed the thematic focus of the library,[3] with LibGen absorbing the overwhelming majority of works in other disciplines in 2011 or later. Before the Gigapedia material arrived, LibGen was a mostly Russian, natural sciences-focused collection that incorporated the various scientific corpuses developed in Russian universities and scientific institutes. The post-Gigapedia LibGen became a much broader archive with reach into the much larger English-reading public for scholarly work.

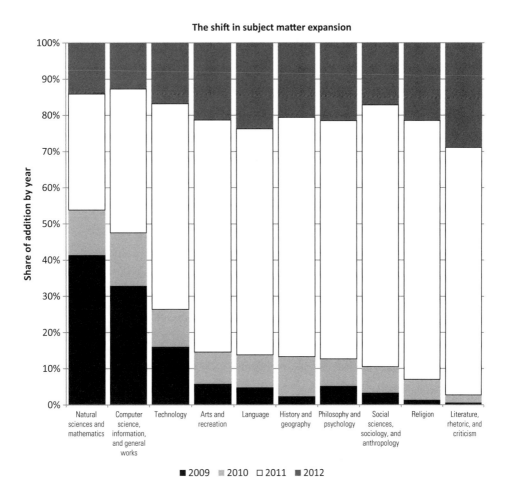

Figure 3.3
Each column represents one top-level Dewey subject category. The shading shows what percentage of all documents was added to the catalog in a given year (identified dataset).

Publishers

More than fifty-five thousand publishers are represented in the LibGen collection, though the exact number is difficult to pinpoint due to both the large number of records without publisher information (in the full dataset: 27 percent; among the texts we've identified: 3.2 percent) and the noise in the existing data. The distribution, as expected, is very concentrated, with the top 100 publishers accounting for somewhere between one-third and one-half of all documents in the catalog (full dataset: 34 percent, identified dataset 50 percent). The top ten publishers' share of the identified catalog and the average downloads per document are visible in table 3.1.

The major Western academic publishers dominate the catalog. Nevertheless, we the catalog also contains thousands of smaller publishers, with just a few titles each, and although there are documents in more than a hundred different languages, the collection predominantly represents the Western, English-language, scholarly mainstream. This focus has an impact on demand, as we will discuss later.

As the last column of table 3.1 shows, publishers with the highest number of works in the catalog are not necessarily the most popular ones. Supply and the demand do not perfectly overlap. The ten most popular publishers in terms of the number of downloads per title (based on publishers with more than a hundred titles in the catalog) account for only less than 0.8 percent of the catalog, but more than 2.2 percent of

Table 3.1
The document share of the top ten publishers in the identified dataset, with average downloads/title figures per publisher (the average downloads/title in the whole identified dataset is 3.1)

Publisher (ISBN based)	Share of catalog	Downloads/title (catalog average: 3.1)
Springer	6%	3
Cambridge University Press	4%	6
Routledge	4%	5
Wiley	3%	4
Oxford University Press	3%	5
Palgrave Macmillan	1%	3
Harper & Row	1%	2
Springer Verlag	1%	6
McGraw-Hill	1%	4
Academic Press	1%	4

all the downloads. These publishers are among the smaller ones with, on average, only 300 works each in LibGen. Most specialize in mathematics and social sciences: Verso (12.58 average downloads per document), The Society for Industrial and Applied Mathematics (10.76), Benjamin/Cummings Pub. Co. (9.81), The Mathematical Association of America (9.76), Попурри (9.70), Polity Press (9.58), John Benjamins Publishing Company (8.74), Blackwell Publishers (8.26), The American Mathematical Society (8.18), and Birkhäuser (7.92).

The same divergence between supply and demand is present in subject matter, as seen in table 3.2. Social sciences are the leading category in the archive, both in terms of volume and demand, representing 15 percent of identified titles, and with slightly higher-than-average downloads per title. Social sciences are followed by technology and engineering texts (14.5 percent), natural sciences and mathematics (9.3 percent), and literature and criticism (8.6 percent). While these latter two categories account for more or less the same share of the catalog, they cannot differ more in terms of demand. Natural science titles on average see almost three times higher demand than literary works.

Drilling down further into the second- and third-level Dewey Decimal Classification (DDC) classes offers a more detailed map of the thematic composition of the collection and the focus of demand. Due to their length, we limit the lists to the ten most frequent classes in tables 3.3 and 3.4.

Table 3.2
Subject matter share and demand in Library Genesis by top-level DDC classes

Top-level DDC classes	Share of titles	Downloads/title
Unclassified	31%	3
Social sciences, sociology, and anthropology	15%	3
Technology	14%	3
Natural sciences and mathematics	9%	5
Literature, rhetoric, and criticism	9%	2
Computer science, information, and general works	6%	3
History and geography	4%	2
Arts and recreation	3%	2
Philosophy and psychology	3%	5
Religion	2%	3
Language	2%	6

Table 3.3

The thematic composition of Library Genesis by second-level DDC classes

Second-level DDC classes	Share of identified dataset	Downloads/title
Medicine and health	6%	2
Computer science, information, and general works	5%	3
American literature in English	4%	1
Economics	4%	3
Mathematics	4%	8
Engineering and allied operations	3%	4
Social sciences, sociology, and anthropology	3%	4
Management and public relations	3%	3
Social problems and social services	2%	2
English and Old English literatures	2%	2

Table 3.4

The thematic composition of Library Genesis by third-level DDC classes

Third-level DDC classes	Share of identified titles	Average downloads/title
American fiction in English	4%	1
Diseases	3%	2
Computer programming, programs, and data	3%	3
General management	2%	3
Applied physics	2%	4
English fiction	1%	2
Special computer methods	1%	3
Data processing and computer science	1%	2
Production	1%	3
Culture and institutions	1%	4

Based on the Dewey subject categories, LibGen has a wide supply of works in American fiction, health, computer science, and natural sciences. It is also apparent that the most populous subsections are not necessarily the most popular ones. The most popular subject matter in terms of average downloads per title are: English grammar (10.29 downloads per title), standard usage and applied linguistics (10.13), analysis (9.87), French philosophy (9.30), algebra (8.67), numerical analysis (8.05), general principles of mathematics (7.99), topology (7.99), probabilities and applied mathematics (7.44), geometry (7.34), German and Austrian philosophy (7.33), modern Western philosophy (7.33), other philosophical systems (7.25), philosophy and theory (7.22), social sciences, sociology and anthropology (7.19), and logic (7.07).

The data indicates pretty clearly that the subjects in highest demand in the LibGen shadow library are books used for learning or working in English, mathematics, and philosophy. English language resources point to the international reach of the archive. As we discussed in chapter 2, mathematics was one of the first disciplines to be extensively digitized and the first discipline to be integrated into LibGen. These parts of the collection were probably more carefully selected and curated by a specialist group than, for example, those that were ingested en masse from publisher e-libraries. LibGen probably also inherited the readers along with the collections, leading to relatively steady demand. Readers of Western philosophy probably arrived later, when the relevant works were integrated from the Gigapedia collection. Whether the high level of interest in Western philosophy is a function of the quality of the collection, of broader awareness of LibGen in these fields, of ethical norms specific to these fields—as one commentator has suggested (Schwitzgebel 2009)—or some combination of the three is a question we must leave open.

The Age of Works in Library Genesis

LibGen also contains information about the date of publication of the documents in its collection, allowing us to make some observations about the age of the collection and the factors that affect it. As seen in figure 3.4, although the collection has a large number of classics, it is heavily skewed toward recent work, which is more likely to have a digital version and thus easier to include than scanning a version by hand.

The Legal Supply of Works in Library Genesis

We measured the legal availability of the titles in the LibGen catalog by collecting data from two additional sources: Amazon.com (in September and October 2013) and

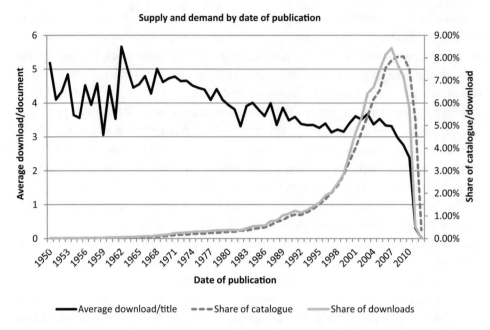

Figure 3.4
The share of catalog and the share of downloads by the date of publication (right axis), and the average download/title/date of publication (identified dataset, average download/title: 3.01).

WorldCat.org (November 2013). We used Amazon.com for data on legal market access, and WorldCat.org for e-library availability. Price information in some categories (such as used book prices or rental prices) should be treated with caution due to their extreme volatility on Amazon.[4] Table 3.5 shows the availability and price information for all the identified documents in all categories.

Based on the Amazon data, it is clear that while print availability is generally high, with nearly 83 percent of titles in LibGen available in some sort of print format (new or used, purchase or rental), there are huge gaps in electronic availability.[5] As figure 3.5 shows, electronic availability figures are dramatically improving for works published more recently. Still, on average, only a third of the identified catalog is available as a Kindle e-book (to buy or rent). E-repository availability seems to be higher, but this result should be treated with caution.[6]

Further analysis reveals that different subject matter has different legal availability rates: Natural sciences and mathematics titles, which form the core of the LibGen collection, have much lower e-book availability rates than literary works, for example.

E-libraries could, in theory, successfully compete with shadow libraries. Institutional subscriptions allow affiliated individuals to access a relatively wide range of titles, at no

Table 3.5

Price and availability information for the identified dataset, based on Amazon.com (prices in USD)

	List price	Sold by Amazon	Sold second hand	Sold as new	Available for print rent	Available on Kindle	Available for Kindle rent	Available through e-libraries
Available	46.74%	53.82%	80.93%	79.07%	1.46%	31.62%	6.26%	64.83%
Not available	53.26%	46.18%	19.07%	20.93%	98.54%	68.38%	93.74%	35.17%
Mean price	87.19	69.43	54.44	62.46	30.73	46.64	28.07	
Median price	57.00	41.40	15.98	29.19	24.94	23.99	14.93	
Mode price	24.95	7.19	0.01	0.01	17.00	9.99	11.61	
25 percentile	28.95	20.95	2.50	11.43	17.18	9.99	10.23	
75 percentile	125.00	89.99	48.24	63.75	37.51	59.99	34.26	

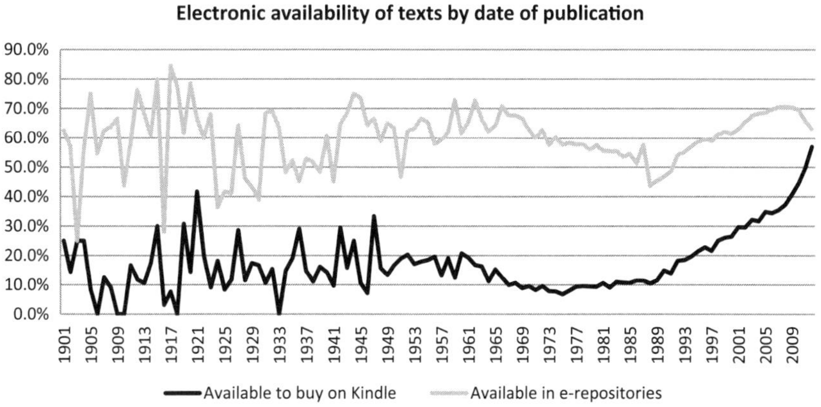

Figure 3.5

Electronic availability of titles in the identified dataset by date of publication.

Note: The sudden drop in shares between 1988 and 1989 can be attributed to political change in the Soviet Union. In 1989, Perestroika was in full swing, resulting in the publication of important long-suppressed works in Russian. Few of these are translated or available in digital formats.

direct cost. In principle, e-library availability is outstanding compared to other forms of electronic access. But actual access to these repositories is sharply limited by a number of factors, beginning with the cost of institutional subscription, and including the necessity of being affiliated with an institutional subscriber, either as faculty or as a student. Basic technical difficulties in accessing e-library catalogs also remain commonplace, making crude but free an effective competitor to even subsidized legal channels.

The analysis of prices suggests that academic publishers tend to price their titles with the library market in mind. A quarter of the titles have a list price over $125, and both the mean and the median prices are well above the $20 to $40 range, which is the usual price for a fiction title. The secondhand and e-book market prices (both targeting individual rather than institutional buyers) are much closer to this price range, suggesting that the primary target for print editions is not the individual buyer and that, accordingly, the effect of pirated copies on sales is not readily measured by conventional estimates of "substitution effects."

The Demand Side

Who uses these shadow libraries? To what extent do they compete with legal sources? There are many theories that link the demand for pirated content to the availability of legal alternatives. Theories of substitution argue that unauthorized file sharing services directly compete with legal alternatives (Dejean 2009; Fink Maskus, and Qian 2010; OECD 2009; Smith and Telang 2012). Other studies find evidence that unauthorized file sharing networks correct the shortcomings of legal markets by providing access to otherwise inaccessible works (Bodó and Lakatos 2012; Bodó 2011; Karaganis 2011). The two accounts are not incompatible, but have tended to be very difficult to reconcile empirically. Markets for media goods are changing rapidly as technologies enable both new forms of intermediation and access (including, in the publishing field, the emergence of a superintermediary in the form of Amazon.com) as well as new practices of consumption (such as bibliophilia freed from the constraints of income and shelf space). The majority of studies from the last decade have focused on disentangling these issues in the music and audiovisual sector. Although there has been some recent work on the unavailability of copyrighted works on legal markets—the so-called "orphan works" problem (Heald 2014; Rosen 2013)—studies of unauthorized downloading in the book market have been few and focused primarily on trade sales (Hardy, Krawczyk, and Tyrowicz 2014; Reimers 2016). Most of the evidence on the effects of piracy in the book industry remain anecdotal (Laskow 2013; Pogue 2013).

Among the academic communities that form the primary audience for the LibGen sites, we are clearly discussing a phenomenon of some global size: on average: 43,500 documents per day were downloaded from B—one of the many mirror sites that incorporate the LibGen catalog—during the three-month period of study in 2012.[7] Positively identified LibGen items were downloaded on average 24,000 times a day—indicating substantial demand for titles from B's large catalog of popular, non-LibGen materials. Since B is only one of the many mirrors of LibGen, overall use within the ecosystem can be assumed to be much higher.[8]

One of the most persistent questions about digital piracy is its impact on legal markets. Demand for pirated materials can compete with legal sales, or it can be driven by market unavailability. If we compare the average download figures for works (un)available in various formats (table 3.6), we can make two claims. First, LibGen clearly plays an archival function in contexts where works are out of print. Although the absolute number of such titles is relatively low, our dataset from B records hundreds of thousands of downloads of such texts. This archival function is almost certainly more pronounced for the nonidentified part of the collection (some 30 percent), which is made up of predominantly harder-to-access, older, non-English works.

Table 3.6
Descriptive statistics of global downloads by legal availability (all means have a statistically significant difference on a 0.05 level)

		Share of titles	Average downloads/title
Available in used copy?	No	19.10%	2.28
	Yes	80.90%	3.29
Available in new copy?	No	20.90%	2.27
	Yes	79.10%	3.32
Available to buy on Kindle?	No	68.40%	3
	Yes	31.60%	3.36
Available to rent on Kindle?	No	93.70%	3.01
	Yes	6.30%	4.51
Available to rent in print?	No	98.50%	3.05
	Yes	1.50%	6.28
Available in e-repositories?	No	35.20%	2.55
	Yes	64.80%	3.4

Yet, in general, as table 3.6 shows, demand on LibGen correlates with legal availability: if a title is legally available in any format, it enjoys higher downloads. The explanation of this correlation is, in our view, unremarkable and somewhat circular: texts are both kept in print by publishers and downloaded via LibGen in function of demand. By the same token, texts are more likely to appear on LibGen when they are in publication in print or digital form. This correlation is consistent but shows some noteworthy variations depending on the nature of the supply channel. The very high per-title demand for titles available as rentals, for example, probably denotes high student demand for textbooks. The high average demand for titles not available on Kindle probably reflects the fact that relatively few scientific books and articles are available in this format. The relatively high demand for titles that are also available through institutional archives suggests the importance of the academic and scientific user community in institutions and countries with little access to paywall services. Through these partial indicators, a picture of the LibGen community begins to emerge.

Library Genesis's administrators stress that they focus on collecting only works that are relevant to the heavily academic community they serve, irrespective of their legal availability. Although large categories of popular work are excluded from these criteria, the definition of relevance clearly piggybacks on the gatekeeping function of publishing itself. What's relevant, broadly speaking, is what's in print. Both the high degree of availability of in-print (if not digitally available) titles and the higher demand for those titles support this general connection. While LibGen certainly has a strong archival function, its main function is to address the lack of access to digital copies, especially outside the communities that have access to large university libraries and publisher e-catalogs.

Demand by Country

This role in expanding access beyond privileged universities is reflected in differences in country-level demand. Table 3.7 contains country-level transaction data for both the B dataset overall and for the identified documents within it.[9]

We will make no strong effort here to disentangle the developmental issues, cultural issues, and other factors that might account for these differences. At a very basic level, B may simply be better known in some national academic communities than in others. But we will venture some observations. We see three broad categories of countries among the largest downloaders.

Table 3.7
Top users of the Library Genesis catalog via the B mirror

Country	All B downloads			Identified document downloads		
	(1) net downloads (without proxy traffic)	(2) share of proxy traffic in country traffic	(3) country share of all net downloads	(4) net downloads (without proxy traffic)	(5) share of proxy traffic in country traffic	(6) country share of all net downloads
Russia	861 865	1%	31%	168 863	1%	12.8%
Indonesia	175 234	2%	6%	135 961	2%	10.3%
United States	222 373	5%	8%	133 827	4%	10.2%
India	129 679	6%	5%	86 817	6%	6.6%
Iran	96 836	1%	3%	67 084	1%	5.1%
Egypt	96 302	0%	3%	55 468	0%	4.2%
China	77 065	0%	3%	55 458	0%	4.2%
Germany	96 618	35%	3%	54 516	33%	4.1%
United Kingdom	61 772	10%	2%	41 065	6%	3.1%
Ukraine	135 726	2%	5%	32 246	2%	2.5%
Turkey	42 637	0%	2%	31 836	0%	2.4%
France	56 131	13%	2%	31 720	10%	2.4%
Poland	48 525	0%	2%	27 925	1%	2.1%
Italy	41 659	0%	2%	26 550	0%	2.0%
Canada	34 393	5%	1%	21 400	3%	1.6%
Spain	30 874	2%	1%	19 691	1%	1.5%
Sweden	35 117	5%	1%	18 229	5%	1.4%
Romania	26 419	3%	1%	18 159	2%	1.4%
Greece	25 161	8%	1%	17 791	5%	1.4%
Netherlands	29 405	45%	1%	16 306	42%	1.2%
Australia	19 988	1%	1%	12 002	1%	0.9%
Algeria	17 747	0%	1%	11 772	0%	0.9%
Hungary	13 988	0%	1%	10 072	0%	0.8%
Czech Republic	17 762	39%	1%	9 431	36%	0.7%

First, Russia and other post-Soviet countries are, predictably, heavy traffic sources, with significantly more downloading of Russian-language content than of material from the rest of the collection.

Second, developing countries such as Indonesia, India, and Iran are also major traffic sources. These countries have in common relatively low per-capita GDP, underdeveloped electronic text markets, and rapidly growing student populations—all factors that we would associate with high shadow library use.

Third, developed countries such as the United States, Germany, and the UK are also represented at or near the top, and require a somewhat different explanation. All of these countries have highly developed print markets, comparatively well-developed electronic book markets, dense and accessible library systems, and otherwise good infrastructures for higher education, science, and research. Nevertheless, for many categories of both scholarly works and users, similar barriers of price and availability come into play: legal access to scholarly works in digital formats is still generally poor and pricing (for any format) is often set at levels that target libraries rather than individual buyers. From the perspective of students, the conflict between personal library building and economic constraints are particularly sharp. As we see elsewhere in this report (and parallel to developments in music downloading), collecting is a powerful motivation in and of itself, and in the downloading era has become increasingly divorced from intentions to read or consume.

A somewhat different global picture emerges if we adjust these results for population size, and only account for the identified documents (see table 3.8). The top of this list is dominated by small, relatively poor countries at the edges of the European Union. All have highly educated populations, dense cultural, political, and economic ties with the West, and—in the case of the Eastern European countries and crisis-ravaged Greece—diminished resources and educational infrastructure compared to the core European countries. Most, moreover, are under obligations to implement EU educational standards established by the 1999 Bologna Accords, which promote compatibility with Western European and North American degrees (Keeling 2006; Reinalda and Kulesza-Mietkowski 2005). The effort to establish such degree and accreditation systems, in turn, has required the rapid transformation of the *content* of education within these systems, ranging from the curricula, to the acquisition policies of university libraries, to the corpuses of knowledge that faculty and students need to be competitive in Western-centric disciplines.[10] Given the limited financial (and sometimes also human) resources available for such transitions, many libraries cannot meet faculty and student demand. Such contexts provide fertile ground for shadow libraries like Library Genesis.[11]

Table 3.8
Document downloads per 1,000 inhabitants (without proxies)

Country	All B downloads per 1,000 persons	Identified document downloads per 1,000 persons
Lithuania	5.5	2.9
Estonia	4.2	2.3
Sweden	3.7	1.9
Greece	2.2	1.6
Barbados	2.9	1.5
Latvia	3.4	1.5
Slovenia	2.2	1.5
Iceland	2.6	1.3
Luxembourg	2.5	1.3
Croatia	1.6	1.2
Russian Federation	6.0	1.2
Macedonia, Fyr	1.5	1.1
Hungary	1.4	1.0
Bulgaria	1.8	1.0
Netherlands	1.8	1.0
Israel	2.1	0.9
Armenia	2.0	0.9
Czech Republic	1.7	0.9
Iran	1.3	0.9
Romania	1.2	0.8
Montenegro	1.1	0.8
Cyprus	1.4	0.8
Malta	1.1	0.8
Finland	1.4	0.8
Poland	1.3	0.7
Portugal	1.0	0.7
Ukraine	3.0	0.7
Egypt	1.2	0.7
Moldova	1.8	0.7
Germany	1.2	0.7
Albania	0.8	0.7
United Kingdom	1.0	0.7

Country-Level Knowledge Diets

Finally, and more speculatively, we can look at the distribution of top-level Dewey subject headings in country-level downloading—a step that allows us to develop a rough sense of the "knowledge diet" of LibGen users in different countries.[12] This analysis revealed three major clusters (mapped to geography in figure 3.6), representing significantly different consumption patterns of subject matter (mapped to subject matter in figure 3.7).

The simple clustering approach had some surprising results. It clearly identified the post-Soviet republics as one group (cluster 3). These countries are differentiated by their large share of unidentified documents in their diet. As we have indicated earlier, the documents we were not able to identify via ISBN-based WorldCat services tend to be older, Russian-language titles. LibGen's Russian collection is actively used by countries that share a common Soviet past.

We also find significant differences among the rest of the countries in the analysis. The clustering algorithm identified two relatively homogenous groups. Countries belonging to cluster 1 have higher levels of social sciences, literature, history, and philosophy, and lower levels of natural sciences and technology in their overall consumption than countries that belong to cluster 2.

There might be many reasons why a country would prefer downloading social sciences to downloading hard sciences, or the other way around. One such explanation is

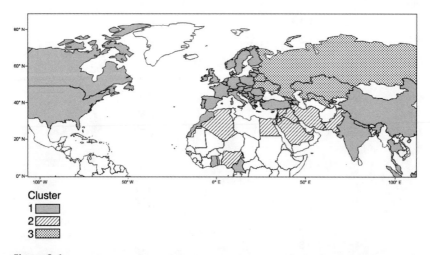

Figure 3.6
Country clusters based on their "knowledge diet." Shading corresponds to that used in figure 3.7.

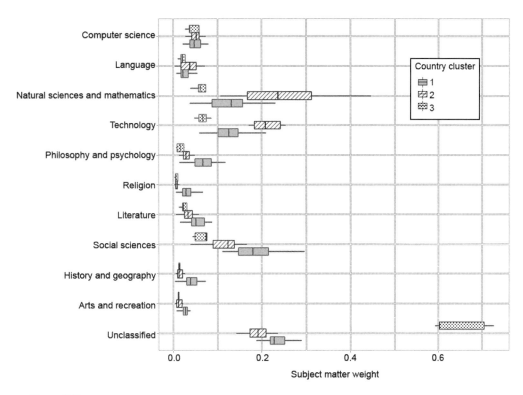

Figure 3.7
The mean weight (and quartiles) of each subject matter in the science diet of the three country clusters. Shading corresponds to that used in figure 3.6.

institutional: based on UNESCO and OECD data, the share of social science, business, and law graduates in the cluster 1 is nearly twice the share of social science graduates in cluster 2 (7.85 percent vs. 4.58 percent), while the difference in the share of science graduates is significantly smaller (OECD 2016; UNESCO 2016). But the existence of the two clusters may also reflect some inherent internal characteristics of the two types of scientific discourse. On the one hand, the hard sciences of use and interpretation relies on the lingua franca of logics and mathematics, which are the least determined by the cultural context in which such interpretation takes place. The social sciences, literature, history, philosophy, and psychology sections of LibGen, on the other hand, are made up of the mainstream of Western thought, and they strongly reflect the conditions that produced that corpus of knowledge. This corpus, contrary to hard sciences, does not in itself constitute a universal interpretative frame, nor can it rely on one. The culturally strongly situated Western social science corpus may not enjoy the frictionless diffusion that hard sciences rely on due to the existence of the universal language of mathematics.

Most of the Latin American and African countries are conspicuously missing from this chart. We could not find any data-related explanation for this phenomenon, so we have to assume other factors explain the dearth of users, such as the lack of substantive Spanish and Portuguese collections in LibGen, and the Russian, Eastern European, and respective ex-pat social networks through which LibGen and similar sites operate.

Because these libraries are frequently penalized by or excluded from search engine indexes, these networks depend heavily on dedicated online discussions and word of mouth. The strong presence of Russian-speaking users may be a self-limiting factor in this regard—as visible to Russian-speaking users as it is invisible to Latin American ones. Other factors, such as differences in Internet penetration and the nature of other informal distribution channels (such as photocopying) almost certainly play a role as well.

Conclusion

In key respects, Library Genesis is the product of social, cultural, and historical circumstances specific to post-Soviet Russia. These circumstances initially gave rise to a shadow library that catered primarily to Russian materials and users—one of many such libraries that digitized and collected books and made them freely available in the 1990s and early 2000s in Russia. By 2014, LibGen was the leading shadow library in both Russian and English for Western science, complemented by a sizable collection in German and smaller collections in other languages.

Eventually, most such libraries must either limit their growth, reach, and relevance, or accept a higher profile and increased risk of prosecution. The current shadow library landscape has many small, specialized collections that operate largely under the radar of the major copyright enforcement efforts in publishing.

Library Genesis is an exception in that it is both big and, to date, enduring. The generally permissive legal environment in the early and mid-2000s in Russia provides some of the explanation for this persistence. And despite signs of stronger enforcement, this is probably still a factor: the limited reach of Internet enforcement into not just Russia but also the array of post-Soviet states linked by Russian-language social and academic networks still provides a wider margin for gray and illegal services than the core European countries. The social norms and legal disarray that shaped LibGen's open policies may or may not ensure its long-term survival, but as a manifestation of broader social pressures they are almost certain to ensure its reproduction.

LibGen's open approach suggests affinities with bottom-up collaborative projects that rely on many small contributors—the classic conception of the peer-produced commons. In reality, and like many of these projects, LibGen neither pursues nor realizes this vision. The impressive growth of the collection is driven by the efforts of a very small community that seeks out and integrates other digital collections en masse, whether derived from long-term scanning and collecting by other academic and quasi-academic communities or, more recently, from the large-scale copying of publisher catalogs.

B and other mirror sites of the LibGen network have developed substantial side interests that extend beyond the original LibGen collection (of which B's massive collection of literary works is perhaps the most prominent example). LibGen itself does not purport to be a universal library—rather, it is strongly grounded in a conception of quality and relevance to academic disciplines, which in turn maps closely to the gatekeeping role of the major publishers. Accordingly, LibGen is made up of mostly in-print but undigitized works.

Given the rapid pace of digitization and the porous borders of the academic community in the United States and Europe, continued leakage of publisher catalogs into shadow libraries is a virtual certainty. Furthermore, given the expansion of Internet access and markets for cheap readers into large parts of the developing world (and the comparatively slow pace of expanded site licensing of publisher databases), we should expect continued high demand for these works at the peripheries of these university and publisher ecosystems. The role that these services play will continue to depend on a balance of forces between legal market development, the viability of highly organized libraries like Library Genesis in the face of stronger enforcement, and the backup plan when both fail: the "sneaker net" of portable media libraries and small-group student and faculty exchanges. Inside the United States and EU, where most of the academically "relevant" work is at least in print, there is still considerable scope for the improvement of digital catalogs, expanded site licensing, and open access models, which can undercut the main functions of the pirate library.

Notes

1. The analysis is based on multiple datasets from different sources. The LibGen catalog is freely accessible through its website, including many bibliographic and file-related metadata. We refer to this dataset in the subsequent analysis as the full catalog. This data was subsequently enriched with metadata from the WorldCat database, and market accessibility data (prices and formats) by collecting additional data from Amazon.com. In the analysis, this enriched, positively identified, de-duplicated subset of the catalog from the second half of 2012 is referred to as the *identified*

dataset. The demand-side analysis is based on web server logs acquired from the administrators of B, a commercial LibGen mirror. It contains author, title, and partially redacted IP address information from between March 2, 2012 and May 27, 2012. The cleansed log data is referred to as *all B downloads*, while the dataset in which the log records were linked to the identified dataset is referred to as *all identified downloads.* Data on the catalog of Gigapedia/Library.nu come from late 2011. The author would like to thank the Online Computer Library Center (OCLC) for providing access to the WorldCat services, and the B administrators for sharing the web server logs.

2. For the sake of comparison, at the time of the last review of this chapter, in February 2016, LibGen contained more than 1.6 million records.

3. We limited the analysis to the identified dataset, since Dewey subject categories are not reliably present in the full LibGen catalog.

4. Availability is subject to strong seasonal fluctuations as semesters start and end, while price, especially for the used book market, is subject to strong, often software-aided competition among different sellers, resulting in constant adjustments and discounting.

5. Because we rely here only on the U.S.-based Amazon, the actual availability rates in all categories (new, secondhand, e-book) are probably overestimated. Though Amazon ships new books globally, it is used only infrequently by consumers outside of the United States—primarily in contexts where the title is not available through local retailers. For our purposes, we assume that if a title is not available on Amazon, it is less likely to be available via other, local channels, especially for English-language titles. For other formats, such as Kindle, book rental, and used books, Amazon has an even more limited global reach. E-book distribution rights are regional: even if there is a Kindle version in the Amazon store, it may not be available beyond U.S. borders. Many second-hand book dealers who offer used books do not ship outside the United States, and textbook rental (both electronic and print) is certainly unavailable for most markets. In these cases, Amazon-based accessibility data represents the best-case scenario, and almost certainly overestimates the actual availability of titles in most local markets.

To further explore these estimation errors, we compared the harvested data with a dataset provided to us by a prominent academic publisher with a significant number of publications in the LibGen collection. We harvested list prices with near perfection. E-book availability was correctly identified in 69 percent of the cases, while the share of false positives and negatives was around 15 percent for each. Since publisher-provided e-book availability data does not perfectly coincide with the date of data collection from Amazon, and includes other e-book providers besides Amazon, we concluded that the Amazon-gathered data adequately represents the actual facts on the ground in terms of theoretical availability, but overestimates actual availability in local, non-U.S. markets.

6. E-libraries are electronic text collections available through university libraries or publisher portals, such as Oxford Scholarship Online. The 60 percent number requires some methodological caveats. E-repository availability is based on WorldCat library records, which may note if a book has an electronic document version. On manual inspection of the records, it turned out that many of the links to electronic versions point to a limited preview Google Books entry, or a

"table of contents" published as a PDF on the publisher's website. The comparison of our collected data with a publisher-provided dataset showed that we falsely assumed the existence of an e-repository copy in 14 percent of the titles. As a result, e-repository availability in fact may be much lower than indicated.

7. The demand-side analysis of LibGen is based on a log file we acquired from the administrators of the B mirror. The log contains 7.990.130 records from between March 2, 2012 and May 25, 2012. The records contain a document identifier unique to B, the title and author information as well as the partially redacted IP address of the downloader. We discarded log records that could not be positively and unambiguously associated with an LibGen catalog entry. We successfully mapped 54 percent of the identified dataset to the cleaned B log, accounting for 1.399.278 (47 percent) of the transactions.

After cleaning the dataset from bot traffic, we identified the countries and ISPs associated with the IP numbers, we marked those records that could be associated with known proxies (such as Tor and VPN exit nodes, Opera mini proxies), and anonymized the dataset by discarding the IP addresses. We then matched the author and title information with the appropriate fields in the LibGen catalog.

Excluded log entries are either Russian-language scientific books/periodicals (without or with more than one corresponding item in the identified dataset) or Russian- and English-language nonscientific material (such as song lyrics, comics, and literary works) included in the B database, but not included in the LibGen scientific catalog.

8. Each successful LibGen search lists LibGen as well as the official LibGen mirrors as download options. Since the download links that point to B are second behind LibGen's own (but superior in download speeds), we are safe to assume that the analysis based on the B logs correctly represents the structure of demand, and seriously underestimates its size. We don't have up-to-date usage numbers from LibGen, but forum discussions suggest that in June 2013, a year after our observation period, LibGen registered 40,000 daily users and 1,230,000 page views.

9. The first thing to note about table 3.7 is that a substantial share of traffic for certain countries comes from *proxy relayed traffic*—i.e., the use of Tor exit nodes or other VPN services to disguise the user's IP address. Luxembourg (44 percent), the Netherlands (42 percent), Denmark (41 percent), Germany (33 percent), and Switzerland (29 percent) all have high shares of proxy traffic, due to the many Tor exit nodes located at local ISPs. Iceland (86 percent proxy traffic) is a special case, as the traffic of the mobile version of the Opera browser flows through proxy servers with Icelandic IP addresses. For our purposes, we have subtracted proxy traffic from country traffic, since a request made via a Germany-based Tor exit node, or an Iceland-based Opera mini proxy most probably does not originate in those countries. Overall, 6 percent of the traffic comes through known proxies. This finding fits in the more general trend of pirate traffic being increasingly conducted through VPNs and other privacy-enhancing technologies (Bodó 2015).

10. See, for example, Abramitzky and Sin 2014 on how these demands play out in relation to legal publishing.

11. The place of Sweden probably requires a different explanation. One obvious factor might be Sweden's pioneering role in file sharing, grounded in the creation of services like The Pirate Bay

in the early 2000s and in wider norms that made file sharing the basis of an actual political movement (The Pirate Party). The other reason for Sweden's high rank might be that the actual share of proxy traffic is higher than what we were able to detect. In large part because of the prominence of file sharing, Sweden is a market leader in VPN adoption, and non-Swedish traffic may inflate the Swedish numbers to a considerable extent.

12. We used hierarchical clustering to check whether there are significant differences between the diffusion of different subject matter. For the process, we only included countries with more than a thousand nonproxy downloads from the identified subset of the catalog.

References

Abramitzky, R., and I. Sin. 2014. "Book Translations as Idea Flows: The Effects of the Collapse of Communism on the Diffusion of Knowledge." NBER Working Paper No. w20023. http:// papers.ssrn.com/abstract=2421123 (accessed August 18, 2017).

Bodó, B. 2011. "Coda: A Short History of Book Piracy." In *Media Piracy in Emerging Economies*, ed. J. Karaganis, 399–413. New York: Social Science Research Council.

Bodó, B. 2015. "Piracy versus Privacy: An Analysis of Values Encoded in the PirateBrowser." *International Journal of Communication* 9:818–838.

Bodó, B. 2014. "Set the Fox to Watch the Geese: Voluntary IP Regimes in Piratical File-sharing Communities. In *Piracy: Leakages from Modernity*, ed. M. Fredriksson and J. Arvanitakis, 241–264. Sacramento, CA: Litwin Books.

Bodó, B., and Z. Lakatos. 2012. "P2P and Cinematographic Movie Distribution in Hungary." *International Journal of Communication* 6:413–445.

Dejean, S. 2009. "What Can We Learn from Empirical Studies About Piracy?" *CESifo Economic Studies* 55 (2): 326–352. http://ssrn.com/paper=1219442 (accessed August 18, 2017).

Fink, C., K. Maskus, and Y. Qian. 2010. *The Economic Effects of Counterfeiting and Piracy: A Literature Review. Advisory Committee on Enforcement.* Geneva: WIPO.

Hardy, W., M. Krawczyk, and J. Tyrowicz. 2014. "Internet Piracy and Book Sales: A Field Experiment." Faculty of Economic Sciences, University of Warsaw Working Papers, no. 23.

Heald, P. J. 2014. "How Copyright Keeps Works Disappeared." *Journal of Empirical Legal Studies* 11 (4): 829–866.

Karaganis, J. 2011. *Media Piracy in Emerging Economies*. New York: Social Science Research Council.

Keeling, R. 2006. "The Bologna Process and the Lisbon Research Agenda: The European Commission's Expanding Role in Higher Education Discourse." *European Journal of Education* 41 (2): 203–223.

Laskow, S. 2013. "Book 'em: Piracy.lab Is Gathering Data on Digital Book Sharing." October 2. *Columbia Journalism Review.* http://www.cjr.org/cloud_control/piracylab.php?page=all (accessed June 30, 2014).

OECD. 2009. *Piracy of Digital Content.* Paris: OECD Publishing.

OECD. 2016. "Education Database: Enrollment by Field." OECD Education Statistics (database). doi:10.1787/33c390e6-en (accessed January 25, 2016).

Pogue, D. 2013. "The E-Book Piracy Debate, Revisited." *Pogue's Posts,* May 9. http://pogue.blogs.nytimes.com/2013/05/09/the-e-book-piracy-debate-revisited/ (accessed June 30, 2014).

Reimers, I. 2016. "Can Private Copyright Protection Be Effective? Evidence from Book Publishing." *Journal of Law and Economics* 59: 411–440. doi:10.1086/687521.

Reinalda, B., and E. Kulesza-Mietkowski. 2005. *The Bologna Process: Harmonizing Europe's Higher Education.* Farmington Hills, MI: Barbara Budrich Publishers.

Rosen, R. J. 2013. "The Hole in Our Collective Memory: How Copyright Made Mid-Century Books Vanish." *The Atlantic,* July 30. http://www.theatlantic.com/technology/archive/2013/07/the-hole-in-our-collective-memory-how-copyright-made-mid-century-books-vanish/278209/ (accessed August 18, 2017).

Schwitzgebel, E. 2009. "Do Ethicists Steal More Books?" *Philosophical Psychology* 22 (6): 711–725.

Smith, M. D., and R. Telang. 2012. "Assessing the Academic Literature Regarding the Impact of Media Piracy on Sales." SSRN. http://papers.ssrn.com/sol3/papers.cfm?abstract_id=2132153 (accessed August 18, 2017).

UNESCO. 2016. "Distribution of Tertiary Graduates by Field of Study." UNESCO Institute for Statistics (database). http://data.uis.unesco.org/index.aspx?queryid=163 (accessed January 25, 2016).

4   Argentina: A Student-Made Ecosystem in an Era of State Retreat

Evelin Heidel

In Argentina, access to educational materials has been shaped by a combination of factors that are relatively unique in Latin America, including a long tradition of free public university education, extended periods of public investment in libraries, a publishing industry well established by the beginning of the twentieth century, and literacy rates well above Latin American norms. It has also been shaped by features more common to Latin America in the latter half of the twentieth century—most important, the retreat of the state as a guarantor of educational and other rights, beginning under the dictatorships of the mid-1960s.

Our story traces a path through these major chords of Argentine history to provide a context for understanding the student-based practices and networks that provide the main form of access to materials in Argentine universities today. Broadly, this history has three parts:

• The emergence of institutional strategies to increase access to educational materials during the post–World War II "golden age" of the university system, exemplified by the creation of the university press, Eudeba, in 1958.
• The often violent attacks on these institutions by the dictatorships of the 1960s and 1970s, and the subsequent failures of both the democratic state and the publishing industry to formulate alternatives under the pressure of the economic crises of the 1980s, 1990s, and 2000s.
• The primarily student-organized efforts to ensure the availability of inexpensive course materials in this institutional vacuum. Most of this activity passes through organized photocopying, more recently complemented by the emergence of online digital archives.

A caveat: much of the study focuses on the University of Buenos Aires (UBA) and on the School of Philosophy and Letters in particular. This focus obviously limits any claims to representativity in the study—even students in other parts of the university system may have very different experiences. Yet there are reasons to draw more general conclusions from the history and experiences described here. The UBA is overwhelmingly the largest Argentine university and—in light of its location—among the most directly implicated in and affected by conflicts with the state. It is home to nearly 20 percent of Argentine university students from across the socioeconomic spectrum; it was the seat of Eudeba and where many of the legal battles between publishers and students and faculty took place.

Eudeba: The University Press as Democratizer of Knowledge

In her research on the cultural impact of publishing policies between 1880 and 2000, Amelia Aguado (2006) identified seven "phases" in the history of Argentine publishing, which she maps loosely to corresponding political periods.

This chapter will not explore this commercial publishing history in any detail. It is important to note, however, how the growth of the industry in the early twentieth century helped prepare the way for the educational agenda that emerged in the post–World War II period. Like so much else in Argentina, the "Golden Age" of publishing had strong political determinants—in this case the rise of Francisco Franco in Spain, which pushed Spanish publishing into decline and many Spanish intellectuals into

Table 4.1
Periodization of Argentine publishing

Years	Publishing history	Argentine history
1880–1899	Emergence of the commercial market	The generation of 1880
1900–1919	Organization of the publishing market	Centennial of the May Revolution
1920–1937	Emergence of modern publishing	
1938–1955	The "golden age"	The first and second Peronist regimes
1956–1975	Consolidation of the internal market	The military dictatorships (La Revolución Libertadora, 1955; La Revolución Argentina, 1966)
1976–1989	The publishing industry in crisis	Third Peronist regime. "Process of National Reorganization" (dictatorship). Democracy
1990–2000	Concentration and polarization of the publishing sector	Menem's Peronism

Source: Amelia Aguado, "Políticas editoriales e impacto cultural en la Argentina (1880–2000)" [Publishing policies and their cultural impact in Argentina (1880–2000)], *Información, Cultura y Sociedad*, no. 15 (2006): 95–105, http://eprints.rclis.org/17132/1/ics15p95-105.pdf.

exile, to the general benefit of Argentine literary culture and publishing. Argentine publishers became leading forces for the translation of European literature and philosophy into Spanish, both fueling and responding to the growth of a domestic intellectual scene. At the same time, they successfully managed the shift from a domestic to an export-driven market—trailing only Mexico in the export of books within Latin America. Rapid growth continued through the two Peronist governments of the 1940s and 1950s, and remained stable under the dictatorship of the "Bureaucratic Authoritarian State" (organized by Onganía) from 1966 to 1973. The economic crisis and political repression that accompanied the next military dictatorship in 1976, however, damaged the industry and ended its preeminence. The economic chaos of the 1980s weakened it further, leading to a wave of closures and buyouts by foreign multinationals in the 1990s.

There was no equivalent transformation of the university presses in the Golden Age. Although most universities had publication or print units, these were small-scale, sometimes departmentally based operations that specialized in publishing the work of local faculty. None sought wider audiences. None published textbooks or other course materials. Yet the universities they served were changing rapidly. The university system underwent rapid expansion in the post–World War II period, tripling in size between 1945 and 1955 to over 140,000 students. As in other countries, this expansion dramatically altered the composition and mission of the university—no longer limited to the professional training of elites but, increasingly, to the education of large sectors of the population.

The founding of the University Press of Buenos Aires in 1958, better known as Eudeba, was in large measure an effort to reimagine a university press adequate to these changes.[1] Boris Spivacow, an editor and mathematician at the UBA, was appointed to manage the new effort.[2]

As an editorial project, Eudeba was the first university press to develop an explicit strategy of serving the public beyond the university and other specialized communities. Eudeba published in each of the scientific disciplines at multiple levels, including materials aimed at teachers and researchers, required texts for different grades and undergraduate courses, books about science for the nonspecialized public, and finally, literary and artistic texts for the general public.[3] As Eudeba's board characterized it: "Eudeba understands that one of its fundamental objectives is to make books—those instruments of material and spiritual progress—a basic necessity. For that purpose, it uses—and will continue to use—all the available strategies to familiarize people with books."[4]

The publishing policies implemented by Eudeba emphasized large print runs of books targeted at the general public, sold at low cost. At one level, this strategy was fundamental to Eudeba's mission of cultural democratization. At another, it permitted the subsidization of smaller print runs of books intended for more specialized publics, which the press viewed as essential to the research mission of the university.

Eudeba complemented this editorial approach with distribution strategies that brought books to newsstands and other unconventional outlets. In 1965, Eudeba had 1,163 distribution points across the country,[5] in addition to a branch in Chile and distribution deals in Latin America, Spain, the United States, France, Germany, Japan, and Israel. By the mid-1960s, these strategies had made Eudeba the second-largest university press in Latin America, after the Fondo de Cultura Económica (FCE) in Mexico.[6]

The impact of Eudeba's policies is visible in many revealing anecdotes about books, book markets, and literary culture from the period, but one in particular is worth recounting here. In 1963, the Federation of Books, based in Cordoba, announced that booksellers in Cordoba and Rosario had stopped selling their books because they were no longer competitive with the steep discounts offered by Eudeba to students and teachers. Spivacow, writing about the situation in 1963, argued: "The leadership [of Eudeba] holds that it is natural that the university press provide students and professors with special conditions of sale; that the university bookshops capture some of the direct sales from booksellers as a result; … and that this greater diffusion translates, in the last instance, into much higher sales for the booksellers than what they have lost."[7]

By "in the last instance," Spivacow meant that the deals for students and faculty incentivized reading in general, which in turn acted to expand the overall book market. Eudeba's operating theory was that selling more books at lower prices was a more effective strategy in all respects—both in regard to social and economic outcomes—than selling fewer books at higher prices.

In 1966, General Juan Carlos Onganía overthrew the president-elect, Arturo Illia, in a military coup. Among the early targets of the new regime were the universities, which had emerged as vocal centers of political opposition. A month after taking power, Onganía abolished the system of university governance created by the University Reform of 1918. Under Decree 16.912, political activities at universities were prohibited and a government official was appointed to run the university. This decision produced a strong reaction in the university community, and led to the occupation of several of the schools in protest. In response, Onganía sent the federal police to retake the buildings, resulting in the arrests of 400 members of the university and the injury of many others, including several deans. "La noche de los bastones largos" or "Night of the Long Batons," as it became known, produced mass resignations of thousands of university staff. Those who identified with the opposition but chose to remain in their posts were soon fired. The leadership of Eudeba announced its resignation en masse with a letter that emphasized the connection between low-cost books, the democratization and self-governance of the university, and freedom of thought and expression.

For eight years a book cost less than a kilo of bread, less than a pack of cigarettes, less than a bottle of ordinary wine. … How did this cultural phenomenon, with no precedent in the country or the world, emerge and grow? Because it was the product of a university, open to all intellectual currents and in the service of the country. A university that brought to the people who sustained it one of the oldest and most powerful tools: the book. Today, this university no longer exists. Its professors have been beaten and humiliated, its students struck down, its classrooms and laboratories closed. Without authorities arising from within, without collegial bodies to discuss its problems, what university do we pretend to create? Of what university would Eudeba be the press?" (Maunás 1995)

Eudeba suffered under the dictatorships. Under the "Bureaucratic Authoritarian State" organized by Onganía (1966–1973) and later the "Process of National Reorganization" (1976–1983), Eudeba's leadership positions were given to faculty close to the dictatorship. The directorship created lists of censured titles[8] and pulled numerous previously published works out of circulation. In 1976, the new dictatorship took this practice to its logical end by organizing book burnings of censored titles. The return of democracy in 1983 allowed Eudeba to resume some of its former activities, but the crisis had greatly damaged its finances and the press never regained its former stature.

From Public to Private: El Centro Editor de América Latina

After the attacks on the university, Spivacow left Eudeba with the entire directorship and staff to start a new project: el Centro Editor de América Latina (CEAL). CEAL was an effort to create a private entity that could advance the public interest agenda that was no longer possible at Eudeba. The initial capital for the enterprise came from Spivacow's friends and colleagues. CEAL's editorial and distribution strategies followed many of the same principles as the predictatorship Eudeba, including distribution via magazine shops and newspaper stands. For Spivacow, the project was not a traditional business, but—under the political and social pressures of the dictatorship—a "cultural enterprise" that would continue the cheap books tradition. With the same goals of quality and low prices, CEAL edited general interest collections and instructional materials for primary and secondary students.[9]

In 1969, the Onganía dictatorship passed Law 17.401, which banned a wide array of "communist activities." The law was soon brought to bear against a number of CEAL titles, including especially the world history series "Siglomundo: The Documentary History of the 20th Century." Responsibility for such censorship fell to the State Intelligence Service (SIDE), which acted repeatedly to block or truncate CEAL publications during the Onganía regime.

With the consolidation of a new dictatorship in 1976, verbal and physical threats to CEAL leadership grew more frequent and intense. Military commando units harassed and, on one occasion, fire-bombed CEAL offices, outlets, and printing presses. In December 1978, police closed CEAL offices in Avellanada, outside Buenos Aires, and arrested fourteen employees.[10] Spivacow appeared before a judge to declare himself solely responsible for the crimes attributed to his employees. On March 25, 1980, the military judge Hector Gustavo de la Serna ordered that, in order to comply with the law, 30 percent of the materials characterized as "questionable" by the intelligence services[11] needed to be burned—a number representing around 1.5 million books. As part of his sentence, Spivacow was ordered to attend the burning, in a waste dump in the Buenos Aires neighborhood of Sarandí.

CEAL found itself caught in a more or less continuous struggle with political repression and financial insolvency. The press experienced a brief resurgence after the return of democratic rule in 1983, but the continuing economic crisis did not permit it to regain its footing. Devaluation, massive external debt, and hyperinflation put enormous pressure on the organization, and the press did not survive Spivacow's death in 1994. Despite the often-extreme difficulty of their work, CEAL edited 5,000 titles and 78 collections over nearly thirty years.

These conditions also affected the sector more generally. After the return to democracy, many publishers and printers discovered that the lack of capital investment over the past decades had left them with obsolete technology, incapable of competing in an increasingly global market. Many had invested in financial instruments promoted by the dictatorship as a way to combat devaluation, inflation, and the outflow of capital. Some of these strategies led to bankruptcy when economic conditions changed again in the 1980s.[12] The resulting weakness doomed much of the independent publishing sector. The subsequent economic boom of the 1990s did not lead to its recovery, but to its consolidation and sale to multinational publishers.[13]

As publisher-based strategies collapsed and libraries suffered under the weight of the dictatorships and the economic crises, the problem of access to materials was left largely to the students.

How Students Survived Changes in the Ecosystem

One of the few available sources of information about what Argentine students need is a general survey conducted each year by the University of Buenos Aires, in which students are asked questions about their satisfaction with the provision of course materials.[14] In 2011, the survey reported that "67 percent of students, on average, are satisfied, with the top of the range in the School of Natural Sciences (86.2 percent) and Law (85.1 percent) with the School of Social Sciences occupying the low end (46 percent)" (UBA 2012, 45).

With respect to the "[a]vailability and access to library materials," the survey stated that "76.7 percent of students on average are satisfied (the average rating for this aspect is 7.4 [out of 10]). Responses on this question across academic units are without noticeable differences" (UBA 2012, 46).

One of the major assumptions of the survey is that the university plays the central role in providing access to materials, leading to the conclusion that, for most students, it does so adequately. The reality is more complicated. At nearly all UBA units, such access passes primarily through photocopiers located in student centers and neighborhood copy shops. Most academic materials are not provided by the university or its schools.

We conducted an online survey in the School of Philosophy and Letters at the University of Buenos Aires in 2013 to better document this fuller array of strategies.[15] We received 322 complete responses—primarily from undergraduates in literature and history, the two largest majors at the school. Although the sample is self-selected, in important ways it is broadly consistent with the overall student body, including by range of majors and years of study.

With a wider range of options, the formal providers fared poorly. Of the 322 students surveyed, only 30 percent (98) had a library card—a prerequisite for borrowing books. Only 4 percent of those surveyed (12) indicated that they borrowed books "frequently" (the rest of the card holders did so "occasionally"). The library appears to occupy a mostly aspirational space in our results: 77 percent recognized that the library had books that were important to their studies. Seventy percent of students had never borrowed a book from the library.

When asked whether they consulted the library for such books, only 7.5 percent (24) said they did so regularly; 35 percent (113) did so occasionally and 57 percent (184) never did so. The findings suggest very little correlation between library holdings, student interest in searching for relevant books, and the subsequent act of borrowing them. The role of the library—the principal institutional mechanism for providing access to course materials—is marginal to the actual practices of students.

The universal response to problems of cost and accessibility is photocopying. Over half of students get all or nearly all of their materials this way. Around 90 percent get at least the majority of their materials this way.

With roughly two-thirds of students photocopying between 60 percent and 100 percent of their materials, we asked where they obtained these materials.

The student center is heavily preferred to commercial copy shops because it is cheaper—at UBA and at other universities, student centers have few of the infrastructural costs (such as rent) associated with the commercial shops. The problem with this solution is that, with rare exceptions, photocopying in Argentina is illegal.[16]

Our survey also asked students about the circumstances in which they bought materials. Responses were again revealing. *Nearly two-thirds of students buy none or almost none of their materials new.* Only around 10 percent buy the majority of their materials new.

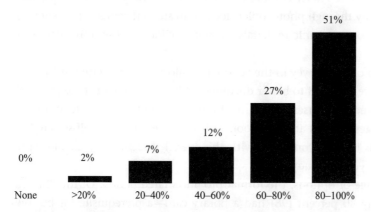

Figure 4.1
How much of your material do you acquire by photocopying?

Table 4.2
Place of acquisition

Place of acquisition	Percentage
Commercial copy shops near the university	28%
Student Center	72%

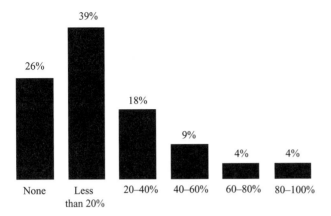

Figure 4.2
How much of your material is purchased new?

Why do students buy materials? We invited them to rank their reasons. Thirty-seven percent indicated that the most important was to keep or collect the material for use beyond the class. Only 16 percent listed availability or reasonable pricing as first answers.

It's worth reflecting briefly on the kinds of answers included in these categories. "I want to keep/collect the material" encompasses a range of different motives, including perceived utility for future studies, personal interest in the topic, or the acquisition of a literary classic that students prefer to own in a more durable, presentable form. "Not available in any other formats" generally reflects an inability to find the text in either the used market or in photocopied form. The baseline for determining whether a new text is reasonably priced is, in most cases, the price of the photocopy, and in a minority of cases the price of a used copy. "Other" includes a diverse range of reasons, including books authored by faculty members or concern with the quality of photocopies.

As with new materials, the percentage of materials bought used was quite low. Roughly a third of students reported buying no used materials; another third bought less than 20 percent used. Only 11 percent were in the top two quintiles. Although there is a sizable market for used trade books in Buenos Aires, it does not extend to textbooks and other classroom materials. In short, students mostly buy new materials when (and in a majority of cases only when) they are interested in preserving them beyond their classroom use.

When we asked students an open-ended question about the "things you see as help-ing you to access the materials you need," answers gravitated toward digital access outside formal channels, sharing via social networks, and—above all—photocopying:

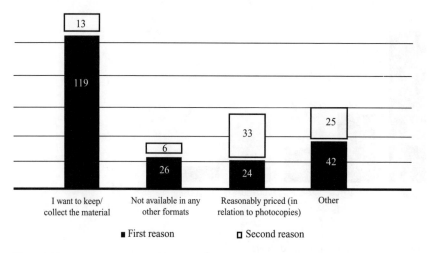

Figure 4.3
What are your easons for buying new?

- 27 percent mentioned photocopying
- 21 percent mentioned the Internet in general
- 13.5 percent mentioned file sharing sites in particular
- 10 percent mentioned student center CDs
- 6 percent mentioned other groups of students;
- 4 percent mentioned faculty members.

In contrast, only 4 percent mentioned the campus learning management system (LMS), 4 percent referred to the library, and less than 1 percent cited scholarly databases. The publications department for the school, the OPFyL, was not mentioned at all.

We also asked students to identify the main obstacles to access to the materials they need. High costs and lack of availability (either in the marketplace or at the Student Center) were the top-cited obstacles by a wide margin, with cost appearing in 29 percent of responses and lack of available translations in 18 percent. Among the most frequently cited problems was not lack of availability of materials, per se, but lack of capacity to copy them: 25 percent of students complained about long lines at Student Center photocopy machines.

The striking finding in both results is the minimal role of the university overall, either as a means of or an obstacle to access. The 67 percent "satisfaction" rate found in the 2011 UBA survey appears to have little to do with university policies or efforts. In contrast, it has a lot to do with the strengths, weaknesses, and responsiveness of students and student centers, copy shops, faculty members, and the anonymous Internet

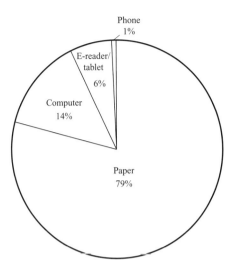

Figure 4.4
How do you do most of your reading?

users who circulate materials on the web. The high level of dissatisfaction with the Student Center—long lines, late availability of material, poor coordination with faculty—is an indicator of where the actual intermediaries are found.

The paradox, if there is one, is that while the Internet and digital media play a large role in the acquisition of materials, they appear to play a relatively minor role in the actual work of most students. In response to a question about how students do most of their reading, reading on paper was the overwhelming favorite.

These answers are not necessarily mutually exclusive. Clearly many students print out materials based on digital copies. Over time, these numbers will probably shift toward all-digital reading. But for now the photocopy still rules.

The Losing Battle against Copying

Student-organized photocopying has largely circumvented price and availability barriers to access at the UBA. With rare exceptions, this solution is illegal in Argentina. Argentine copyright law has no provisions for educational exceptions, library limitations or exceptions or fair use, putting it in the company of only twenty-one other countries worldwide (Crews 2014). This prohibition extends to any copies—including digital copies—made without permission of the rights holder. Violations are not only civil matters, but also criminal ones that can result in incarceration.[17]

Copy machines—first mimeographs and later more efficient photocopiers—began to be widely used in Argentina in the early 1970s. As the first photocopied texts began to circulate, publishers were quick to invoke Article 72, paragraph A of the copyright law, which establishes criminal penalties for those who "edit, sell, or reproduce, by whatever means or instrument an unpublished work or a published work without the permission of the author or rights holder."

Among the first targets was Maria de las Mercedes Jáuregui de Canedo, by then president of the Student Center at the School of Philosophy and Letters at the UBA. In 1972, Jáuregui was charged with violating Article 72 for mimeographing and selling materials for sociology classes. She was acquitted by a lower court, but the public prosecutor in the case joined the plaintiff in an appeal. In November 1973, the appellate court ruled 2–1 for acquittal. Writing for the majority, Judge Prats Cardona argued:

I share the view expressed by Judge Rojas Pellerano [the dissenting vote] regarding the extent of protection afforded by Law 11.723 ... [but] in relation to this concrete case [...] which involves two mimeographed documents of 13 and 90 pages, destined to facilitate the understanding of specific themes and copied by students at the UBA School of Philosophy and Letters without intent of public or indiscriminate sale ... I think that the accused, in her capacity as a representative of the Student Center, could think with some reason that the nature, purpose, and limited scope allowed for publication, and introduce a reasonable doubt as to the illegality of such action.

In 1975, a second case was brought against a UBA student, Carlos Ladowski—this time from the School of Economics. Ladowski led a small group of students who photocopied textbooks in a classroom, on a machine given to them by the school administration for that purpose. Like Jáuregui, he was charged with criminal copyright infringement under Article 72.

The judge, James Fuentes, found Ladowski guilty and sentenced him to a one-month suspended sentence (with the additional requirement to pay court costs). In his ruling, the judge made an argument that would later become common in publishing enforcement efforts: a purchased photocopy is a lost sale for the publisher: "We must conclude that [economic harm] exists in the case in question since the active participation of Ladowski in publishing the photocopy of the textbooks in itself constitutes economic harm to the authors of the respective works, given that some of the students might prefer to acquire those copies and thereby diminish the author's sales." On appeal, however, the appellate judges overturned Fuentes, finding—as in the Jáuregui case—that the circumstances of the case merited acquittal.

Publishers continued to bring cases against students and faculty under Article 72 and they continued to lose them.[18] In 2007, philosophy professor Horacio Potel was sued by the Argentinean Chamber of Books (CAL) for making texts by Heidegger,

Derrida, and Nietzsche available on websites he had built to support his teaching—a practice he had begun in 1999. The suit was initiated at the behest of Les Éditions de Minuit, a publisher of Derrida's work, and was promoted by the French Embassy, which invoked "the golden rule" of intellectual property (Hax 2009). (The Nietzsche component was dropped when someone pointed out that Nietzsche's work had entered the public domain decades earlier).

The case moved forward slowly, then quickly. In Potel's account: "I didn't hear a word about any of this until 2009, when the police banged on my door in the middle of the night to check my address. It was a terrible situation. All the police said was: "You already know what this is about." It was not until the next day that we were able to find out what the charges entailed. I, a philosophy professor, was charged with disseminating philosophical texts for free."[19] The circumstances of the case produced a significant public outcry. Under pressure, CAL decided not to pursue the case. Because this was a criminal matter, however, the withdrawal of the plaintiff did not end it. The public prosecutor decided to continue the case. Potel's motion to dismiss was rejected, and Potel was required to post a bond of 40,000 pesos. While waiting for trial, however, the State Prosecutor reversed course and dropped the charges, observing: "Although the behavior displayed by the accused fits without difficulty into the penal framework … the insignificant harm that may have been caused to the property of the rights holder does not warrant the severe sanctions of this judicial process."[20]

Where a profit motive could be more easily established, publisher campaigns had somewhat more success. In 1999, actions against a group of twelve copy shop owners near UBA campuses resulted in a mix of probation, community service, and small fines. The faculty and students identified in the investigations were not pursued (Clarín 1999). In 2001, publishers succeeded in passing a bill to raise fines for unauthorized copying—the "Law to Promote Books and Reading" (Law 25.446). In 2002 and 2003, cases were brought against two more copy shop owners, Juan Mogus and José Luis Sanchez, resulting in prison sentences of eighteen months.[21]

Despite the protection that judges afforded students and faculty, educational limitations and exceptions did not coalesce into a clear or consistently reproduced doctrine. None of the acquittals addressed the issue. On several occasions, judges found technicalities that allowed them to avoid sentencing students under criminal law, such as the argument that "to photocopy a photocopy is not a crime."[22] Although such decisions favored the students and established increasingly elaborate precedents against the use of Article 72 in such contexts, they skirted the underlying question of the role of copyright law and of university policies in enabling affordable access to educational materials. Instead, what began as more or less informal practices and forms of complicity between students and universities became more formalized and widespread. Student responsibility for organizing access to materials for their peers became a norm and ultimately a duty assumed by student associations. In some cases, the universities provide the space or other forms of subsidies to sustain this practice. The result is a de facto rather than de jure set of educational exceptions, more or less recognized and tolerated by the major institutional players.

This system of subsidized and unlicensed copying continued until 2009, when the UBA announced that it had entered into a blanket licensing agreement for photocopying with an organization representing some authors and publishers, CADRA.[23] Under the agreement, the university would pay a little more than $2 per student, or a total of around $700,000 per year when multiplied across the 300,000 students in the UBA system. The agreement had a four-year term, after which it could be renewed or renegotiated. With Horacio Patel facing criminal charges, student leaders saw a process of shakedown by the publishers and university capitulation. Every year for the next four years, the student leadership at the School of Philosophy and Letters and the School of Social Sciences unanimously passed statements repudiating the agreements. In 2013, after a lengthy process of review and continuing concerns about the transparency of the arrangement, the university decided not to renew the agreement.

Toward Online Digital Libraries

Until he was singled out for prosecution, Horacio Potel was typical of many of the early student and faculty experimenters with scholarly communication on the Internet. For many, it was a natural step from sharing photocopies within campus networks to posting digitized texts on personal or class websites. As Internet adoption increased in the early 2000s, small-scale, disorganized, public, noncommercial posting of materials flourished, racing ahead of legal online availability, norms around digital use, and enforcement.

In a few cases, these small-scale and personal efforts grew into more ambitious programs of collection and distribution—acquiring catalogs and search functions that allowed them to play larger roles in addressing the problems of access to books and other materials. For the most part, these sites emerged in parallel to the larger file sharing communities that developed around music, software, and film.

There is little systematic information about these Spanish-language online digital library projects; most keep low profiles to avoid attention from rights holders and police. But the largest is almost certainly Hansi Libros, a collection of more than eighty thousand titles that dates back to the early 2000s. Many of the Hansi collaborators were veterans of earlier online book-sharing communities such as FTP de Michel, a book-hosting site that closed in 2005 after receiving threats from CEDRO, the collective rights management organization for the Spanish publishing industry.

Hansi is the progenitor and, in many respects, the source of texts for most of the Spanish-language online digital libraries. It was the first to make a concerted effort to pull together all the digitized books available through the other channels and mediums, such as personal websites, IRC channels, FTPs archives, and so on. It was the first to gather them into a user-friendly website and among the first to develop (and share) a content management and cataloguing system specially designed to handle texts.

In a 2013 interview with the author, one of the Hansi collaborators described how the core group worked: "We have two or three basic tasks. There are people looking for material. When a new book appeared that we don't have, we got it, check to see if it is complete, categorize it, and try to add a review. Month after month, these titles are added to the site. Then we create lists of the books of the week or month, depending on how the fishing went."

Others saw their participation as a continuation of their student experiences:

I began typing copies on a Lexicon 80 typewriter for the student center at the University of La Plata in the 1970s. When the Internet emerged, it was easy for me to start scanning, using OCR software, and correcting the results. I always read a lot and was interested in the free circulation of culture. It hurt when I couldn't read books because of their high prices, and even more knowing that the authors didn't see this money. I scanned books that didn't sell—Herman Boch, for example. And I had a team of scanners—a librarian in Navarra, an Argentinean with a bookstore in Stockholm who sent me stuff.

Hansi Libros changed its name and domain several times in order to avoid enforcement efforts directed against its hosting providers. On more than one occasion, it lost gigabytes of information due to changes in hosting policy. As with LibGen in Russia, this pressure has pushed Hansi to become more a distributed network of collaborators and systems, with greater redundancy. As one collaborator put it (in an IRC interview with the author):

Resiliency comes from rapid dissemination and replication. Now, something new is made available across twenty sites within hours. There are metanetworks—every shared interest unconsciously forms a network—and there are dozens of sites that do this. It doesn't matter if one is erased. Even though the law is becoming less flexible, I don't think this dynamic will change. Either new business models will emerge that are fairer to the consumer, or this activity will continue underground.

BiblioFyL

At the UBA, students began to experiment with collaborative, organized digitization and archiving of classroom materials in the mid-2000s. The most prominent of these projects was BiblioFyL, which began in 2007 and continues today, in spite of various difficulties. The early days of the project followed a familiar trajectory of student self-organization, facilitated by listservs and forums. BiblioFyL began as a small-scale Internet forum for the exchange of course materials at the School of Philosophy and Letters. Over time, this exchange became more organized, reaching more students. As its catalog of materials and audience expanded, BiblioFyL moved to a dedicated content management system and website.

Like many other shadow libraries, BiblioFyL had its origins in a classroom community. In 2001, a professor of linguistics and grammar, started Kleopatra,[24] a mailing list devoted to sharing materials for his classes and for fielding questions about the curriculum. Said the professor: "From the beginning, what I tried to do was ensure that the course materials circulated, so that people brought them to class, always thinking about how I could optimize class time. Unlike the virtual libraries of today, there was no wider or more open agenda."

Because linguistics and grammar are among the required classes in the School of Philosophy and Letters, participants on the list tended to be recent entrants into the major. At the time, the school had not yet introduced an LMS or other official channels of electronic communication.[25]

Although there were other mailing lists for other subjects, such as history and anthropology, none had as much traction in the community as Kleopatra. Soon, Kleopatra became the principal means of communicating many types of information at the school, spanning numerous disciplines. The breadth of the resource ensured that students stayed on the list even after the completion of their studies in the field. Between 2004 and 2007, the list averaged 300 messages per month, ranging up to 900 messages in busy months.

Support for more systematic digitization and distribution of course materials began to grow in 2006 and 2007. In 2007, the Student Center began to digitize required readings for distribution on CDs, though Student Center leaders disavowed any intention to put them online. The discussion about what to do with digital materials nonetheless grew on Kleopatra and on other disciplinary listservs. Anthropology students convened a meeting to discuss the issue. Others—primarily from the Kleopatra list—jumped straight to implementation.

In 2007, two students set up a forum designed to address the technical limitations of Kleopatra and provide a more structured space for discussion and the exchange of course materials. In the words of one of the administrators: "It seemed to me that we had discovered a missing space for students, especially as I wasn't one who hung out on campus to talk. I went to campus, took my classes, and went home. This didn't allow for a lot of connections with people or opportunities to ask questions and discuss things. It seemed to me that this space was missing, and so I said, ok, let's make it."

This effort grew into ForoFyL—the Forum for Philosophy and Letters—which was hosted on a free server. In its inaugural email, ForoFyL described its mission as digitizing "texts of various kinds, daily publishing of recorded lectures, books, and resource sites." It proposed to be a place for "discussion, play, learning, and teaching" and for "satisfying the academic and human needs for communication among students."[26] As one of the founders put it, the site "quickly established itself as a destination for this little world of digital humanists, who were interested in books and who had grown up with digital technologies. There was a ready community."

"My participation in ForoFyL started after I offered digitized materials on Kleopatra," one student explained. "I had digitized them in order to print out copies for a colleague, and took advantage of this to share them with others as well. But the system was impractical because one couldn't add files to an archive—one had to send them individually to whoever asked for them. ForoFyL solved this problem."

"It wasn't as if we had these files and said, whoever wants them should ask me for them," another student recalled. "At some point the idea emerged that we could upload them to a place where anyone could access them without asking permission. This was good because it worked without there being someone in charge."

Another forum participant came to the project with experience in a different digital library effort, la Biblioteca Recargada (the Library Reloaded), which operated primarily via Yahoo Groups. The student gave details of this experience:

When I began my courses at the School, I had less time for the Biblioteca Recargada. But I discovered the possibility of collaborating with my classmates. I was able to bring things that I knew were on the Internet, or that I had already digitized. So I created two mailing lists called los Altillos (the Attics). The Attics were a bunch of texts that I had digitized for my own pleasure, but which served to catalyze some of the things that gave rise to BiblioFyL.

This convergence of interests reached critical mass in 2007 with the founding of ForoFyL. Many of the participants had experience in other online digital library projects—la Biblioteca Recargada, Libros Gratis, Hansi Libros, and others that lived on IRC—contributing variously as editors, submitters, or re-uploaders who ensured that the archives survived takedown notices and other threats.

Over time, the collaboration around ForoFyL produced a division of labor. Some searched Student Center computers for digitized files. Others had access to industrial scanners, with automatic document feeders, and digitized materials that their classmates gave them. Others worked with scanners at home. Others scoured the Internet for material relevant to their majors, including IRC-based libraries and other sites.

In general, these materials shared two features: they were important to the curriculum at the School of Philosophy and Letters, and they were, in the great majority of cases, impossible to find on the commercial market. Following the student center practice of building from course syllabi, many of the materials were single chapters or excerpts of longer works, which were otherwise especially expensive to acquire.

The sharing and organizing of this material followed the strategy adopted by many file-sharing link sites. Materials were uploaded to external storage services, such as—at the time—Esnips and 4shared. Links to those materials were organized and shared in the "files" section of the forum. As one collaborator recalled: "It was a random concatenation of materials, built from the things people were exchanging. But rather suddenly, it had a lot of texts, which people began to organize within the framework of the forum."

By the end of 2007, ForoFyL had outgrown the capabilities of its free hosting service and soon moved to a paid service. As the files section continued to grow, it also became clear that the file exchange functions needed to be disentangled from the conversational functions of the forum. In early 2008, several of the collaborators rebuilt the files section into a dedicated site. This was BiblioFyL—a library of links to external services that hosted the files, supported by a community of collectors, scanners, uploaders, and site editors. In the early days, said one of the founders, "We grabbed all the files we had already uploaded [via ForoFyL] and systematized everything on a spreadsheet. Then we started manually adding new texts. The new file manager launched with 5,000 texts. By late 2009 we had 10,000."

The new file system changed the nature of the collaborative enterprise. Management of the system required greater differentiation of responsibilities. Administration increasingly focused on the acquisition and improvement of texts, while technical contributions involved streamlining of the experience for contributors. Both, in practice, became concentrated in fewer hands.

The BiblioFyL example proved attractive to other student groups. In 2009, members of the School of Social Sciences launched BiblioSoc, the first of several BiblioFyL clones at the UBA. One of the collaborators in BiblioSoc characterized the effort this way:

The thing that got us interested in the topic was the notice of the agreement between UBA and CADRA. We asked ourselves: what is the UBA doing? It's trying to regularize a situation that was the product of the dismantling of EUDEBA, that is to say the rise of photocopying but also the commodification of knowledge, which requires that faculty publish certain kinds of books in order to increase their professional ratings. It creates the paradox whereby their own students have to illegally photocopy their books or those of investigators in their own academic units.

Other shadow libraries began to appear in 2011, created by students in other schools within the UBA, with varying grades of success. Thus was born BiblioPsi in the School of Psychology and BiblioCEN in the School of Natural Sciences. With more or less success, these started from the same principles that had animated BiblioFyL, despite significant differences in the composition and organizational agendas of these groups. Like BiblioFyL, the participants understand their work explicitly as a response to the failure of the university to implement access policies that support the university's democratic ideals. As one student noted, "The school administration can't even put doors on the bathroom stalls and the students have to upload their own materials."

Notice and Takedown

In September 2009, the administrators of BiblioFyL received a notification from El Server, the host of both ForoFyL and BiblioFyL, informing them of a takedown notice directed against their sites. If the students did not take down the sites, El Server warned, the data would be turned over to the sender of the notice. According to an admin,

When we got the notification, it seemed to me like a good moment to separate the forum from the library, which had continued to be closely linked. BiblioFyL was a subdomain of ForoFyL, and I thought it likely that if the library was taken down the forum would be as well. The Potel case was happening at the same time and seemed to set a bad precedent.

Just the week before, the rights' management organization, CADRA, had held a public talk at the university. So it wasn't as if no one was aware of what was happening with copyright issues. But when I had to take down the library we got lots of complaints. The users didn't care what had happened. They only cared when the library would be back online—without consideration of who would put it back up or what kind of work it would require. Getting so many complaints was completely demoralizing for me.

However, there were signs of support, including among the faculty.[27] After the library was taken down, BiblioFyL participants met to discuss possible next steps. The issue came to the attention of the school's Academic Secretary, who tried to help find a way through the impasse. One of the collaborators remembered it this way:

I think they [the administration] did not comprehend the problem until that moment because, for them, the question of access to materials was answered by the Student Center. What could go wrong? In theory, professors came, left materials, people came and took them and everything was fine. In an ideal world that's enough. In theory everything was organized, and the remaining problems were the little ones, the day-to-day ones.

In the course of the meetings, however, it became clear that the school did not have much to offer. Most of the time, it shielded itself in legal arguments.

That is where things stood at the beginning of 2010. BiblioFyL returned to operation on a different server—severed from ForoFyL. Relations with the Student Center were formalized, and the administration of BiblioFyL passed to Student Center staff.

Although there were no major changes at the institutional level, the fall and restoration of BiblioFyL coincided with the gradual adoption of other technologies for sharing materials, including growing use of the university's virtual campus platform[28] and increased use of Facebook by students. Both the forum and the library lost some of the intense participatory dynamic that had made them essential in earlier years, when other tools did not exist. If the virtual campus succeeded in playing some of these roles for some faculty, it was largely in contradiction with the law and stated policies of the university. As with the photocopiers and later BiblioFyL at the Student Center, the policy was laissez-faire. As a result, access to materials still depends on Student Center photocopies, off-campus copy shops, files uploaded by faculty to the LMS, and other shadow libraries.

Reintermediation

Given the Argentine tradition of policy and institutional responses to the problem of access to materials, it is remarkable that responsibility devolved so completely to students. This delegation or neglect reflected a transformation in understanding of the educational mission at the highest levels. The "golden age" of the Argentine university system produced a philosophy of access built around the extension of the publishing model—the "good, handsome, and cheap" and above all *widely available* catalog of educational titles that formed the core of Eudeba's mission. But when that model was crushed in the political and economic crises of the 1960s, 1970s, and 1980s, nothing took its place.

The university publishing sector is more complex than in the early 1960s, and also far less ambitious. There are more than forty recognized publishers (the precise number is difficult to estimate because of the number of subunits or publishing offices operating more or less autonomously within universities).[29] Nearly all focus on publishing research produced by the local faculty rather than attending to the needs of students, much less the general public (De Sagástizabal 2002, 13). University press contributions to the publication of scientific and technical books are also marginal.

The libraries were also unable to adjust. Budget problems across the university system were chronic from the 1960s on. Space constraints affected the ability of libraries to serve large student bodies—especially in relation to the waves of growth in the public university system in the 1960s and 1980s. With the restoration of democracy in 1983, the character of the student body also changed dramatically, with many more part-time working students for whom having time to spend in the library is at a premium. By the time of our study, the role of the library as an intermediary for materials was minimal.

Yet the transformation of the print ecosystem promised, if not yet broadly imposed, by digital technologies has forced some rethinking of university publishing and library roles. These efforts—some dating back over a decade—have had mixed success.

In 1995, university publishers formed the National University Press Network (la Red de Editoriales de Universidades Nacionales, or REUN) in an effort to address chronic problems with distribution and low-margin, low-print-run publishing.[30] REUN's efforts focused on physical, printed books, although as the Internet grew, it was the logical body to establish digital standards for the sector. Like every other university press system, it lagged severely in doing so. The network was not able to establish uniform policies for Internet sales or digital distribution of their books, though several member presses moved forward with their own efforts.[31]

This lack of a common "digital strategy" for university presses led, in 2012, to an effort to develop a shared digital distribution platform, with participation by the Ministry of Education, REUN, the Secretary of Culture,[32] and the National Institute for Industrial Technology.[33] As Rudolfo Hamawi, then director of Cultural Industries at the Ministry of Culture put it, the effort was needed to "break the blockade on distribution" of digital materials. The result was the Portal for Argentine University Books (Portal del Libro Universitario Argentino), launched in 2013 and currently inactive.[34] The Portal allowed for downloading of university titles, but the participation of universities has been limited to date.

University libraries had (and have) similar coordination problems. Many have identified open access to university research as an important part of their digitization strategies, but few have succeeded in shifting their universities toward open access policies or in developing digital repositories capable of managing the resulting inflow of materials.[35] Some progress is being made: the SEDICI[36] at the University of La Plata, Memoria Académica at the Faculty of Humanities and Science Education of University of La Plata,[37] the Digital Library[38] of the Faculty of Natural Science of the University of Buenos Aires,[39] the repository of the University of Córdoba,[40] and the repository of the University of Mendoza[41] are working to develop university policy and technical infrastructure. But overall, practices remain inconsistent, poorly connected across services,[42] and focused on the research of faculty members rather than the curricular needs of undergraduates.

By the late 2000s, however, librarians had partly succeeded in making access to research a public policy issue: nearly two-thirds of investment in academic research in Argentina was attributable to public funding.[43] At the librarians' urging, the Ministry of Science, Technology and Innovation drafted Law 26.899, governing the "Creation of Institutional Open Access Digital Repositories, Owned or Shared." Passed in 2013, the law required that all publicly funded research be made available online under an open access license through digital repositories maintained by the national universities and their research institutes.[44]

While promising, it will be some years before the law is fully implemented, and longer until the archives achieve sufficient critical mass to become important teaching resources. There are also technical and cultural hurdles. Some institutions have struggled to build digital repositories; most have faced difficulties in changing faculty habits.

It is unclear how these forces will play out. The open access movement continues to rely on Creative Commons and other voluntary licensing schemes that—for now, at least—do not address the problem of access to the vast majority of materials used in the classroom. Publishers, for their part, lack consensus about a digital business strategy, with some struggling to preserve the status quo while others move toward mixed models of open digital licensing and physical sales. Despite some progress on digital access models, universities continue to rely on student-organized access to materials, while remaining largely silent on the copyright issues that make such activity illegal.

Notes

The author would like to thank colleagues at BiblioFyL for their work over the years and for their generous contributions of time and testimony to this project. I would also like to thank Guido Gamba for helping me systematize the results of the survey and for his observations; Ezequiel Acuña and Matías Raia for their corrections; and Pablo Ortellado for his attentive reading. The remaining errors are mine. Unless otherwise noted, access dates for all URLs in the notes are August 31, 2017.

1. The main instigator of this shift was Risieri Frondizi, who was elected president of the University of Buenos Aires in 1958. One of Risieri's first steps was to open a publishing unit, and to task members of the university faculty led by Antonio Orfila-Reynal—at the time, director of the Argentine branch of the Fondo de Cultura Económica (FCE), then the most important university

press in Mexico and one of the most important in Latin America—to explore the possibility of converting the unit into a large-scale university press.

2. Regarding the fascinating career of Boris Spivacow, see *Boris Spivacow: Memorias de un sueño argentino*, a long interview conducted by Delia Maunás (1995) months before his death, and *Boris Spivacow: el señor editor de América Latina*, by Judith Gociol (2009), a book filled with anecdotes and stories about the editor.

3. Among the examples of this politics of publishing were collections like *Arte para Todos, Cuentistas y Pintores* [Art for everyone: Artists and painters], which sought to "bring art out into the streets," or the edition of the Argentine classic *Martín Fierro*, by José Hernández, with illustrations by Castagnino, which sold 30,000 copies in its first four days and which ultimately ran to 250,000 copies.

4. From Article 69 of the minutes of Eudeba board meetings, compiled in *Libros para todos* (2012).

5. According to the 1965 proceedings, Eudeba counted 830 distributors and bookstores that offered Eudeba materials; 103 news and magazine stands; 40 stands installed in universities; 41 street kiosks; 7 kiosks in hospitals; 140 sales agents, and two of its own bookstores.

6. The FCE is no longer a university press.

7. From article 68 of the minutes of Eudeba board meetings, compiled in *Libros para Todos* (2012).

8. A good reference book on censorship during the dictatorships is *Censura, autoritarismo y cultura: Argentina 1960–1983* (Avellaneda 1986).

9. In 1967, less than a year after the formation of the press, Spivacow launched its signature collection *Capítulo: Historia de la literatura argentina*, which was a literary work accompanied by a collectible booklet written by academics and intellectuals. Through such initiatives, Eudeba and later CEAL became poles of attraction for teachers, professors, and intellectuals in the period. Other equally memorable collections from the period included *Historia del movimiento obrero* [History of the workers movement], *Biblioteca política Argentina, La historia popular, Cuentos del Chiribitil* (for children), *Siglomundo, Nueva Enciclopedia del Mundo Joven, Transformaciones, Historia de América en el siglo XX, Los hombres de la historia*, and *Mi país, tu país* (Argentine geography).

10. The order came from Héctor Gustavo de la Serna, a retired military chief who acted as a federal judge, and who justified his action under National Security Law 20.8404, which covered "Penalties for all subversive activities in all of its manifestations." To read the text of the law, see http://www.infoleg.gov.ar/infolegInternet/anexos/70000-74999/73268/norma.htm.

11. The intelligence report can be read in "Proyecto de Reconocimiento a la Labor del CEAL" (Bill for Recognizing the Work of CEAL), developed by Antonio Morante (who additionally recounts a large part of the history of CEAL). http://www1.hcdn.gov.ar/proyxml/expediente.asp?fundamentos=si&numexp=5296-D-2010.

12. See Gettino 2008 for a deep account of these strategies.

13. According to an analysis conducted by El Centro de Estudios para la Producción (2005), a unit of the Ministry of the Economy.

14. Although the survey is annual, results are published only every four years.

15. Our survey was conducted via an online form, circulated through email lists and online forums. Most respondents were undergraduates from the nine majors available at the Faculty: history, literature, geography, library science, anthropology, philosophy, education science, publishing, arts, with literature and history—the largest majors—predominating. Nearly all students (97 percent) have computers and Internet access at home. Around a quarter (26 percent) had tablets or e-reading devices.

16. According to Article 72 and 72bis of Law 11.723, http://www.infoleg.gov.ar/infolegInternet/anexos/40000-44999/42755/texact.htm. The main exceptions involve books in the public domain or distributed under a Creative Commons license, or the reproduction of news stories.

17. According to Article 72 and 72bis of Law 11.723, http://www.infoleg.gov.ar/infolcgInternet/anexos/40000-44999/42755/texact.htm.

18. In 1995, Eudeba sued UBA student Elias Litman for photocopying coursepacks. Litman was acquitted. See "Litman, Elias D. s/inf, Art.72," 1995.

19. The full interview can be found here: http://www.signandsight.com/features/2102.html.

20. The news about the charges being dropped and also the full argument can be found here (in Spanish): https://www.vialibre.org.ar/2009/11/21/sobreseen-a-horacio-potel/.

21. See, respectively, CNCP, sala II, del April 22, 2002, "Mogus Juan V.," LA LEY 2002-E, 198; and CNCP, sala III, "Sánchez José Luis," July 10, 2003.

22. In the Litman case, the Fifth Chamber of the National Criminal Court absolved Litman on the grounds that his behavior was inconsistent with the offense described by the statute because it involved reproductions of coursepack materials and that a photocopy of a photocopy could not be considered criminal. The plaintiff (in this case, Eudeba) appealed to the Supreme Court, resulting in a narrow administrative criticism of the Fifth Chamber's interpretation of the law.

23. CADRA is a nonprofit organization founded in 2002. It is not a collecting society—a role that in Argentina requires presidential authorization. On the agreement, see Reynoso 2009 and Reggiani 2009.

24. See https://groups.yahoo.com/neo/groups/Kleopatra/info.

25. For example, the School of Philosophy and Letters had no mailing lists or information about majors available on the website. For such information, students had to go in person to the relevant departments.

26. See https://groups.yahoo.com/neo/groups/Kleopatra/conversations/topics/11570.

27. For example, the article by literature professor Daniel Link in *Perfil*, a daily newspaper, entitled "Una pena extraordinaria": http://linkillo.blogspot.com.ar/2009/11/una-pena-extraordinaria.html.

28. The virtual campus (http://campus.filo.uba.ar) is a tool intended to support classroom teaching. It has been inconsistently adopted—although probably with the greatest frequency in the School of Philosophy and Letters.

29. On this subject, see De Sagastizábal 2002 and De Sagastizábal, Ramo, and Uribe 2006.

30. The statute incorporating REUN is available at http://www2.biblio.unlp.edu.ar/jubiuna/Members/elofie/EstatutoREUNreformado2007.doc.

31. Among the notable examples: the University of Quilmes Press, the Publication Center at the National University of the Litoral, and—since 2011—Eudeba Digital. Eudeba Digital made a number of controversial decisions, including the use of Adobe digital rights management and requiring that users have a bank account to obtain a discount on a reading device—a step that excluded many students (Vallejos 2011).

32. Now the Ministry of Culture.

33. See Saavedra 2012.

34. See the Portal Universitario del Libro Argentino, http://plua.educ.ar/. This link worked until 2014; the program has since been dismantled.

35. A short overview regarding Open Access in Latin America can be found at http://www.unesco.org/new/en/communication-and-information/portals-and-platforms/goap/access-by-region/latin-america-and-the-caribbean/.

36. See http://sedici.unlp.edu.ar/.

37. See http://www.memoria.fahce.unlp.edu.ar/.

38. See http://digital.bl.fcen.uba.ar/gsdl-282/cgi-bin/library.cgi.

39. A comprehensive list of all the digital repositories of Argentina can be found at http://www.biblioteca.mincyt.gob.ar/sitio/page?view=repositorios-nacionales.

40. See https://rdu.unc.edu.ar/.

41. See http://bdigital.uncu.edu.ar/.

42. For example, few repositories are connected with broader Latin American Open Access repositories like REDALyC (http://www.redalyc.org/), leading to inconsistent records. For a good overview of the many Open Access initiatives in Argentina, see Miguel et al. 2013.

43. Albornoz, Macedo, and Alfaraz 2010.

44. And other members of the National Science, Technology and Innovation System. See http://www.ip-watch.org/2013/12/16/argentina-passes-open-access-act-making-publicly-funded-research-available/.

References

Aguado, Amelia. 2006. "Políticas editoriales e impacto cultural en la Argentina (1880–2000)." *Información, Cultura y Sociedad* 15: 95–105. http://eprints.rclis.org/17132/1/ics15p95-105.pdf (accessed August 31, 2017).

Albornoz, Mario, Mariano Matos Macedo, and Claudio Alfaraz. 2010. "Latin America," in UNESCO Science Report 2010—The Current Status of Science around the World," dir. L. Brito. UNESCO, 77–101. http://www.unesco.org/new/fileadmin/MULTIMEDIA/HQ/SC/pdf/sc_usr10 _la_EN.pdf (accessed August 31, 2017).

Avellaneda, Andrés. 1986. *Censura, autoritarismo y cultura: Argentina 1960–1983*. Buenos Aires: Centro Editor de América Latina.

Crews, Kenneth. 2014. *Study on Copyright Limitations and Exceptions for Libraries and Archives*. SCCR/29/3. OMPI, Geneva.

Clarín. 1999. "Probation a libreros por fotocopiar libros." *Clarín*, June 21, https://www.clarin.com/ sociedad/probation-libreros-fotocopiar-libros_0_rkAlwITlRKg.html (accessed August 31, 2017).

De Sagastizábal, Leandro. 2002. *Informe sobre la situación y perspectivas de las editoriales universitarias en Argentina*. Buenos Aires, Instituto Internacional para la Educación Superior en América Latina y el Caribe (IESALC) y Ministerio de Educación, Ciencia y Tecnología de la República Argentina, Secretaría de Políticas Universitarias. http://unesdoc.unesco.org/images/0014/001494/ 149476so.pdf (accessed August 31, 2017).

De Sagastizábal, Leandro, Claudio Ramo, and Richard Uribe. 2006. *Las editoriales universitarias en América Latina*. Bogotá, Instituto Internacional para la Educación Superior en América Latina y el Caribe (IESALC) y Centro Regional para el Fomento del Libro en América Latina y el Caribe (CERLALC). http://www.cerlalc.org/secciones/libro_desarrollo/Editoriales_universitarias.pdf (accessed August 31, 2017).

El Centro de Estudios para la Producción. 2005. "La industria del libro en Argentina."

Gettino, Octavio. 2008. *El capital de la cultura: Las industrias culturales en Argentina*. Buenos Aires: Ediciones Ciccus.

Gociol, Judith. 2009. *Boris Spivacow: el señor editor de América Latina*. Buenos Aires: Capital Intelectual.

Hax, Andres. 2009. "Francia impulsó la baja de un sitio argentino que difundía obras filosóficas." February 28. http://edant.clarin.com/diario/2009/02/28/sociedad/s-01867515.htm (accessed August 31, 2017).

Libros para todos. Colecciones de EUDEBA bajo la gestión de Boris Spivacow (1958–1966). 2012. Buenos Aires: Biblioteca Nacional.

Link, Daniel. 2009. "Una pena extraordinaria." *Diario Perfil*, June 11. http://www.perfil.com/ columnistas/Una-pena-extraordinaria-20091106-0055.html (accessed August 31, 2017).

Maunás, Delia. 1995. *Boris Spivacow: Memoria de un sueño argentino*. Buenos Aires: Ediciones Colihue SRL.

Miguel, Sandra, et al. 2013. "Situación y perspectivas del desarrollo del Acceso Abierto en Argentina." *Palabra Clave* 2 (2): 1–10. Universidad Nacional de La Plata, La Plata. April. http://www.palabraclave.fahce.unlp.edu.ar/article/view/PCv2n2a01 (accessed August 31, 2017).

Reggiani, Federico. 2009. "Las malas ideas: 'Centros de administración de derechos reprográficos' y servicios bibliotecarios" [En línea]. Curso-taller El acceso a la información en el contexto de la Ley 11.723: Una mirada desde las bibliotecas. November 20, La Plata. http://www.fuentesmemoria.fahce.unlp.edu.ar/trab_eventos/ev.514/ev.514.pdf (accessed August 31, 2017).

Reynoso, Susana. 2009. "La UBA pagará derechos por las fotocopias que usen sus alumnos." *La Nación*. May 14. http://www.lanacion.com.ar/1127847-la-uba-pagara-derechos-por-las-fotocopias-que-usen-sus-alumnos (accessed August 31, 2017).

Saavedra, Agustín. 2012. "Una sala virtual de lectura." *Página/12*. April 24. http://www.pagina12.com.ar/diario/universidad/10-192553-2012-04-24.html (accessed January 28, 2015).

UBA. 2012. Coordinación general de planificación estratégica e institucional. *Resultados finales: Censo de 2011*. Buenos Aires, Universidad de Buenos Aires. http://www.uba.ar/institucional/censos/Estudiantes2011/estudiantes2011.pdf.

Vallejos, Soledad. 2011. *Eudeba, en el mundo del libro electrónico. Página/12*. June 24. http://www.pagina12.com.ar/diario/sociedad/3-170736-2011-06-24.html (accessed August 31, 2017).

5 Access to Learning Resources in Post-apartheid South Africa

Eve Gray and Laura Czerniewicz

Any inquiry into how university students get the learning resources they need for their education in post-apartheid South Africa must deal with three interrelated subjects: the legacy of apartheid, which continues to structure educational opportunities in important ways more than twenty years after the first democratic election; the organization and increasingly radical transformation of the commercial publishing market, which has been the primary source of textbooks and other materials in the system; and—common to all of the chapters in this book—the mix of new-technology-enabled strategies through which students do their best to get the textbooks and other materials they need.

We track three decades of tensions around these issues, as post-apartheid leaders struggle to reform an educational system originally designed primarily to control and oppress rather than educate the majority population. Because the old system had grown up around numerous (and often colonially grounded) accommodations of the global publishing business, international copyright law, and—most important—a structural disregard for whether the system worked in more than a minimal sense, the pressure for reform has produced tensions on all of these fronts.

The end of apartheid began a process of reconnecting South African higher education to the international community and to a publishing environment that had selectively shunned the old regime. This process was shaped by the financial crisis of the South African state as well as by larger global crises. It involved students taking seriously the "right to education" enshrined in the constitution concurrently with the consolidation of the publishing and bookselling industries at home and abroad. Throughout, the new democratic government struggled to accommodate two distinct concepts of reform: the desire to restructure higher education to improve global competitiveness—a market-driven approach—on the one hand, and on the other a more developmental approach coupled with demands by student movements and radical academics for a more complete "decolonization" and Africanization of higher education.

During most of this period, the competitive, market-focused view of the university has prevailed, resulting in the steady reduction of government subsidies in spite of massive increases in student numbers. With public support diminishing, universities have been hard-pressed to seek alternative funding to meet student needs, while students are protesting, with increasing levels of violence, in favor of free higher education. This is, of course, consistent with broader trends in higher education worldwide. What sets the South African situation apart are the extremes of inequality and the concomitant levels of student poverty—both educational and financial—that have needed to be addressed in the wake of apartheid.

The role of shadow libraries in the South African context, during apartheid and after, has to be understood in the light of this dichotomy. On the one hand, extensive photocopying practices, including increasingly sophisticated pirated textbooks, have been the most common practice, rather than comprehensive digital sites. The demand for a decolonized curriculum, on the other hand, looks back to a tradition of subversive production of anti-apartheid content by radical student movements and "oppositional" publishers, as well as collaborative approaches to compiling resources. This was perceived as an "alternative curriculum" by anti-apartheid students who drew on a range of resources to compile their publications, while publishers tried to keep their publications out of the eye of the regime, often distributing them through informal networks.

Higher Education under Apartheid

The control of access to education and to different levels of knowledge was a central pillar of the apartheid state—a way of enforcing the subjugation and difference of the majority black population. This was not a simple matter of a binary divide between black and white, but a complex spatial and ideological mapping of race, class, and geography.

Most of the core practices of segregation in South Africa predated the consolidation of the apartheid state after World War II. Separate schools for white and black South Africans began to appear in the 1910s, after the creation of the Union of South Africa (Jansen 1990). Separate curricula dated from the mid-nineteenth century, with the education available to black South Africans oriented primarily around industrial training.

From these practices, the apartheid regime developed a much more thorough application of racial ideology to the structure of higher education. The resulting system was baroque in its complexity, using tribal identity and rural geography to enforce what the National Party government saw as a "natural" separation and hierarchy. With the passage of the Extension of Universities Act No. 45 in 1959, fully segregated higher education became the law of the land.[1] Henceforth, it was a criminal offense for a "non-white" student to register at an "open" (i.e., white) university without the permission of the minister.

The 1959 Act reshaped the university system around this complex racial vision. Different institutions were created for the several recognized racial groups (white, colored or mixed race, Indian, and black) with different government departments responsible for each. A number of notionally "independent" tribal areas were also created—the so-called Bantustans—each with its own government and separate university system. Some racially segregated colleges were started de novo; others emerged from branches of the distance education provider, UNISA, which later grew into the largest provider of higher education in the country. Among the casualties of these policies were the handful of high-quality colleges that served black students, including the University of Fort Hare, founded by Scottish missionaries in 1916 as the South African Native College. The education Fore Hare offered was elite and Eurocentric—in Nelson Mandela's words, "For young black South Africans like myself, it was Oxford and Cambridge, Harvard and Yale, all rolled into one" (Mandela 1994, 7). It was not a large institution, yet by the time that the apartheid regime reclassified it as a Bantu tribal university, its alumni included a long list of African heads of government and future leaders of the apartheid struggle.[2]

White South Africans attended urban English or Afrikaans universities, perceived as liberal and conservative, respectively. The seven Afrikaans institutions were aligned with the apartheid regime and were authoritarian in their approach, seeing themselves as the providers of civil servants and professionals in the service of apartheid.

The four English universities regarded themselves as international institutions with a strong commitment to academic freedom. Blue-sky research was important and international donor funding helped insulate the institutions from some forms of government pressure. Below the top-tier institutions were fifteen "technikons" or polytechnic schools, divided into eight white institutions and seven black ones. These tended to have a more conservative and instrumentalist orientation than the universities.

For black South Africans, the primary aim of the apartheid education system was to maintain the rigid separation of class and power, in which the majority population served either as low-level workers in the economy or as apartheid civil servants.[3] These objectives were driven at the outset by the needs of the mining sector for a compliant migrant labor force.

Overall, the education system strove to replace individual identity with collective racial and tribal identities—a goal that predicated the location of black universities in remote rural areas. This separation was intensified by the underresourcing of these universities, in spite of steady increases of student numbers, resulting in inadequate facilities, library resources, and underqualified teachers (Jansen 1990). Libraries tended to be stocked with unlicensed photocopies and students relied extensively on copied textbooks and compilations in the absence of a functional and affordable textbook supply chain.

In the apartheid era, the intellectual environment was severely constrained by restrictions on freedom of information, enforced through extensive censorship and a system of "bannings" of authors and works, imprisonment of offending authors, and, in some cases, assassination of activists. Geographic isolation and the poverty of the teaching and learning environment, among other factors, resulted in what Soudien (drawing on the theories of Sen and Ostrom) described as "a massive capability deprivation machine" (Soudien 2013, 57), in which education provided little basis for control over the future. As the newly democratic government set out in the 1990s to reverse the effects of apartheid on higher education, this physical, economic, and psychological deprivation has proved to be a lasting heritage.

Student Resistance and the Publishing Underground

Given the extent of repression in the educational sector during apartheid, it is not surprising that student and faculty resistance emerged as a countervailing force in the apartheid years. This radicalization intensified in the 1970s—the beginning of the end of apartheid. The South African Students Organization (SASO), led by Steve Biko, broke away from the predominantly white, liberal National Union of South African Students (NUSAS) to mobilize black university students against the regime. In the less-resourced black universities, this split aligned many students with the Black Consciousness movement, which promoted a radical break with both the service-oriented curricula imposed by the state and Eurocentric intellectual traditions. Biko was beaten to death by secret police in 1977, but the Black Consciousness student movement continued.

In 1976, around ten thousand high school students in the huge Soweto township outside Johannesburg took to the streets in protest, triggered by an attempt to enforce the teaching of key subjects in Afrikaans—considered the language of repression—rather than in English. When the students were attacked by heavily-armed riot police, the event became a national and international media event and a seminal moment in the anti-apartheid movement. In the protests that followed, hundreds were arrested or killed and a new phase of resistance and repression began, in which the killing, arrest, and torture of students became commonplace. The event proved a watershed for student radicalization across the country, with student protests playing a central role in anti-apartheid activism and large numbers undertaking the risky journey to neighboring countries to join the African National Congress (ANC) (Hyslop 1988; Swilling 1988, 93).

The intellectual underpinnings of the regime also came under fire as a generation of academics argued for a more Afrocentric and class-centered basis for research and teaching. The illicit production and circulation of texts played a large role in this activism. SASO compiled and circulated a wide range of materials, including compilations drawing on Frantz Fanon and the Negritude tradition of Léopold Senghor and Aimé Césaire (and the writings of local Black Consciousness leaders like Biko and Barney Pityana. The smaller but better resourced movement in the white English-speaking universities adopted similar tactics, producing protest literature on their own printing presses and helping to build a radical intellectual alternative to apartheid discourse focused on the history of opposition to colonialism and apartheid, worker rights, and trade union development (Kell 1991; Hofmeyr 2013; Berger 2000; Moss 2014).

These student movements and academic oppositional presses confronted the intense censorship imposed by the apartheid government. The chief vehicles for this censorship were the Publications and Entertainment Act of 1963, which provided for the seizure of "undesirable" publications, and the Suppression of Communism Act of 1950, which prohibited quoting or publishing the work of those on a list of "banned" individuals. The publishing networks thus faced considerable threats of harassment, police violence, "banning orders" (which involving restrictions on movement, association, and communication), imprisonment, torture, and even death.[4]

A wide range of counter-strategies emerged to mitigate these risks while also maintaining the circulation of critical materials. These included the extensive use of informal publishing genres and distribution networks; the willingness of local radical publishers to defy the rules; and radical publishers and university presses in the UK and United States publishing South African works in exile. Banned publications then became objects of smuggling and reprinting through the student and academic networks.

For many student leaders, these underground publications operated as an alternative curriculum, delivered through student magazines and serialized publications and pamphlets. They provided students with access to knowledge relevant to the realities of South African life—something not available in more "neutral" international (or even local) publications and learning resources. Lectures and papers on the political situation and the history of the opposition reached large audiences. On one occasion, University of Witwatersrand students printed 100,000 copies of a protest pamphlet overnight for Soweto student protesters (Moss 2014). These activities aligned with the rise of an alternative radical scholarship that began to be absorbed into the curriculum in the 1980s and 1990s as these students moved on to become faculty members.

Throughout this period, local university presses played a relatively small role in this process. Most were cautious or, in some cases, politically conservative. A small group of independent publishers, however, had closer connections to student radicals and gave voice to academic opposition to the apartheid order. The publishers David Philip, Ravan Press, Skotaville, Taurus, and Ad Donker specialized in radical and anti-apartheid writing and scholarship—subjects whose publication could invite raids and confiscation of stock by the police and banning orders amounting to home imprisonment for publishers (Philip 1991; Evans and Seeber 2000).[5] Early versions of digital typesetting were used in house by Ravan Press and Taurus to prevent linotype compositors from warning the police about "deviant" books in production.

These informal and formal publications effectively made up a shadow library of a different kind, in varying degrees defying copyright conventions and censorship to advance a decolonized curriculum. The impact is epitomized by an anecdote from a former staffer at Ravan Press, who described a street vendor selling Ravan Press's radical *Staffrider* magazine by standing on a corner in Soweto, holding the publication aloft, and shouting "Knowledge! Knowledge!"[6]

The Anti-apartheid Academic Boycott and the Rise of a Copying Culture

Photocopying was the basis of the other form of shadow library common in South African higher education. Whole books and extracts were widely copied in the face of inefficient supply lines and the unavailability of required reading because of censorship. This tendency was further fueled by the international academic boycott of South African universities, which had been launched by British academics in 1957 at the request of the ANC (Haricombe and Lancaster 1995, 31). The boycott movement expanded slowly in the academic community in the next two decades, only gaining widespread political support in the 1980s with the passage of the Anti-Apartheid Act in the United States in 1986. After its enactment, a number of U.S. publishers withdrew textbooks and scholarly publications from the South African market (ibid., 43). However, this strategy was not universally accepted. The Association of American University Presses (AAUP) and the Association of American Publishers (AAP), for example, rejected the boycott, characterizing access to information as a force for change.

The boycott did not have a large impact on the general book trade, but the tertiary and scientific departments of booksellers felt the effects markedly (Philip 1991, 18). Some publishers, like McGraw Hill, pulled out of the country altogether in response to U.S. trade sanctions, selling its local list to Lexicon Publishers. Haricombe and Lancaster, discussing a survey of faculty, reported that 49 percent of their sample complained of the lack of access to textbooks or journal subscriptions or both (Haricombe and Lancaster 1995, 44; Gray 2000, 176). The book boycott was clearly a factor, but not the only one: financial sanctions and a weak exchange rate "doubled or even trebled the prices of books and journals from abroad. ... Required textbooks priced themselves out of the student market. As a result, the university library sometimes became a textbook repository, and students copied the required sections from the textbooks" (Haricombe and Lancaster 1995, 89).

The combination of the boycott, local censorship, and—throughout the 1970s and 1980s—the introduction of affordable photocopy machines, combined with inefficient distribution networks, produced a steady rise in the role of photocopied coursepacks. Later, as copy machines became more efficient, there was wide-scale copying of textbooks by copy shops and temporary commercial operations set up at the start of the academic year in shipping containers close to campuses, particularly those situated outside the main cities, where distribution was problematic.

In this environment, photocopies became the dominant form of classroom material in many settings, especially in the rural black universities, where published materials were scarce. In the better-resourced universities, photocopied coursepacks included extracts from textbooks as well as radical local publications. This set of practical workarounds against censorship, the boycott, high costs, and inadequate distribution systems became one of the major forms of curricular continuity between the apartheid and post-apartheid periods.

Post-apartheid Higher Education Policy

The announcement of the end of apartheid came suddenly and, to most South Africans, unexpectedly, in a speech by President F. W. de Klerk in February 1990, which lifted the ban on the African National Congress, announced the release of Nelson Mandela from prison, and opened the way for negotiations for democratic elections. General elections, with full enfranchisement of black South Africans, took place four years later, resulting in a major victory by the ANC.

Higher education policy development at this stage grappled with two distinct—though often intertwining and sometimes contradictory—challenges. The first was a development agenda aimed at reversing the damage done by apartheid and realigning the curriculum to address the needs of the country and its disenfranchised community. The second challenge aimed at regaining international recognition for South

African higher education, with an emphasis on international competitiveness and prestige.

Some of the challenges facing post-apartheid higher education were widely understood. The new education policy would have to accommodate very rapid growth in the number of black students, nearly all of whom suffered from serious economic and educational disadvantages in the wake of apartheid policies and in a country with one of the highest income gaps in the world. Many of the large numbers of new students entering university would not be able to afford fees, accommodation, textbooks, or digital learning aids. Also needed was the transformation of the racial profile of the faculty, which, following the division of educational opportunity under apartheid, was overwhelmingly made up of the minority white population. And policy would have to include changes in curriculum design to better reflect national development concerns and the cultural politics of the new South Africa (Gray 2000; Bunting 2002; Jansen 2003).

The Right of Access to a Locally Relevant Education: Aspirations and Realities

Many of these ambitions drew on the liberation rhetoric of the ANC, which focused on education as a human right. The Freedom Charter, an important 1955 manifesto adopted by the Congress movement[7] early in the apartheid period, states under the heading *The Doors of Learning and Culture Shall Be Opened*: "Education shall be free, compulsory, universal and equal for all children; Higher education and technical training shall be opened to all by means of state allowances and scholarships awarded on the basis of merit."[8]

In 1996, the new South African Constitution granted the right to a free basic education and an opportunity for "further education, which the state, through reasonable measures, must make progressively available and accessible."[9] Thus, although access to university education was not given the compulsory, free-of-charge status that school education was, the policy documents of the ANC and the new democratic government made democratic access a key goal, initially supported by student loans and bursaries. A National Student Financial Aid Scheme (NSFAS) was established in 1997, expanded in 1999, and has grown rapidly since. By 2017, 175,000 students received NSFAS funding.

Many universities took up the need for access and student success through the provision of academic support programs designed to address the "inadequate articulation between the secondary/further education system and higher education in its existing forms" (Soudien 2013, 62, 64). Multilingualism was encouraged through a number of programs and policies, such as the use of Sepedi at the University of Limpopo and the introduction of compulsory Zulu at the University of Kwa-Zulu Natal. These efforts were broadly aligned with the ANC push for a more Afrocentric curriculum, in line with the liberation vision articulated by the radical student movements, academics, and publishers of the 1970s and 1980s.

National Education Policy—A Divided Agenda

The implementation of post-apartheid higher education reform started in earnest with the National Commission on Higher Education, whose 1996 report and 1997 white paper outlined the proposed transformation of the system, from changing student and faculty composition to reforming curricular and research agendas (Badat 2009). At this stage, policies favored institutional autonomy. The result was an uneven state of transformation and institutional development, complicated by migration of students to the metropolitan, historically white universities. The black universities created by apartheid fared especially poorly under this model, with "financial deficits, high failure rates, managerial ineffectiveness and poor students unable to pay for higher education"—all worsening as additional funding for redress did not materialize (Jansen 2003, 305).

With the National Plan for Higher Education in 2001, the government adopted a much more interventionist approach. The plan identified a need for more accommodation of the multilingual student population, in which the majority of students spoke English as a second, third, or even fourth language. It argued for adoption of a locally appropriate and Afrocentric curriculum, with more locally produced materials and capacity to adapt international content to local case studies and African perspectives (Soudien 2013, 55). In the language of the National Plan: fields of study would need to include "African languages and culture, African literature (and not only in its English form), indigenous knowledge systems, and, more generally, the transformation of curricula to reflect the location of knowledge in the context of the African continent" (DHET 2001, 27).

The major pressure against this agenda came from economic liberalization policies, negotiated by the ANC in parallel with the more public deliberations on the post-apartheid future of the country. Most directly, the financial requirements of the transformation agenda were inconsistent with the budgetary discipline needed to tie South Africa to the WTO, the IMF, and the World Bank, including the commitment by the Mbeki government to repay the apartheid government's national debt (Cloete and Gillwald 2014). More generally, it was inconsistent with pressure to reframe South African higher education around the market-driven goal of greater competiveness in international higher education.

As Badat observed, the different values and goals that interest groups assigned to higher education led to contestation:

These could include social equity and redress on the one hand, quality on the other. Focusing on transformation at the expense of quality could compromise the production of graduates with the necessary skills for national economic development. Competing in the process were questions of national redistributive reconstruction and global competitiveness, a debate in which questions of differentiation become important. (Badat 2009, 461–462)

In the university sector, these pressures exchanged the vision of generous government support for higher education, as articulated in the Freedom Charter and Constitution, for a more market-driven and commercialized model. Despite the booming student population, government subsidies in real terms decreased as a component of total university income, from 49 percent to 40 percent while the contribution from student fees, in turn, rose from 24 percent to 31 percent (CHE 2015, 95). Universities were encouraged to seek "third-stream funding" from corporate partnerships and other university-supported commercial activity, including catering to the still-powerful mining sector.

In contrast to the highly segmented system under apartheid and also to post-apartheid proposals to recognize the different roles played by different types of institutions, post-apartheid higher education policy consolidated around a vision of a relatively undifferentiated institutional landscape.

At the same time, as part of the targets built into higher education policy, the higher education system has seen continuous pressure to bring the demographics of students and staff into line with national profiles. There has been a rapid and substantial increase of black students, although white students remain overrepresented in the elite institutions and the rural black universities remain overwhelmingly black. As a result of the rapid increases in black students, the student population doubled between 1994 and 2015, from under half a million to just over a million (HESA 2014; DHET 2015).[11]

Efforts to transform the demographics of faculty, particularly at the elite levels, have been less than successful. Black faculty, and particularly black women, remain underrepresented, especially at the professorial level. This is also reflected in the production of classroom materials, with authorship of locally published textbooks by black authors standing at only 22.6 percent in 2012 (PASA 2013).

Within this ecosystem, the distance education university UNISA has emerged as the dominant institution in terms of student numbers, with 400,000 students in 2015. The next-largest institution has 74,000 students.[12] UNISA thus has considerable influence on the textbook market, both in terms of the books published and the threats that it can pose for the local industry in relation to the development of digital materials and open education resources.

Completion Rates

The expansion of the student population in the sector took place against a background of financial distress and poor preparation of students in schools, which resulted in high dropout rates (Cloete and Gillwald 2014). Secondary schooling remained sharply divided, with high-performing schools in formerly white middle-class areas attracting the learners more likely to succeed and the poorer schools in black townships and rural areas remaining underresourced in terms of infrastructure, libraries, and teaching skills.

As a result, low completion or "throughput" rates at UNISA and other institutions became a major concern for post-apartheid educational planning. The National Plan for Higher Education (DHET 2001) aimed at the throughput rate of 75 percent for the completion of undergraduate degrees in three years, achievable in part through greater investment in remedial education and corresponding "bridging" materials designed to ease the transition to higher education.

By 2011, however, throughput within three years averaged 25 percent for face-to-face courses and 15 percent for distance education, with UNISA achieving a throughput rate of only 7 percent (DHET 2012, 11). Put differently, of all students enrolled in three-year degrees in 2006, only 53 percent graduated within five years, with an extra estimated 41 percent dropping out completely.

This lack of articulation between high schools and universities remains a profound problem that affects all students. In the international competitiveness rankings for education, South Africa ranks very low. Particularly in language and mathematics, students coming through the secondary school system demonstrated serious deficits in basic knowledge, especially with regard to university expectations.

Throughput rates this poor pose serious challenges for the provision of learning materials. With dropout rates this high, the argument that a good textbook would ensure academic success is unlikely to apply on its own: the failure is clearly deeper and more endemic. This has meant that higher education institutions have needed to develop high levels of expertise in understanding the complex reasons for dropouts and the pedagogical and social approaches that can help address the problem.

The inability of the education system to manage linguistic diversity further depresses these statistics. There are eleven official languages in South Africa, yet education beyond elementary school level and in higher education takes place in English and Afrikaans. A high proportion of students, therefore, study in their second, third, or fourth languages.

Locally published university textbooks are also overwhelmingly in English, with a few Afrikaans titles and nothing at all in the other nine official languages.

This gap between plans for transformation of the system and the laissez-faire reality has had a variety of implications for scholarly and academic textbook production. The post-apartheid transformation agenda called for a locally relevant African vision of research and research publication, yet textbooks published by the major U.S. and UK publishers seldom had any references to Africa. South African textbooks were often favored for this reason, but as another legacy of apartheid and the neocolonial trading environment, these rarely discussed the regional environment (although this is changing as publishers move to more flexible digital delivery methods that allow for localization and customization). The creation of appropriate bridging materials to help deal with underprepared students was, with a few exceptions, avoided by local publishers and left to universities to develop themselves.

The Academic Publishing Sector in a Period of Change

The dominant story of textbook publishing in the English-speaking world in the second half of the twentieth century was one of consolidation, as educational publishers were bought up, merged with, or driven out of business by a shrinking number of multinational conglomerates. By 1996, the seven largest college textbook companies accounted for two-thirds of the global market (Worth 1996). By 2014, three companies—Pearson, McGraw-Hill, and Houghton Mifflin Harcourt—controlled more than half the market.

In South Africa, this process was delayed by the rise to power of the apartheid government after World War II. The process of internationalization experienced in much of the rest of the world was matched by increasing parochialism at home. Where conglomerates did arise, they did so primarily on the basis of locally owned enterprises. The apartheid government was an active supporter of Afrikaner business and encouraged the creation of powerful national corporations, particularly in the media industries. Nasionale Pers (or Naspers, as it is more commonly known); Perskor, which had close links to Verwoerd; and De Jager HAUM, a right-wing press with church connections, were all able to gain dominant positions in the elementary and high school publishing market, building on their lucrative relationships with government (Mpe and Seeber 2000, 19–20; Badat 1991).

The academic textbook market was—and post-apartheid, remains—a much smaller industry sector than trade or schools publishing, characterized by lower profits and considerable participation by overseas publishers. By the end of the apartheid period, more than 65 percent of academic textbook sales were estimated to be in the hands of international publishers. At that stage, these companies included Pearson, Hodder Headline, Wiley, Heinemann, McGraw Hill, Macmillan, and Butterworths, among others.

The largest of the local players in the academic market was Juta, a legal and academic publishing and bookselling company founded in 1853 by Jan Carel Juta, who happened to be married to Karl Marx's sister. Juta's entry into academic publishing came in 1857 when he won the right to supply reference books to the examining board of the University of Good Hope (the precursor to the University of Cape Town). The company ultimately grew into a solid school and university educational publisher and bookseller, alongside its legal business.[13]

The other dominant local academic textbook publisher was Van Schaik, which was founded as a privately owned bookseller in 1914, moved into trade publishing, and began to develop its academic textbook business in the 1960s. The company was taken over by in 1986 by Naspers—a rapidly-expanding conglomerate supportive of the government in the apartheid years—and became a higher education-focused business.[14] Companies like Longman and Oxford University Press, which had a local office, published some academic works but focused predominantly on the primary and secondary schools market.

An unusual facet of the South African higher education textbook market was the dominance of large distance education institutions—UNISA and TechnikonSA—which later merged into one institution. Created as an examining body in 1873 and expanding to correspondence course delivery in 1946, UNISA was granted dominant status as a distance education provider by the apartheid government in 1959. Ultimately, it grew into the largest university in South Africa by a wide margin, becoming one of the bigger distance education providers in the world.[15]

The draw of UNISA and Technikon SA for academic textbook publishers was their large first-year classes and potential for direct supply—bypassing booksellers to achieve higher levels of sell-through and bigger margins. Local publishers, who were otherwise vulnerable to small market size and tenuous profitability, gravitated toward subjects where local case studies were important and distance classes were large—particularly in areas such as commerce, marketing, business studies, and communications. In practice, however, the geographical remoteness of the rural "black" universities and absence of local bookshops resulted in a very weak supply chain for these institutions, leading—as we will see in more detail—to a wide array of informal copying practices organized by students and faculty, and resulting publisher complaints.

Post-apartheid Market Consolidation

The toxicity of the apartheid regime afforded South African publishers a certain degree of insulation from multinational pressure. South African publishers were not attractive targets for takeover in an era of academic boycotts and government censorship, nor did many international companies seek to set up local publishing operations.

This changed with the end of apartheid: some South African publishing and bookselling industries had consolidated in the apartheid years into large media holding companies, such as the local conglomerate, Nasionale Pers, which has a wide range of media, publishing, electronic, telecommunications, and broadcasting interests—including in China, where it owns the large instant messaging business Tencent. Naspers is now one of the biggest global multinationals. Other companies experienced a roller-coaster ride as national and international corporations invested and disinvested in different segments of the industry. Juta, the family-owned educational, academic, law, and professional publisher and bookseller, withdrew from higher education publishing, later sold off its school textbook division after incurring losses in the new curriculum, and, in 2013, scaled back and then sold its bookselling business to Protea booksellers.

Trade bookshops underwent a parallel process of consolidation. Specialty independent bookshops faced increasing competition from expanding shopping mall trade book chains, which focused on the popular mass-market end of the international market and tended to favor international bestsellers, often consigning South African books to the back shelves of the store.

The Demise of the Radical Publishers

In this changing context, the independent anti-apartheid publishers established in the apartheid period, such as Ravan Press, Ad Donker, and David Philip, saw sales fall off as their outlets narrowed and then largely disappeared. A watershed moment came in the late 1980s, when de Jongh's Bookshop, near Wits University, closed its doors when its owner returned to the Netherlands. This was the last bookshop in the country that specialized in both international and local intellectual trends.

The mainstream university textbook booksellers, by that stage, had largely limited their stockholding to high-volume undergraduate textbooks—further undermining the distribution of more specialized and localized learning resources. Together, these developments effectively killed off the market for "recommended reading" prescribed for students, substantially reducing the sales levels of South African-focused social science and humanities books. Today, only a handful of bookshops—like Clarke's Bookshop in

Cape Town and Thorold's in Johannesburg, which are also second-hand and antiquarian bookshops—widely stock the kinds of books on South Africa and the rest of the continent that were published by the anti-apartheid radical publishers.

The Rise of the International Mega-textbook

By the end of the apartheid era, the nature of the "product" had also changed in ways that reflected wider patterns of consolidation. Increasingly, the market was shaped by the rise of international mega-textbooks, characterized by extreme length (800–1,400 pages), authoritative tone, high production values, color illustrations, and multimedia support packages for lecturers. This became the aspirational standard for local publishers and, indeed, for lecturers who pushed for adoption of the new "global" textbooks as a form of competitive alignment with international standards of teaching and learning. As in other countries, the marketing of these mega-textbooks focused primarily on the lecturer delivering the course, not on the students, creating markets in which price sensitivity could not be easily expressed.

These developments presented a problem for local publishers, who typically had lower profit margins than their international counterparts, but also little or no ability to amortize investment across large export markets. They could not afford, in most cases, to compete with the mega-textbook—with its international prestige, extreme length, color printing, and multimedia enticements.[16] The new model also produced steep price increases: between 1980 and 1992, textbook prices increased by 250 percent in the United States, compared with a 70 percent increase in the consumer price index (Worth 1996). These costs were passed on in international markets like South Africa, ensuring low classroom adoption, with adoptions excluding poorer students. This mismatch, in turn, encouraged sharing, photocopying, and other strategies designed to mitigate the cost.

Supply Chain Problems

The stockholding habits of bookshops also changed as they absorbed the profit-maximizing strategies of the global chains (Horvath 1996). In order to lower the risk of returns, bookshops—both trade and academic—introduced low stockholding strategies, relying on reorders when stock ran out. Academic textbook booksellers developed estimates for the sell-through they expected in particular courses—often as low as 35 percent of students—and stocked this number or less at the beginning of the academic year. As in other developing countries, the supply chain was generally inadequate to support this model, leading to badly synched supply and demand and fueling student reliance on photocopying for access to materials.

This tendency to limit bookshop stocks at the beginning of university semesters was—and is—especially problematic for books ordered directly from the United States or UK (as distinct from those held in stock by South African-based publishers or distribution agencies). In 2013, these direct imports represented around a third of the turnover in the sector—some R230 million in retail sales (PASA 2014, 91). If stocks of these books run out, reordering can take six to ten weeks. For poorer students, this can pose serious challenges beyond the obvious financial ones: for reasons of geography and poor transportation, many can't go from bookshop to bookshop seeking available copies.

Cross-national Pricing: Territorial Markets and Parallel Importation Prohibition

One way that poorer countries mitigate the high prices of imported textbooks is by publishing locally licensed editions of popular international titles. This has been a particularly effective strategy in India, where the huge market base and potential for competition from state-subsidized or state-owned publishers have pushed the major international publishers to seek local partners. The effective use of this mechanism, however, is highly dependent on the size of the local market. In South Africa, the local market has proven too small to create adequate incentives for many licensed local editions.

Indian editions reach very large markets and tend to be considerably cheaper than the U.S. or UK versions of the book. However, Indian editions have rarely been available in smaller markets like South Africa, due to a combination of territorial limitations written into the licenses and parallel importation prohibitions written into South African copyright legislation. A UK publisher, for example, could license an edition of a book to an Indian publisher with the contractual limitation that this edition could only be sold in India. The ban on parallel importation prevents a third party from buying the books in India and importing them into South Africa.[17] South African booksellers could therefore legally import the original high-priced edition from the United States or UK, but not the cheaper version from India.

Prohibitions on parallel importation were introduced into the copyright law of most of the ex-British colonies at the behest of UK publishers and remain common in African copyright regimes. They are not, however, required by international copyright treaties such as the Agreement on Trade Related Aspects of Intellectual Property Rights (TRIPS). In South Africa, the ban secured British dominance of the local market. More generally, it continues to protect a complex network of cross-national territorial deals—extending the territorial reach of a publication while protecting the publisher's ability to set different prices in different markets. The resulting fragmentation of the book market, however, is becoming an anachronism in an increasingly digital world.

International Student Editions

As a way to address these problems in smaller markets, the international publishers developed International Student Editions (ISEs) for selected titles, which they made available on a discretionary basis in certain countries. These titles often fell between the U.S./UK price and the price of the equivalent Indian edition. The International Student Editions were mostly targeted at the larger undergraduate classes and were indistinguishable from the full-price editions, although they often had a simpler cover. International publishers with a local presence in the South African market and distributors of imported books were likely to have large numbers of ISEs.

These international editions were sold through the bookshops. ISE prices were roughly comparable with South African textbooks, or slightly more expensive, but considerably cheaper than the more specialized textbooks used in the senior years of the curriculum, which were imported at the full U.S. or UK price.

The Impact of *Kirtsaeng v. Wiley*

This entire system has been thrown into disarray by the 2013 U.S. Supreme Court decision in *Kirtsaeng v. Wiley*—a case concerning parallel importation and its intersection with first sale rights. First sale or "exhaustion" is an important adjacent principle in copyright law that limits rights holder control of the circulation of the work to its *first sale*, after which the buyer may dispose of it as he or she wishes. This principle of full transfer of ownership after sale underpins major features of the learning ecosystem, including both library lending and the used book market.

The Supreme Court case arose from the activities of a Thai student, Supap Kirtsaeng, who purchased international editions of textbooks in Thailand, brought them back to the United States, and sold them to U.S. students at lower prices than the domestic editions. Kirtsaeng, in this context, was one of the more entrepreneurial representatives of a larger trend, as American students sought ways to game territorial licensing in order to lower textbook costs.

Kirtsaeng was sued by the publisher of some of the textbooks, John Wiley & Sons, for copyright infringement. The publisher won the first round of the case, resulting in a stiff fine for Kirtsaeng for violating parallel importation restrictions. The Supreme

Court, however, agreed to hear Kirtsaeng's appeal and ruled the other way. The court said that Kirtsaeng was entitled to first sale rights in books that he had purchased legally in another country, and that there is simply "no basic principle of copyright law that suggests that publishers are especially entitled to" [sell books for differential prices in different geographic markets].[18] In so finding, the ruling undermined the long-established differential pricing structure on which the international textbook market is based (and indeed the world book market as a whole).[19]

The effects of the Kirtsaeng ruling are still playing out in international markets, but the short-term outcome was not, as it ought to have been, the elimination of parallel importation prohibitions to allow for a freer and more equitable market. Although Australia proposed lifting parallel importation prohibitions on books in 2016, there is no sign yet of South Africa following suit. Rather, there was a rise in prices in most developing countries as U.S. publishers began withdrawing International Student Editions. In South Africa, these had largely disappeared by 2014, although some UK editions were still available. The standard editions could still be ordered, but at higher prices.

As the chair of the SA Booksellers' Association put it, at the time, in response to the Kirtsaeng case: "U.S. publishers are unwilling for the most part to forego the profits they earn on higher priced editions to continue supporting third world learners with cheaper ones. At present a number of prescribed texts are available in South Africa at prices over R1,000 ($99), which students will resist. How this will play out in the coming year will remain to be seen."[20]

A key tactic in limiting the fallout has been a tendency for international publishers like Pearson in South Africa to fast-track the publication of local South African editions of high-selling textbooks, priced for the local market.

Although these price increases did not take effect immediately, by 2016 prices of international textbooks had risen dramatically, with some undergraduate textbooks selling for over R3,000 ($230)—an unaffordable price in the South African context. Not all of this rise is attributable to Kirtsaeng: falling exchange rates have also played a role. In general, South African publishers agree that the Kirtsaeng case will be beneficial in the long run as the cost of imported books becomes prohibitive. Such a shift should, in theory, diminish the power of the multinationals and increase domestic publishers' share of the local market.

South-South Trade in Textbooks: South Africa and India

The absence of South-South trade in textbooks in this context is striking, particularly in the case of India, which has longstanding historical links with South Africa (Hofmeyr and Deverakshanam 2009; Hofmeyr 2013) and a large low-cost publishing sector (Bhattacharji 2008). The possibility of such a relationship was not lost on the Indians. After the end of apartheid, in 1994, a high-level Indian publisher delegation visited the country to explore the potential for collaboration in higher education textbook publishing.

The South African universities and their faculty were cautious of these approaches, articulating concerns about Indian copyright infringement and copyright violations in Indian textbooks—both stories strongly promoted by the British and U.S. publishing industries. At the publishers' request, India was regularly placed on the "Special 301 Watch Lists" by the U.S. Trade Representative—the main mechanism for signaling U.S. displeasure with levels of IP protection and enforcement in other countries. Indian publishers saw this as a moral panic propagated by the United States and UK in the face of potential competition.

The U.S. and UK arguments were persuasive to academics and to an industry that appeared to place its global aspirations above questions of lowest-cost sourcing of materials (to say nothing of the potential advantages of trade with partners in emerging economies that might share common interests with South Africa). To this day, South African college textbook publishing has resolutely faced North, with serious price implications for students and, ultimately, for South African publishers that might have had opportunities to expand access into the Indian market.

Price and Affordability of International Textbooks

Because ISEs enjoyed economies of scale from being sold across a number of countries, ISE prices fell more or less into line with locally priced books. An American undergraduate textbook in media studies, for example, might sell in South Africa as an ISE for $53 (R690), compared to a full price of $119 (R1,555)—or $170 by 2017. An ISE science textbook might be $80 (R1,045) and a popular medical textbook $58 (R745) as opposed to $90–$150 (R1,175–R1,960) at full prices.

Because Kirstsaeng was a U.S. judgment, U.S. publishers have been the fastest to drop the ISE model. Cheaper editions were still available in some cases for a while after the judgment, notably for UK editions, where parallel importation restrictions remain in place, or when they were purchased through independent international wholesalers, or, possibly, because of deals made with local publisher branches. A brief pricing survey conducted in 2015 found major, and not always clearly explicable, variations in pricing, suggesting an environment in transition.

However, by 2017, prices had risen even further, making imported books unaffordable to most students. An increasing range of electronic media are being used in conjunction with printed books and e-books, providing a bewildering array of options for faculty and students and rendering comparisons—and for students, comparison shopping—difficult or impossible. Increasingly, publishers are pushing digital course-ware rather than books, an indication of the shift in strategy on the part of the academic publishing industry.

The implications of these increasing price levels for South African student budgets are nonetheless significant—especially given the government interest in expanding access to education. Over 40 percent of households headed by black South Africans, for example, are categorized as "poor," with *annual* incomes under R33,000 (roughly $4,700 in 2011) for a family of five.[21] In such contexts, the difference between a $10–$20 textbook, a $50–$70 textbook, and a $100–$130 textbook, let alone a $300 textbook, multiplied across multiple classes and potentially multiple children, can be enormous. In practice, as we will see, even "moderate" South African prices frequently represent no choice at all: students do without.

Growth in Local South African Textbook Publishing

Pressure for lower prices and greater South African content has contributed to substantial growth in locally published academic and professional books. The sales percentage of locally produced textbooks has steadily grown since the advent of a democratic government, from a 65/35 percent split in favor of imported texts in the early 1990s to a roughly 60/40 percent split in 2013 in favor of local books, published either by South African publishers or by the local branches of international publishers, such as Pearson and Oxford University Press (PASA 2013).[22] There has also been a steady increase in the number of locally produced academic e-textbooks produced, year on year, perhaps reflecting greater potential for e-textbook growth in the wake of rising local investment in electronic products, such as Vital Source.

In fields where local content is at a premium, such as the teaching of law and accounting, South African publishers completely dominate. Ninety-one percent of law and accountancy textbooks are published locally, with most of these supplied to practitioners rather than students. Overall, the output of academic and professional books by local publishers stood at 284 new titles in 2011, of which 150 were academic textbooks and 78 professional books. Imported textbooks, on the other hand, saw a net decline in sales of a cumulative 37.7 percent in the 2008–2011 period.[23]

On the whole, there has been evolution in the sector rather than a radical transformation in products and market strategies. What has changed most, arguably, is the level of responsiveness to market realities: publishers are reporting closer relationships with students and greater investment in development to ensure language appropriateness and pedagogical soundness; and publishers are trying, without much success, to change the racial profile of authorship. Local publishers are very aware of price sensitivity among students and tend to cap their prices at levels that will not meet with customer resistance—claiming that profits are falling as a result.[24]

Of the international publishers with a local presence in the South African market, Pearson Education is the largest player, with a dominant position in the supply of international textbooks and an expanding list of locally published books and local editions of international titles. In the early years post-apartheid, Pearson developed specialized materials for the learning gaps that undermine graduation rates—much of this via the local branch, Pearson Education South Africa (PESA). Other international companies publishing in the local market include the local offices of the Oxford University Press (South Africa). OUP, post-apartheid, publishes an increasingly substantial list of academic textbooks in South Africa, having considerably expanded its medical and legal textbook lists, among others. The take-up of the medical textbooks, in particular, has succeeded in supplanting more expensive international titles.

Despite government statements in favor of greater Africanization of the university system and some successful efforts by publishers to introduce a more locally relevant curriculum, books published by local publishers tend to be written almost entirely in English—96.7 percent according to 2013 industry statistics—complemented by a niche market in Afrikaans (3.3 percent) and nothing at all in African languages (PASA 2013). Contributing factors to this dominance are the widespread use of English as the language of instruction and, among students, the aspirational association of English with job opportunities.[25]

Scholarly Publishing and University Presses

University presses provide a framework for scholarly communication in South Africa, but this sector is not a major contributor to student learning materials (Pascal 1996). With nearly all science and engineering research published overseas, press output focuses on the humanities and social sciences, where South African themes and content are important. It is these titles that, in theory, ought to have produced the alternative curriculum advocated by student radicals in the 1970s and 1980s and articulated in the higher education policy drawn up by the new ANC government.

The overall number of titles produced by South African university presses is low. According to a study by the Academy of Science of South Africa (ASSAF 2009) and bibliometric studies by CREST at the University of Stellenbosch in 2009, and being followed up by ongoing research, 389 monographs were published by authors in South African universities between 2001 and 2006, with the larger university presses accounting for around ten to fifteen titles per year. Sales are also low. Consistent with the experience of small U.S. and UK university presses, most titles can expect lifetime sales of 200 to 500 copies; very few titles sell more than 1,000.

As in other countries, the university presses have struggled to develop a new business model that addresses either the weaknesses of the traditional distribution model or the opportunities of the digital transition. There are, however, three areas where national policymakers have stepped in to create solutions to perceived weaknesses of the ecosystem.

The first and, at this stage, the most promising, is the Department of Science and Technology's support for the creation of a publicly funded national open access platform for South African scholarly journals, called SciELO South Africa, managed through the ASSAF.[26] The project is a collaboration with the successful publicly funded Latin American journal platform of the same name, based in Brazil and now the second-largest national provider of open access scholarly journals in the world. Scholarly books have been included in the SciELO platform in Latin America since 2012, but not yet in South Africa.[27] A venture such as this could well provide a conducive environment for addressing the demand for African-relevant titles that could be used as textbooks in the social sciences and humanities.

The second policy intervention is the system of financial rewards instituted by the Department of Higher Education and Training, whereby universities and departments receive substantial per-article grants for articles published in "recognized" journals (around \$9,100/R120,000 per article at the time of writing) and starting in 2016, for scholarly books. The money goes to the institution, which, at its own discretion, can pass on a part of the grant to the author, rather than directly supporting publication or authorship (and most universities do so).[28] It has also fueled the scramble for prestige through journal articles published in ISI-ranked international journals rather than local content and has tended to discourage faculty from top research universities from investing in textbook writing.

However, in spite of these grants, and in the face of declining government subsidies for universities, there is a general lack of financial support from universities and the government for the production of scholarly books, as opposed to authorship by faculty. Instead, the presses are expected to be "profitable" or, at the very least, able to operate with diminished levels of financial support from their host university. This is an increasingly unrealistic expectation even in the richer markets of the United States and UK, where university presses have traditionally been perceived as an investment in prestige by their home institutions. As in those markets, the South African university presses have responded by trying to focus on broader scholarly and trade markets, rather than on scholarship per se. As the ASSAF study on scholarly books puts it: "The paradoxical outcome of this logic is that scholarly publishers can only remain in the field if they are able successfully to move beyond it. They have to operate in adjacent fields in order to generate the required revenue to sustain the scholarly publishing programme" (ASSAF 2009, 66).

A complicating factor in the availability of books for prescription from the humanities and social sciences is an increasing trend for local authors to seek prestige by publishing overseas with publishers like Routledge and Palgrave, which produce high-quality books in small runs, sold at very high prices by South African standards.

The third high-level intervention in the publishing ecosystem was the establishment of the Human Sciences Research Council Press in 2003—an offshoot of the research funding body—on an open access model. In 2008, HSRC Press books were distributed in 11 countries, but were being read online in 184 countries (Rosenberg 2008). Its successful titles could reach 1,000 downloads a month, and its publications were widely used as teaching materials.[29] In the face of budgetary constraints in the organization, and under the common misapprehension that scholarly publishing should be profit-making, the HSRC reduced its output, retreated from its fully open access mandate in 2012, and substituted a delayed open access of six to nine months or, in some cases, no open access provision at all, thus considerably reducing its impact. In a recent speech at an HRSC Press book launch, Science and Technology Minister Naledi Pandor criticized the move, stating, "The HSRC Press has done much to decolonize that link in producing new knowledge. It's all very well for me to pronounce on our need to train more and more PhDs in the social sciences. But that call is pointless if candidate and graduate PhDs have nowhere to publish other than to go abroad."[30]

A key question is who will anchor the next curricular paradigm: the universities or the publishing sector? Here, answers are shaped in part by South African copyright law, which creates the legal environment in which alternative models of provision are emerging.

Copyright Meets the Right to Education

Debates about access to learning materials now refer, in part, to the South African Constitution of 1996, which makes explicit the right to both basic and higher education. Largely a nascent proposition in the 1990s, debates over the meaning and scope of this right sharpened as student numbers increased and as the system, in significant ways, continued to fail large numbers of them. Better implementation of this right has tended to focus on two mechanisms for expanding access to materials: South African copyright law, which structures both the formal marketplace and informal means of acquisition of books and other materials, and government-supported student loans, which have a broader remit to support educational success, but which have consistently focused on the cost of materials.

The Copyright Act

Copyright in South Africa is governed by the Copyright Act No. 98, passed in 1978, originating in the British Copyright Act of 1911, which was incorporated wholesale into the first South African Patents, Designs, Trade Marks and Copyright Act of 1916. The official title, of the British Act, the "Imperial Copyright Act," identified the role of this original legislation as a mechanism to protect British copyright in a colonial country.

In spite of some amendments to the South African Copyright Act of 1978, there is general agreement that copyright law in South Africa is badly out of date and needs a thorough overhaul. It makes no provision, for example, for the management of digital copyright. Longstanding questions about educational exceptions, liability, and enforcement in the era of photocopying and now digital reproduction remain unresolved. Plans for revision have been on the legislative calendar for several years but the issue has been repeatedly deferred, with extensive proposals for copyright reform only emerging in the Copyright Amendment Bill B-13-2017, still in the process of public discussion. This long delay reflects a political hesitancy that most observers attribute to the late 1990s debacle around anti-retroviral AIDS medications, which put South Africa at odds with the United States over the parallel importation of generic medicines from India (Armstrong et al. 2010; Schonwetter, Ncube, and Chetty 2010; Gray and Seeber 2004).

One of the benefits of this inaction is that South Africa has not adopted the levels of protectionism and enforcement associated with much of the "TRIPS Plus" agenda set out in international treaties and built into legislation in the United States in particular. Whereas the "Agreement on Trade Related Aspects of Intellectual Property Rights" (TRIPS 1994) set down minimum standards for international intellectual property rights, the expansion of these rights (TRIPS-Plus) that has taken place in bilateral agreements, has come to dominate international copyright debates. These have led to U.S.-style notice and takedown requirements accompanied by high penalties for even minor infringements, or copyright term extensions beyond "life plus 50 years" (Schonwetter,

Ncube, and Chetty 2010). From the print industries' perspective, the main problems with South Africa's Copyright Act of 1978 have to do with the absence of provisions for digital media and weak enforcement measures to deal with piracy. In reports drafted by the industry, such as the PICC Report (Gray and Seeber 2004) and in other public statements, publishers have argued in particular for higher statutory damages in cases of copyright infringement in order to create a meaningful deterrent against commercial piracy, and improved provisions for obtaining evidence in order to prosecute cases of commercial-scale infringement (Gray and Seeber 2004). Neither effort has borne fruit.

Enforcement

In the face of legislative deficiencies (from the point of view of the industry) and given the high legal costs of enforcement, rights holders have been reluctant to pursue cases under the copyright statute. As a result, there is very little South African case law on copyright infringement. Instead, the industry has turned to a newer piece of legislation, the Counterfeit Goods Act of 1997, which is designed to protect owners of copyright goods and trademarks from illegal possession, production, selling, and distribution of such goods (De Beer et al. 2010). However, even under the more enabling provisions of this legislation, the publishing industry has pursued very few cases (and when they have, the resulting penalties have been low). The biggest of these cases tackled large-scale copying and distribution of school and university textbooks.

Industry representatives interviewed in the African Copyright and Access to Knowledge (ACA2K) investigation, a continent-wide review of the state of copyright legislation,[31] reported additional resistance from government departments when it came to pursuing cases regarding education, given the emotive status of the debate about access and the cost of textbooks. The perception of the Department of Trade and Industry was that enforcement and anti-piracy cases should focus instead on trademark violations. Access to education in this view trumps copyright as the priority (Schonwetter, Ncube, and Chetty 2010, 263–264).

Exceptions and Limitations

The legislative environment was complicated by disputes about the scope of exceptions and limitations in South African copyright law, particularly with regard to educational use, and two decades after the end of apartheid this is still the case. There are, for example, provisions that cover a variety of library and archival needs, such as the copying of an entire work or substantial parts of works if an unused copy of the copyrighted work cannot be obtained at a fair price (Schonwetter, Ncube, and Chetty 2010, 239).[32] Copying for private use is governed by a "fair dealing" section that allows for the use of literary or musical work "for the purposes of research or private study by, or the personal or private use of, the person using the work" (240). There are also provisions for educational use that allow for use of a work by way of illustration for teaching purposes and for translations of works for educational purposes (ibid.).

A complicating factor in these provisions are the specific exceptions for educational use contained in the Regulations linked to Section 13 of the Act. These allow for copies to be made for classroom use, and the making of a single copy for purposes of teaching. However, these are all governed by a general and overriding principle contained in Regulation 2, which provides that "the cumulative effect of the reproduction does not conflict with the normal exploitation of the work to the unreasonable prejudice of the legal interest and residuary rights of the author" (Schonwetter, Ncube, and Chetty 2010, 241). There is no clarity as to exactly what constitutes a "reasonable portion."[33] In other words, copying for educational purposes can be undertaken—perhaps even the creation of coursepacks, although publishers have frequently contested this— but copying cannot in any way threaten publisher earnings. This raises additional issues in a developing country, where the small market size puts a much lower limit on the extent of copying that could meaningfully erode such earnings (Wafawarowa 2007).

These ambiguities produced circular arguments for and against generous exceptions and disputes about what constitutes "fairness," creating a permanent stand-off between universities and publishers on an issue of fundamental importance to educational access.[34] An attempt by the University of the Witwatersrand in the early 1990s to broker a workable mutual understanding of what would constitute fair use in university copying eventually broke down when the university lawyers concluded that the ambiguity of the legislative environment played to the advantage of higher education institutions. They terminated the negotiations.[35] The first signs of a long-promised overhaul of the copyright act emerged in a Draft National Policy on IP in late 2013 (DTI 2013). Although proposed reforms were not charted in detail, the tone was weighted toward better balance and the exercise of democratic rights in education and health.[36] In 2016, draft proposals for amendments to the Copyright Act led to lively debate with local and international copyright scholars arguing for the introduction of Fair Use provisions in the South African Copyright Act No 98 of 1978, to provide a more robust and effective environment for educational uses.

Collective Licensing

After apartheid, the primary policy goal of the publishing industry was a collective licensing agreement that would establish a flat fee for all photocopying in the universities. This process was undertaken by the DALRO—the Dramatic and Literary Rights Organization.[37]

As before, the negotiations were turbulent. DALRO threatened massive penalties for university departments that had embraced coursepack copying during the academic boycott. Protests erupted across the university sector, especially from the black rural universities that in many cases still stocked libraries with photocopied books and journal articles. Nonetheless, strong government support and EU funding granted to the poorer universities as an inducement produced agreement in 1997–1998. The blanket licensing agreement was fully implemented by 2004–2005.

The blanket licensing system aligned broadly with the UK model, which allows publishers to sign on voluntarily, rather than the Nordic model that compels all publishers to participate. The agreement covers all copying of participating members' work undertaken during the academic year within agreed upon percentage limits with respect to the work. The administration of and reporting on levels of copying is undertaken by the universities. For publishers outside the system, the university consortia that administer the agreement have to obtain separate permissions for any copying of works and pay for these over and above the per-student fee.

What the blanket license provides for is the creation of multiple copies of articles or coursepacks for photocopying, placement on the library short-term loan system, and electronic storage on the university intranet and library electronic reserve, which can then be accessed by students registered for the course in question.[38] Student photocopying beyond these provisions can usually benefit from preferential rates at university-based photocopy shops paid for through credits loaded on student cards. Theoretically, this photocopying should be contained within the limits of fair dealing, but the general consensus is there is little oversight of copying levels, apart from warning signs set up in university copy shops, and few publishers willing to undertake prosecutions for excessive photocopying.

Most publicly available information about the agreement and the way it operates comes from a 2011 government investigation of collective rights management organizations, initiated by criticisms that the music rights organization SAMRO, in particular, had an excessive backlog of unmet payments to artists. The Copyright Review Commission, with Justice Farlam as commissioner, expanded its purview to include a review of the collection of literary rights—in particular the agreements between DALRO and the universities (DTI 2011).

In broad strokes, the agreement made the universities responsible for reporting on the number of copies made for classes and for levying an annual fee from students to cover their copying costs.[39] In 2009, this fee was around $6.50 per student at universities and $5 at the polytechnic schools. It was calculated according to estimates of historical copying levels, but incorporating a reduction to allow for copying undertaken by students and staff that would qualify as fair dealing. (Rates have risen on an annual basis in line with inflation, but have never been renegotiated, unlike in many other countries.) DALRO then distributes the revenue collected to the participating publishers, who are, in turn, responsible for calculating and paying the amounts owed to authors as part of their royalties. These royalties are determined by contracts drawn up between publishers and authors and are therefore not open to public scrutiny.

The Copyright Review Commission reported that "in the 2010 calendar year, the total amount collected from licensing was around $4 million (R28,582,389) and the total amount distributed was $3 million (R21,601,415), of which $1.2 million (R9,477,661) was distributed to local rights holders. The low returns to domestic rights holders, moreover, have led to criticism that the system favors international publishers: most of the licensing revenue sent to DALRO leaves the country.

The IP Unit at the University of Cape Town, in its submission to the Copyright Review Commission, argued that the blanket license agreement does offer efficiencies, but could equally well be charging for the reproduction of materials that should fall under fair dealing provisions.[40] However, DALRO claims that it does not make a profit from its university licenses, and low charges would be to the advantage of universities and their students. The commission determined that DALRO's return to publishers was lower than in other countries, leading to recommendations that it improve its procedures for managing and compensating authors.

In general, when interviewed, parties on both sides of the agreement appeared at this stage to be content to leave well enough alone. As a publishing industry representative put it, in 2013, "DALRO is now doing a marvelous job." Others were less effusive, but tended to be broadly supportive. The license offers revenue, another commented, that boosts the bottom line in markets that would otherwise not have been viable. Other inquiries have found less support, marked by concerns that the blanket license was onerous for the universities that had to undertake the administrative work of monitoring copies, and that the universities had not been aggressive enough in negotiating the rates (Schonwetter, Ncube, and Chetty 2010, 261).

Student Loans and Stipends

Copyright law and curricular mandates remain contentious in part because they affect the publishing ecosystem, altering the balance between buying and copying on the one hand and between domestic and international suppliers on the other. But these are mostly indirect forms of government influence. The state provides no support for the development or publication of learning materials, nor indeed for local publishing as a creative enterprise.

There is a strong government role, on the other hand, in the growth of university stipends that make explicit provision for book purchases. Created in 1999, the National Student Financial Aid Scheme (NSFAS)[41] provides funding for textbook purchases as part of a much broader program for student support through payment of course fees, meals and residency plans, and other allowances, in the form of some student grants but primarily through loans repayable after graduation, when the student secures a job. In so doing, it frames the problem of access to materials as a subset of the larger problem of access to education, particularly in light of the steeply rising cost of university education in South Africa.

The fund has played an increasingly important role in enabling access to learning materials. Between 1999 and 2017, the fund grew substantially, from a base of around $57 million (R441 million). In 2017, NSFAS announced that it would be supporting 400,000 students, on a budget of R15 billion ($1.2 billion). Funding was originally administered through universities, but NSFAS has switched to a system of direct payments to students, not without teething problems.

The levels of funding for books—ranging between $70 (R1,000) and $140 (R2,000) per semester, depending on the school—represents roughly two to three textbooks in most contexts[42] and so rarely covers all assigned books for a particular year of study. But students—according to a leading bookseller—are careful optimizers, selecting those that will best improve their chances of success in their courses. The importance of choosing which courses to buy materials for also strongly emerged in this study's student survey and focus groups.

The bursary (monetary award to meet financial needs) schemes are very popular, but also vigorously criticized as inadequate for student needs as well as being bureaucratically inefficient. The main challenge has been that, except for certain instances, the grants are structured as repayable loans. Combined with the extreme poverty of many of the students, the repayable loan provision has proven onerous and resulted in high levels of unrecovered debt. The situation is made worse by a provision that degree certificates can be withheld if there are outstanding amounts in loan accounts—a result that can also, all too often, be the result of inefficiency in the administration of the system.

The 2014 academic year in South Africa saw a number of sometimes-violent protest actions against the NSFAS across the country. Fort Hare University—located in South Africa's second-poorest province and the alma mater of many South African anti-apartheid leaders—was the site of one such protest. Fort Hare students undertook a four-week strike protesting what they regarded as reneged promises of funding for books, meals, and student fees.[43] The University of Limpopo in the north of the country and Mangosuthu University of Technology outside Durban saw similar actions. The Tshwane University of Technology saw violent protests late in 2014, resulting in closure of the university for a period, with the question of funding for fees and books high on the list of grievances—in particular, student exclusions as a result of failure to pay fees.[44] In 2016, budget shortfalls and the exclusion of some students from funding triggered another round of protests in many universities.

The question of student loans, and particularly the repayment of loans, has proved to be a particularly thorny issue with students due to the weakness of South Africa's employment market. In the wake of these developments, student protests have coalesced around the principle of free tuition—a reasonable reading of the 1994 constitutional right to education but a very ambitious goal given the financial pressure on the state and national governments and the current low levels of funding for the university sector.

Student Practices

The bursary system also enjoys strong support from publishers, largely because funds are reserved for the purchase of new materials. Neither publishers nor booksellers, however, have much information about how students get what they need outside the bursary system. Most of them view photocopying as the main form of student access, and the blanket license with DALRO as a satisfactory way of dealing with copying at this level. They tend to see the license agreement as a source of revenue for the industry that would otherwise be lost to the large informal economy, rather than susceptible to recuperation from students through enforcement or other forms of pressure. Few see much benefit in provoking the powerful student activist movement, which is organized in response to the escalating cost of higher education.

Accordingly, publisher enforcement efforts have largely ignored students in favor of targeting the copy shops that reproduce textbooks on a large scale for sale in peak seasons. As in other countries, these are the easy and preferred targets—vulnerable to raids and operating on a scale that triggers criminal charges. Unauthorized downloading—an obsession among the music and film trade associations—remains a comparatively distant worry, a potentially threatening but not yet a measurable factor.[45] The second-hand market for textbooks is fragmented, with no major commercial players under-cutting the market for new books. Publishers do invest in educational efforts, though less to discourage photocopying than to convince students of the value of owning textbooks. As Juta Academic Publisher's promotional literature at the Vaal University of Technology put it: "Statistically, only one in three students passes each year—and only 15 percent of all students will ever graduate. As research by Juta Publishers shows that a main cause of student underachievement is failure to buy textbooks, the company launched a national Student2book campaign to encourage students to buy textbooks and, therefore, improve their pass rate."[46]

In short, the range of competitive pressures on the industry and the highly regulated structure of the bursary system means that,as one publisher put it, "Piracy is not an issue in South Africa. The issue is rather rethinking what academic publishing is about."[47] The survey and focus groups undertaken for this study confirmed elements of this perspective, but also yielded a more complex account of the materials ecosystem.[48]

Buying Books

The impact of the bursary system is visible in purchases of new books. A third of students surveyed said that they bought 80–100 percent of their textbooks new; 19 percent bought 60–80 percent new. This is a much higher figure than in comparable settings in Brazil, India, or Argentina, where new book purchases are infrequent.

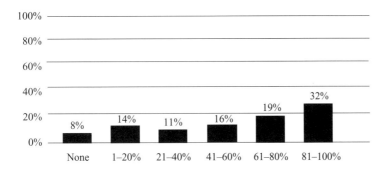

Figure 5.1
How much of your material is purchased new?

Most students (75 percent) reported spending less than $300 (R3,000) per year on new books, while 14.8 percent reported costs of between $300 and $500.[49] Costs were particularly high for law books, with some textbooks costing $100 (R1,000) or more.

Professional students were more likely than others to keep books, citing primarily the value of having a reference collection for later use. In some cases, this was expressed in the strongest terms. Said one student, "When you go into practice one day, and you're in the rural areas where you don't have access to [I]nternet or something, your book is there and you can flip it over and see 'OK, I need to apply this principle to treat this thing.' So for me, selling some books just feels like I'm giving away my life. I can't."

It was clear that, from the students' perspective, there are three main obstacles to buying textbooks: high prices, a fragmented second-hand market (exacerbated by the issuing of frequent new editions), and the move to minimize excess stock, which results in frequent mismatches between supply and demand at the beginning of semesters. Several reported that, in the case of international reorders, books only arrived days before examinations. Bursary students were often the most affected by such practices, as the relatively common administrative delays made them unable to buy books when they were most likely to be available at the beginning of the semester.[50] Poor students were also less likely to be able to compensate for low availability by traveling to find stock elsewhere. Said one such student, "I drive around, you know, because I have a car, but a lot of people can't drive around from bookshop to bookshop."

Student Sharing Networks

The lack of a large, organized used-book market hinders access to previous-year textbooks compared to—for example—the highly organized commercial vendors like Amazon and Chegg in the U.S. market. This is reflected in the relatively small role that used book purchases play in student acquisition practices.

The lack of organization of the used book market is at least partly related to the difficulties associated with student access to online commerce in general. Many students lack access to credit cards and operate with cash, making online purchases difficult. This is, in all likelihood, a temporary problem as e-retail in South Africa expands.[51]

The weakness of commercially organized resale, however, does not mean that used materials play a minor role. Students spoke constantly about practices of informal, locally organized sharing, passing down, and resale of textbooks. This practice is common in student residences and frequently organized across cohorts, in which more senior students support first-years with materials. Explained one first-year student:

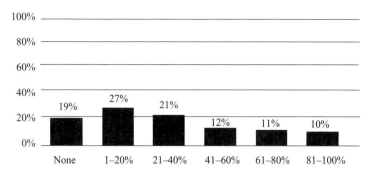

Figure 5.2
How much of your material is purchased used?

Students ... pass down information from one year to the next year, so you actually find that I've got work until the [final] year. You know what I mean? All the stuff that I am supposed to go and research by myself and do by myself. ... So instead of going to consult textbooks and the Internet and go do the research that would require us to use all those resources, senior year students have made it very easy for us.

The library emerged as a relatively strong alternative to buying books, primarily due to the practice of one-day loans of in-demand texts. Seventy-five percent of respondents indicated that they borrowed materials occasionally or often, although large numbers also indicated that availability often broke down during exams and other periods of high demand. Multimedia access, too, was a regularly cited problem among the communications students, with more of the burden falling on lecturers to make the necessary materials available. Faculty members also play a role in facilitating access via lending or copying of materials, or by preparing "updates" that permit the use of older editions of textbooks.

Photocopying

Although the textbook industry perceives photocopying as being the major route for student piracy, survey answers suggested otherwise: 67 percent of students said that they photocopied few to no copies, with only 2 percent admitting to copying over 80 percent of their materials.

In the focus groups, the expense of photocopying was frequently mentioned as a major deterrent. Our survey indicates that a large majority of this copying takes place on the university campus, at the discounted cost offered by on-campus copying. Anecdotally, the cost of photocopying at the better-resourced university where the study

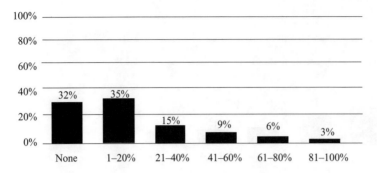

Figure 5.3
How much of your material is photocopied?

was undertaken was cheaper, at $.03 (R0.35) per page, than at poorly resourced universities nearby, where copies were $.05 per page. For students figuring out how to maximize use of a budgeted $70 or $100 per semester on course materials, such differences can be very significant. Only 18 percent of respondents indicated that they use off-campus copy shops, suggesting a relatively minor role in the ecosystem for unauthorized "commercial-scale" copying.

Digital Materials

In practice, student access to materials is cobbled together from a wide range of sources and methods, with none clearly dominant. The bursary system supports new book purchases for some students but is insufficient for student needs. The blanket license legalizes a large portion of student photocopying—that of class-level and coursepack copying—but photocopying remains too costly to be a complete solution for individual students. The organized used book market plays a small role; informal sharing, passing down, and personal resale play a large role. Students make careful decisions about which books to buy or acquire, trying to prioritize those that will have the most impact on their classes and careers. The library provides access in some contexts, but does not scale well for either regular studying or exam times. When these methods fail, large numbers of students simply do without.

The shift toward digital materials and digital reading has begun to have a visible impact on student practices, and produced a further deformalization of the ways in which students get what they need. Although many students expressed a preference for print materials, the cost advantage of digital copies for those with ready access to laptops or tablets is clearly an important factor.[52]

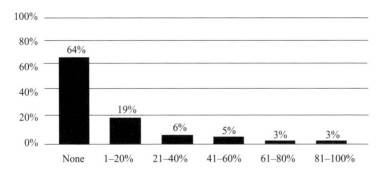

Figure 5.4
How much of your material is downloaded from sources believed to be illegal?

As one student put it: "Well, I know a few kids photocopy stuff, but that's just expensive, printing out stuff. So, I just read everything off my tablet and download PDFs from … you find everything online anyway, so I don't know why the … department was fretting about putting it on the LMS because, you literally just Google whatever title you're looking for .pdf, and it pops up with it. So, it's Google's fault." Here distinctions between sources of digitized material have become relatively fluid, with unauthorized file sharing via peer-to-peer or major file locker services factored in among an array of forms of personal and group exchange. Fewer than 10 percent of respondents indicated that they had downloaded the majority of their materials this way, although this might reflect an unwillingness to admit too readily to online file sharing.[53]

In comparison to perceived illegal downloading, roughly twice as many students (around 70 percent) indicated that they obtained the majority of their materials digitally from other students. The student networks that support textbook sharing and reuse create fertile ground for the sharing of digital materials and students and faculty make use of a wide array of systems. Of the 70 percent who share materials digitally, 80 percent do so via email, 51 percent via thumb drives, 18 percent via file storage services like Dropbox, and 10 percent on social networks like Facebook. Roughly two-thirds described this as organized activity, passing from class to class and from one cohort to the next. Perhaps predictably, 90 percent of these students also share music via the same methods; 71 percent do so for movies.

The legality of copying in these different contexts was a matter of uncertainty for many students, in this respect accurately reflecting South African legal debates. Roughly half said that they believed that copying files from other students is legal. Even among those who viewed it as illegal, indifference was the common response. Students were not very responsive to anti-piracy rhetoric in general (Yu 2012) and much less so in the context of educational materials, where the framing of education as a human right generally trumps other considerations. To deny access, as one student put it: "Simply because of resources; that's ridiculous in this day and age. So, kudos to [the author] for his textbook, but I need a degree. Sorry!"

Another, asked about whether he had any fears about illegal downloading, answered: "No, worried about graduating." Although student opinion was more favorable to authors than publishers, the easiest way to void student sympathy was for teachers to require their own texts in class—a relatively common practice widely condemned by students as profiteering.

The explosion of use of "free" online resources that supplement classroom materials has also blurred lines in the minds of students. For any given class or subject, there are often supplementary materials provided by faculty and always a range of potentially complementary materials available online. Students stressed the usefulness of lecture slides and videos sourced on the university LMS in particular, as well as—among medical students—YouTube for videos of medical procedures. University provision of podcasts or videos of lectures on the LMS also proved popular. Database access at this university is also relatively strong, and law students have joined a professional culture built around online research, with widespread use of LexisNexis and Juta Law.[54]

Overall, the student responses are striking for the seriousness with which they approach the purchase of textbooks (something also commented on by a number of publishers and booksellers); for the wide and inventive array of strategies they deploy when the money for new books runs out; and, notably, for the pervasiveness of a view of learning materials that stresses flexibility, collaboration, and variety in the range of materials used. This move away from a focus on the textbook as the sole instrument of instruction is part of a larger shift away from more monolithic views of institutionalized learning—echoed, among other places, in recent proposals for curricular change advanced by government and university associations, as well as by broader changes in the curriculum provision landscape (Czerniewicz et al. 2014). These strategies also have their analogs in publishing, where the flexibility and additional forms of student support enabled by digital delivery are beginning to undermine the textbook model from the other direction.

The Modular, Flexible Future

In 2013, the Council on Higher Education (CHE) proposed a new round of curriculum reforms to address continued poor graduation rates and ill-preparedness of students from the secondary school system to the Ministry of Higher Education and Training. Policy documents called for greater integration across the different institutions in the higher education sector, a cross-disciplinary approach to the integration of African languages in the curriculum (DHET 2013, 38), and—reflecting earlier approaches to curricular reform—a need for more locally relevant materials. These policies argued for the implementation of elements of the earlier 1997 *White Paper on Higher Education*, which proposed the "development of a national network of centers of innovation in course design and development" and made a strong argument for wider use of open educational resources and open licensing to address the chronic dilemmas of high cost and poor access (DHET 2013, 54–60).

"Flexibility" became the watchword in this current round of proposals, which generally means the need for more modular learning resources that can support a wider range of pathways through four-year degrees, with different routes and different levels of support for students with different degrees of preparation. At present, these plans have not been translated into public policy and have little likelihood of producing major new institutional mandates or funding streams. There is currently no means to financially support the production of learning resources or the publication of locally produced textbooks to meet the requirements of such a system. However, the white papers point in a direction that some of the major publishers and universities are moving already, with the uptake of entirely new strategies. The result is a complex and transitional ecosystem marked by considerable experimentation.

Open Educational Resources (OER)

At the annual publishers' meetings in mid-2008, UNISA was reported—to the consternation of publishers—to be planning a move to consolidate the delivery of learning materials around its own courseware packs, changing and perhaps reducing its reliance on textbooks. Although it then stepped back from this commitment, UNISA continues to develop OER policies and content, as have other universities. If this shift continues, it will mean a very different role for publishers—and not necessarily a diminished one. Pearson is working with UNISA to build new courses on this model, providing publisher support for the development of materials. The institutional infrastructure for large-scale development and use of these materials appears to be emerging via UNISA Open,[55] which includes UNISA Open Courseware and an array of partnerships with open access initiatives.[56]

e-Textbooks

The most direct publisher shift toward digital models involves the sale of what are, essentially, digitized versions of the physical textbooks, enhanced with such features as the ability to take and share notes. Some of these e-books also offer access, via an included code, to a website with additional electronic and interactive services. The main commercial e-textbook solution in South Africa is Vital Source by Ingram, a major international book distribution company with a large catalog of titles drawn from many different publishers. (It is, reportedly, also the most-used digital textbook platform in the United States.) The goal is to provide digital textbook delivery at a lower price than print.

Vital Source launched in South Africa in 2014 with 464 titles from Wiley, at a standard price of $40 per title—at least 30 percent less than the average print price. The launch of this list was complicated by the technical infrastructure needed to restrict access to South African buyers (via digital rights management and geocoding)—in order to avoid both parallel importation and political backlash from U.S. students, who are paying considerably more for the same books.

Vital Source is well integrated into the South African book retailing sector, with a strong presence, in particular, in Van Schaik Bookshops. There are in-store kiosks in its major stores, piloted in field tests with UNISA, which allow students to download and activate e-books without requiring a continuous Internet connection—a critical feature in bandwidth-poor South Africa. Local publishers such as Juta are using the platform to distribute digital versions of their textbooks and the system will eventually integrate with university intranets and libraries, allowing for bulk institutional deals.

Although the Vital Source products are being taken up relatively slowly in South Africa in their initial phase, publishers and booksellers appear confident that they will find a strong position in the learning material ecosystem in the next few years.

Toward a Digitally Mediated Ecosystem

For decades, when academic textbook publishers were asked about their core business, their answer was "content." They meant that they commissioned, developed, published, copyrighted and distributed the materials that would be taught in classes. This business model—as in other so-called content industries like music and film—was lucrative and understood by all parties. Therefore, it is startling, to say the least, to hear leading publishers now say, "Content is not our core business."

The major college textbook publishers in the United States are progressively stepping out of the content role, seeing their strategic role in a larger field of learning delivery and support. The big five—McGraw Hill, Cengage, Macmillan, Pearson, and Wiley—have invested heavily in courseware and online learning environments that are increasingly customizable, interactive, and, from the student perspective, personalized.[57]

The content that used to be at the heart of the business is now secondary to the core business of providing learning support systems, which can include content other than that produced by the publisher. Pearson, for example, is increasingly investing in the creation of Pearson colleges of learning, which have a strong emphasis on electronic learning systems.

The collective impact of these events—including the rise of online university-based course delivery, the used book market, open education resources, and file sharing—has been a sharp fall in the profitability of textbook companies. There has been downsizing, restructuring, strategizing, and, in the cases of Cengage and Houghton Mifflin Harcourt, declarations of bankruptcy.[58]

The change of direction in the large companies is still nascent: teaching methods and practices change slowly and lag well behind the technological curve.[59] But they are having a large impact in the struggle to shape the future of educational publishing. Traditional publishers are becoming full-spectrum service providers for classroom learning and research, encroaching on tasks performed by libraries, bookstores, teachers and administrators, and technology providers, and incorporating a variety of other student support services. Increasingly, educational publishers understand their competition not as other publishing companies, but as telecommunications companies, software companies, information retrieval providers, and the like. Unlike the music and film industries, however, the educational publishers have had more time, less pressure to evolve toward digital media, and markets that remain largely embedded in institutions, which are more resistant to disintermediation and reliance on individual textbooks than the various consumer markets for "content." As a result, they have so far remained in control of these markets even as their roles are changing.

In the student focus groups, OER curricula and resources intersected the paths of only a handful of students—notably those who had experience with the digital commons. In these contexts, OER materials were greeted with enthusiasm by students. But there is a clear disconnect between issues concerning bursaries, which affect students directly, and the production and adoption of OER materials, over which students have little agency. Nevertheless, growing student focus and widespread protests on university campuses about the cost of education and the rising cost of textbooks, as well as the need to transform and decolonize the curriculum, is likely to raise the profile of OER policy debates.

With publishers moving in many of the same directions, the next decade of curricular change looks relatively clear. The main questions relate to the mix of university and publisher control over the ecosystem, the evolution of informal practices where this control fails, and the degree to which the resulting systems internalize the cost of materials to students and address their need for locally grounded materials. As student demonstrations broke out again in 2016, it was clear that the promises of post-apartheid education, much less redress of the larger legacies of apartheid, remain unmet.

Nevertheless, the emerging new models, with their emphasis on flexibility and access, might come closer to providing an ecology of access to learning materials that better accommodates what students themselves described as their reality—one that retains the flexibility of materials drawn from multiple sources and adapted to local contexts, while at least diminishing the ruthless process of selection and deprivation dictated by economic need.

Conclusion

Student protests since 2014 have introduced enormous volatility into the South African higher education system as well as the learning resources ecosystem. While embedded in current realities, the #RhodesMustFall protests at the University of Cape Town in 2015 that demanded the removal of a statue of a colonial-era icon raised echoes of many of the arguments of the 1970s student activists for the transformation and decolonization of the universities and the incorporation of a more Afrocentric curriculum. There followed the #FeesMustFall movement, addressing the financial crises of many students, unable to afford books, accommodation, food and fees, and criticizing the failures of NSFAS, including the exclusion from graduation of students who could not pay their student loans.

It is clear that the conundrum of providing learning materials in South African universities extends far beyond the materials themselves and beyond supply chains, to the complex ecologies of access in general shaped by apartheid separatism and present-day policy disconnects. Student access to resources has been the victim of vacillation between a policy tradition grounded in the "alternative curriculum" principles of anti-apartheid publishing and a developmental approach, and one grounded in a neoliberal market-oriented view of the role of higher education. Despite repeated efforts to build a national education agenda around the former, persistent economic difficulty has been a more fertile climate for imposing and rationalizing the latter view, helping provoke the current protests.

One result of the neoliberal approach is the expectation that universities should be, to an extent, self-funding, with student fees as an important part of this mix. This has been a particularly unrealistic expectation in South Africa as the system expands to serve the disproportionately poor and often underprepared majority population. Expansion of the NSFAS—the national student bursary and loan scheme—has been the primary policy response, but an inadequate one given the scale of student needs.

These problems are exacerbated by the variety of market failures in the book publishing and retailing sectors, including unaffordably high prices and chronic mismatches of supply and student demand, particularly in regard to international textbooks. In this context, many students ration their limited financial resources, making judgments about which books are most important for their studies and doing without the others. They employ a combination of strategies for accessing resources that extends well beyond the commercial market, including the sharing of resources within and across cohorts, photocopying, and relying on downloading—generally with little regard to legality.

These arrangements also reflect the segmented nature of the international market, which is structured by parallel importation prohibitions in copyright law. These prohibitions allowed originating publishers to provide discretionary, cheaper editions for developing countries, while preserving the higher-cost U.S. and UK markets, but they also significantly limited the bargaining power of small-market countries. The *Kirtsaeng v. Wiley* case in the United States in 2013 has begun to unravel these arrangements, leading to market instability and higher prices on imported books as new pricing models are put in place.

The complexities of the system have been deeply shaken by the issues raised during the student protests. The questions being raised refer very directly to the question of student learning resources and their appropriateness to the African context in which their users live. While the university presses have produced readers and republication of the works of African thinkers, the bigger questions of the reform of the university systems and the curriculum remain in abeyance. There is a very real risk of a general failure of the higher education system as a whole, in the face of underfunding and misalignment of policy directions with student aspirations.

It is perhaps serendipitous that publisher strategies have been changing in ways that better support this variegated landscape. Digital delivery is improving across the sector and some of the larger publishers are becoming—in key respects—educational technology companies, focused on not just textbooks and materials but also broader provision of learning design, support, assessment, and evaluation systems and services.

With countries like South Africa facing both growing student numbers and a rapid technological adoption curve with respect to computers, bandwidth, and devices, there are many indications that the developing world is a focus of these developments. In the short term, however, the numerous digital efforts have contributed to the instability of the market overall and to chaos in book pricing in particular. The variety of pricing models; delivery systems; digitized, born digital, and digitally supplemented products; bibliographical management systems; and feedback mechanisms from faculty—all present students with confusing and complex decisions.

Open educational resources look to be likely beneficiaries of these pressures on the system. Although currently fragmented in South Africa, in both policy and practices, OER presents an obvious opportunity in a system that needs less costly, more flexible, and legal solutions. If the current trends hold, solutions will likely emerge from partnerships between government, universities, educational NGOs, and the commercial sector, and ideally will produce effective digital delivery systems that accommodate the wide range of underserved paths through South African higher education.

Acknowledgments

With thanks to Kelsey Merkley for her role in research and data collection and to Havard Overson for his contribution to research and data collection in the student surveys.

Notes

1. The segregation of education in schools had already taken place with the passing of the Bantu Education Act in 1953.

2. See http://www.ufh.ac.za/About/Pages/History.aspx.

3. In the 1960 census, for example, the "Bantu" population was recorded at 68.3 percent of the total population, with the white population at 19.3 percent.

4. These risks were not hypothetical. A number of dissident academics were assassinated by the apartheid regime, including philosopher Rick Turner of the University of Natal in 1978 and anthropologist David Webster of the University of the Witwatersrand, shot in 1989.

5. This type of publishing faded quickly after the end of apartheid. It proved to be both strongly tied to the culture of opposition and highly vulnerable to changes in the book business—especially the consolidation of bookselling in mega-bookstore chains, which we will discuss later.

6. Personal communication, 2017.

7. Members of the Congress movement were the African National Congress, the South African Congress of Democrats, the South African Indian Congress, and the Colored People's Congress.

8. The Freedom Charter was adopted in Kliptown in 1955, after wide-ranging consultation, collecting input from members across the country. http://www.anc.org.za/show.php?id=72.

9. Constitution of the Republic of South Africa, 1996, Chapter 2, Bill of Rights, clause 29 (1), http://www.gov.za/documents/constitution/chapter-2-bill-rights#29.

10. Interestingly, in his analysis of apartheid intellectual traditions, Allsobrook describes the focus on the ISI indexes as a continuation of the positivist thinking underpinning apartheid, with its emphasis on metrics (Allsobrook 2014).

11. Official statistics linked to the national census tend to provide figures that are some years out of date, and it is the commercial analysts that are compiling more up-to-date figures (for example, BusinessTech in October 2015, https://businesstech.co.za/news/general/101412/here-are-south-africas-26-universities/).

12. See https://businesstech.co.za/news/general/101412/here-are-south-africas-26-universities/.

13. Juta also helped begin a tradition of local legal publishing that has set South Africa apart from the many other British ex-colonies that rely on British legal publications. This difference is driven by the fact that law in South Africa reflects not only the British colonial heritage but also the Roman-Dutch tradition of the earlier Dutch colonial regime. See, for example, https://juta.co.za/media/filestore/2013/06/JutaHeritage.pdf.

14. See http://www.vanschaiknet.com/companyhistory.

15. UNISA's early growth as an education provider was associated with Afrikaner conservatism, which gave its academics a dominant role in black universities in the apartheid years. Later, it benefited from the fact that it was the educational provider to many political prisoners who subsequently took up senior roles in the new government, and managed to progressively transform its conservative reputation.

16. Although the cost of textbooks has a variety of determinants, the main price driver is the small size of the local market. The Cost of Books Study reports that average South African print runs are relatively low (at 2,000 copies and below), with only 30–50 percent of books going to reprint. This problem is exacerbated by the low penetration of South African textbooks across African borders due to distribution and currency exchange barriers (Gray 2000). Still another contributor is the relatively high author royalties for textbooks, which as a percentage of net sales rose to 17.3 percent in 2011.

17. For a clear and succinct account of the arcane sphere of territorial rights and parallel importation, see Andrew Rens's chapter on the "Legal Context for Publishing in South Africa and Uganda," in the report on the 2010 IDRC-funded project on Publishing and Alternative Licensing in Africa, https://idl-bnc-idrc.dspacedirect.org/bitstream/handle/10625/45649/132110.pdf?...1.

18. See https://arstechnica.com/tech-policy/2012/10/a-supreme-court-clash-could-change-what-ownership-means/.

19. For an analysis of the judgment, see a KEI posting by Krista Cox, https://www.keionline.org/node/1686; for a more academic discussion of the issues prior to the Supreme Court decision, see John Mitchell, "Trans-Pacific Partnership proposes Suppression of Price Competition," February 21, 2012, in the Infojustice.org discussion forum, http://infojustice.org/archives/8305.

20. See *Bookmark* 35 (Sept.–Nov. 2013): 7, https://www.sabooksellers.com/wp-content/assets/BookmarkVol35.pdf.

21. StatsSA 2014, 53.

22. Local branches of international companies in South Africa, such as Pearson and Oxford University Press, publish locally a number of titles by South African authors or editors, as well as hold stock of and distribute imported books from their overseas branches The books published by the local publisher are included as locally produced books in the statistics, while books published by the overseas branches and held in stock by the local publisher are treated as "imported titles." Reported separately in the statistics are books imported directly by booksellers from other overseas publishers and not held in stock in South Africa.

23. The Publishers Association of South Africa (PASA) produces annual statistics reflecting the activities of its membership, which include the majority of the large industry players and a number of smaller publishers. These statistics are then adjusted to provide a picture of the industry in its entirety, including nonmembers. The PASA turnover figures reflect publisher revenues, not the gross sales revenue generated in the marketplace, and retail turnover is then estimated by adding back the value of the average discount applied by booksellers. Once every three years, the South African Booksellers Association (SABA) conducts a parallel survey of the performance of its members in the bookselling industry, which provides a picture of retail sales revenue. The SABA survey adds an important element to the statistical picture, in the form of figures for direct imports of international titles, not reflected in the publishers' figures. This provides a detailed view of the whole book industry, its players and markets, industry participants, and demographics. A combined report of this kind was produced in 2011, providing an up-to-date industry-wide picture of academic publishing and bookselling in South Africa.

24. Interviews with local publishers, carried out in 2013–2014.

25. Much the same pattern is reproduced in authorship, where on an annual basis, the vast majority of authors are white. Book industry statistics for 2012 reported that only 14 percent of locally published books had black authors. Whether this is owing to the difficulty of recruiting authors to write textbooks due to a reward system organized around journal publication, as some publishers reported, or to the relative lack of seniority of black academics, or to persisting conservatism, or to some combination of factors, there is a continued misalignment of policy aspirations and author demographics.

26. See http://www.scielo.org.za/. There are currently fifty-eight journals indexed in SciELO SA. A concise account of this intervention is provided on the ASSAf web page: https://www.assaf.org.za/index.php/programmes/scholarly-publishing-programme/107-scholarly-publishing-programme.

27. For an analysis of this program, see the report on its fifteen-year development: http://scielo.org/php/level.php?lang=en&component=42&item=31.

28. Historically, books were rewarded at a much lower level in this incentive system. However, as a result of a survey of scholarly book publishing carried out by the Academy of Science of South Africa, the subsidy for peer-reviewed scholarly books is due to rise considerably from 2015 onward.

29. For a case study of the conceptualization, implementation, and strategies of the HSRC Press, see Gray, Van Schalkwyk, and Bruns 2004; to be found at: http://www.codesria.org/spip.php ?article752&lang=en.

30. See http://www.gov.za/address-minister-science-and-technology-naledi-pandor-mp-book-launch -hsrcs-state-nation-1994-2014.

31. The African Copyright and Access to Knowledge research program, in which the author played a part.

32. Section 3 of the Copyright Regulations, 1978, as published in GN R1211 in GG 9775 of 7 June 1985 as amended by GN 1375 in GG 9807 of 28 June 1985.

33. It is to be noted that fair dealing is a narrower concept than that of fair use set forth in U.S. copyright legislation.

34. The African Copyright and Access to Knowledge study of the South African research program provided the following summary of the limitations and advantages of the South African legislative environment in relation to access to learning materials: (1) The ambiguities in the provisions for copying for educational purposes detracts from the potential of these provisions to provide effectively for L&Es for educational access. (2) The Act fails to provide for fair dealing in the case of digital works. (3) There is no provision for the scanning and digitization of works for access by the visually impaired (De Beer et al. 2010). (South Africa has not yet ratified the Marrakesh Treaty, which was concluded in 2014.)

35. The author of this report was involved in these discussions in her capacity as then-director of the Wits University Press.

36. See http://ip-unit.org/wp-content/uploads/2013/10/IP-Policy-Academics-Submission_final17 1013.pdf.

37. DALRO was originally a privately owned company but by the 1990s had become a subsidiary of the South African Music Rights Organisation (SAMRO).

38. See http://www.rcips.uct.ac.za/rcips/ip/copyright/bla (UCT contracts office guidelines on the DALRO license).

39. There are, in addition, limits set on the extent of copying allowed from individual books and journals. The limits for copying and the terms that apply are set out in university guidelines: for example, Wits University, http://libguides.wits.ac.za/c.php?g=145347&p=953449; and UCT, http://www.rcips.uct.ac.za/rcips/ip/copyright/bla. Transactional licenses for extracts from publishers who have opted not to be included in the blanket license have to be negotiated individually with DALRO, at a pre-agreed page rate for publication-by-publication licensing.

40. Listed as Submission 27, from the University of Cape Town in the Commission report, 113.

41. See http://www.nsfas.org.za/.

42. At 2015 exchange rates.

43. Six weeks into the second semester of the 2014–2015 academic year, 2,500 students at the University of Fort Hare campus in Alice who qualified for an NSFAS grant had not received funds. Their Student Representative Council was told there was no money. University management has come under fire from students for charging fees that exceed NSFAS allocations, including a 100 percent increase year on year for residence. Cost of a shared residence for one year on campus in 2013 was R9,000; in 2014, it was R19,000.

44. See https://mg.co.za/article/2014-09-15-tut-management-suspends-src.

45. Some publishers indicated that South African textbooks do not even appear on torrent sites—another dimension of the small-market problem that shapes South African publishing. The publishers' association has begun tracking South African textbooks in international torrent sites, and has signaled readiness to issue takedown notices if and when necessary.

46. See http://jutaacademic.co.za/articles/winners-of-2012-student2book-campaign-announced-at -vut.

47. Author interview with publisher.

48. A questionnaire containing 63 questions was distributed during, before, and after lectures (with lecturer permission) resulting in 1,008 responses. The questionnaire was developed with colleagues across five sites and was divided into sections on access to technology, acquisition of materials, and library databases and online platforms. The survey analysis was undertaken by the data specialist serving the broader project. After the surveys had been completed, six student focus groups were run, two each in three disciplinary areas respectively: law, health sciences and communication studies. Forty-two students were interviewed: twelve male, thirty female. All remained anonymous and their responses were coded by disciplinary grouping, focus group number, and student number. Coding was undertaken by a research assistant and the principal researcher. Among the major demographic features of the survey group: 99 percent were full-time students; of which 50 percent were in their first year, and 67.6 percent said that their first language was English, with the remainder citing predominantly other South African languages. In terms of household income, the students were reasonably well spread across the levels, with a quarter in the highest bracket and a quarter in the lowest bracket. Just under two-thirds said that their parents were funding their studies. The percentage of students surveyed who reported being on financial aid (16.9 percent) was close to the overall percentage in the university (15.6 percent).

Nearly all of the students, except four, owned a cell phone (99.6 percent), a reflection of the high levels of cell phone use in South Africa. Of those with a cell phone, 94.7 percent had Internet access via their phones.

49. Only three students reported costs of over $1,000 (R10,000).

50. The plight of bursary students in the face of this facet of market failure cited here emerged in focus groups with students and in media reports on problems with the NFSAS student bursary scheme.

51. The merger of the two main e-retailers, Kalahari.com and Takealot, approved by the Competitions Commission in late 2014 and have subsequently been implemented. This has accelerated the development of the online market for textbooks, in part via an expansion of alternative payment methods.

52. Our sample drew on a relatively privileged university community on a city campus, and so demonstrated high levels of Internet access and ownership of computers and devices. Of the 1,008 students surveyed, 930 owned a laptop; 276 had a tablet or e-reader, and 908 had Internet access at home. Internet access on campus was available to all the respondents. In remote universities, all of these numbers would likely be significantly lower.

53. When asked which illegal resources they had used, survey respondents cited two categories of websites predominantly. Direct download sites comprised 30 percent of the answers, with Megaupload, 4shared.com, and Library.nu (the book downloading site) receiving the most mentions. Peer-to-peer sites such as torrent providers were also popular, accounting for 37.8 percent of the total, with the sharing software D++ appearing in 16.2 percent of the responses and the well-known Pirate Bay site taking 9.2 percent of the specific answers. The dominance of the dated DC++ file sharing protocol—a Napster-like precursor of BitTorrent that makes use of a centralized server for indexing content—is somewhat surprising. Although we can only speculate, its popularity may reflect the international bandwidth constraints under which South African Internet users labored for much of the past decade. As a centralized archival system, DC++ can be set up and efficiently run on the South African side of the bottleneck.

54. This explosion of sources has also had a secondary effect. In contrast to copyright infringement, fears of inadvertent plagiarism were common and sometimes quite strong. Remarked one student, "I am more worried about university consequences than legal consequences, because a lot of times I like pray with my Turnitin report [an automated plagiarism detection service] just like "please don't be red, please don't be red." So I'm more worried about that, getting called in for plagiarism than going to jail."

55. See http://www.unisa.ac.za/Default.asp?Cmd=ViewContent&ContentID=27721.

56. Including OER University and OER Africa, a project initiated by the South African Institute of Distance Education (SAIDE).

57. Young 2013.

58. See, for example, http://www.thebookseller.com/news/profits-fall-penguin-momentous-year.

59. See Young 2013.

References

Allsobrook, Christopher John. 2014. "A Genealogy of South African Positivism." In *Intellectual Traditions in South Africa: Ideas, Individuals and Institutions*, ed. Peter Vale, Lawrence Hamilton, and Estelle H. Prinsloo, 95–118. Scottsville: University of KwaZulu-Natal Press.

Armstrong, Chris, Jeremy de Beer, Dick Kawooya, Achal Prabhala, and Tobias Schonwetter, eds. 2010. *Access to Knowledge in Africa: The Role of Copyright*. Cape Town: UCT Press, in conjunction with the International Development Research Centre, the Shuttleworth Foundation, and the Link Centre. https://idl-bnc-idrc.dspacedirect.org/bitstream/handle/10625/44667/IDL-44667.pdf.

ASSAF. 2009. "Scholarly Books: Their Production, Use and Evaluation in South Africa." Pretoria: Academy of Science of South Africa. https://www.assaf.org.za/files/2017%20reports/ASSAF%20 Scholarly%20Report%20FINAL%20Proof.pdf.

Badat, Saleem. 1991. "The Expansion of Black Tertiary Education 1977–90: Reform and Contradiction." In *Apartheid Education and Popular Struggles*, 1st ed., ed. Elaine Unterhalter, Harold Wolpe, Thozamile Botha, Saleem Badat, Thulisile Dlamini, and Benito Khotseng, 73–94. Johannesburg: Ravan Press.

Badat, Saleem. 2009. "Theorising Institutional Change: Post–1994 South African Higher Education." *Studies in Higher Education* 34 (4): 455–467. doi:10.1080/0307507090277.

Berger, Guy. 2000."Publishing for the People: The Alternative Press 1980–1999." In *The Politics of Publishing in South Africa*, ed. Nicholas Evans and Monica Seeber, 73–103. Scottsville: University of KwaZulu-Natal Press.

Bunting, Ian. 2002. "The Higher Education Landscape under Apartheid." In *Transformation in Higher Education: Global Pressures and Local Realities in South Africa*, 1st ed., 58–86. Landsdowne, Cape Town: Centre for Higher Education Transformation. http://www.chet.org.za/download/file/fid/216.

Chan, Leslie, and Eve Gray. 2013. "Centering the Knowledge Peripheries through Open Access: Implications for Future Research and Discourse." In *Open Development: Networked Innovations in International Development*, ed. Matthew L. Smith and Katherine M. A. Reilly, 197–222. Cambridge, MA: MIT Press.

CHE (Council on Higher Education). 2015. "Vital Stats: Public Higher Education 2013." Pretoria: CHE. http://www.che.ac.za/media_and_publications/monitoring-and-evaluation/vitalstats -public-higher-education-2013.

Cloete, Nico, and Alison Gillwald. 2014. "South African Informational Development and Human Development: Rights vs Capabilities." In *Reconceptualizing Development in the Global Information Age*, 1st ed., ed. Manuel Castells and Pekka Himanen, 140–174. New York: Oxford University Press.

Czerniewicz, Laura, Andrew Deacon, Janet Small, and S. Walji. 2014. "Developing World MOOCs: A Curriculum View of the MOOC Landscape." *Journal of Global Literacies, Technologies, and Emerging Pedagogies* 2 (3): 122–139.

De Bellaigue, Eric. 1997. "Conglomeracy and the Book Business: Where Next?" *Logos: The Journal of the World Book Community* 8 (3): 127–134.

DHET (Department of Higher Education and Training). 2001. "National Plan for Higher Education in South Africa." National Policy Document. Pretoria: DHET.

DHET (Department of Higher Education and Training). 2013. *White Paper for Post-School Education and Training: Building an Expanded, Effective and Integrated Post-School System.* As approved by Cabinet on November 20, 2013. Pretoria: DHET.

DHET (Department of Higher Education and Training). 2015. *Statistics on Post-School Education and Training in South Africa.* Pretoria: DHET. http://www.dhet.gov.za/DHET%20Statistics%20 Publication/Statistics%20on%20Post-School%20Education%20and%20Training%20in%20 South%20Africa%202013.pdf.

DTI (Department of Trade and Industry). 2011. Copyright Review Commission Report. Judicial Review. Pretoria: DTI. https://www.gov.za/sites/default/files/CRC%20REPORT.pdf.

DTI (Department of Trade and Industry). 2013. "Draft National Policy on Intellectual Property (IP) in South Africa." September. Pretoria: DTI. http://ip-unit.org/wp-content/uploads/2013/09/ DRAFT-IP-POLICY.pdf.

Evans, Nicholas, and Monica Seeber, eds. 2000. *The Politics of Publishing in South Africa.* Scottsville: University of KwaZulu-Natal Press.

Gray, Eve. 2000. "Academic Publishing in South Africa." In *The Politics of Publishing in South Africa*, ed. Nicholas Evans and Monica Seeber, 163–188. Scottsville: University of KwaZulu-Natal Press.

Gray, Eve, and Monica Seeber. 2004. PICC Report on Intellectual Property Right*s in the Print Industry Sector.* Cape Town: Print Industries Cluster Council. http://www.publishsa.co.za/ downloads/intellectual_property_report.pdf.

Gray, Eve, Karen Bruns, and Andrew Rens. 2010. "Publishing and Alternative Licensing Models in Africa." Cape Town: Association for Creative Research and Development. https://idl-bnc.idrc.ca/ dspace/bitstream/10625/45649/1/132110.pdf.

Gray, Eve, Francois Van Schalkwyk, and Karen Bruns. 2004. "Digital Publishing and Open Access for Social Science Research Dissemination: A Case Study." *Conference Proceedings.* Codesria, Dakar. www.codesria.org/IMG/pdf/Eve-Gray.pdf.

Haricombe, Lorraine, and F. W. Lancaster. 1995. *Out in the Cold: Academic Boycotts and the Isolation of South Africa.* Arlington, VA: Information Resources Press.

HESA. 2014. "HESA Response to the Council on Higher Education Task Team on Undergraduate Curriculum Structure (August 2013)," February. 2013_HESA_Response-to-the-CHE-Undergraduate -Curriculum-Structure_Dec-2013.pdf.

Hofmeyr, Isabel. 2013. *Gandhi's Printing Press.* Cambridge, MA: Harvard University Press.

Hofmeyr, Isabel, and Govinden [Betty] Deverakshanam. 2009. "Africa/India: Culture and Circulation in the Indian Ocean." *Scrutiny 2: Issues in English Studies in Southern Africa* 13 (2): 5–15. doi:10.1080/18125440802485961.

Horvath, Stephen. 1996. "The Rise of the Book Chain Superstore." *Logos* 7 (1): 39–45.

Hyslop, Jonathan. 1988. "State Education Policy and the Social Reproduction of the Urban African Working Class: The Case of the Southern Transvaal 1955–1976." *Journal of Southern African Studies* 14 (3): 446–476.

Jansen, Jonathan. 1990. "Curriculum as a Political Phenomenon: Historical Reflections on Black South African Education." *Journal of Negro Education* 59 (2): 195–206. http://repository.up.ac.za/handle/2263/1384?show=full.

Jansen, Jonathan. 2003. "The State of Higher Education in South Africa: From Massification to Mergers." In *State of the Nation: South Africa 2003–2004*, 1st ed., ed. John Daniel, Roger Southall, and Adam Habib, 290–311. Pretoria: HSRC Press.

Kell, Catherine. 1991. "Activists and Academics: The Role of Liberal Universities in Research for the Democratic Movement." In *Apartheid Education and Popular Struggles*, 1st ed., ed. Elaine Unterhalter, 146–155. Johannesburg: Ravan Press.

Mandela, Nelson. 1994. *Long Walk to Freedom*. South Africa: Macdonald Purnell.

Moss, Glenn. 2014. *The New Radicals: A Generational Memoir of the 1970s*. Johannesburg: Jacana Media.

Mpe, Phaswane, and Monica Seeber. 2000. "The Politics of Book Publishing in South Africa: A Critical Overview." In *The Politics of Publishing in South Africa*, ed. Nicholas Evans and Monica Seeber, 15–42. Scottsville: University of KwaZulu-Natal Press.

PASA (Publishers Association of South Africa). 2013. "Annual Book Publishing Survey 2012: Business Economic Report December 2013." Cape Town: PASA. http://publishsa.co.za/file/1441481157ues-annual-publishing-industry-survey-2012.pdf.

PASA (Publishers Association of South Africa). 2014. "Annual Book Publishing Industry Survey 2013." Cape Town: PASA. http://www.publishsa.co.za/downloads/2013_Annual_Publishing_Industry_Survey.pdf.

Pascal, Naomi B. 1996. "Between Academe and the Marketplace: University Presses Face the 21st Century." *Logos* 7 (1): 113–119.

Philip, David. 1991. *Book Publishing in and after Apartheid in Book Publishing in South Africa for the 1990s*. Cape Town: South African Library.

Rosenberg, Garry. 2008. "Broadening the Exchange of Knowledge." *Mail and Guardian*, June 13.

Schonwetter, Tobias, Caroline Ncube, and Pria Chetty. 2010. "South Africa." In *Access to Knowledge in Africa: The Role of Copyright*, ed. Chris Armstrong, Jeremy de Beer, Dick Kawooya, Achal

Prabhala, and Tobias Schonwetter, 231–268. Cape Town: UCT Press, in conjunction with the International Development Research Centre, the Shuttleworth Foundation, and the Link Centre.

Soudien, Crain. 2013. "Regarding the Capability Deprivation Machine: The Pedagogical Deal for Post-Apartheid Young South Africa." *CriSTaL* 1 (1): 53–79. doi:10.14426/cristal.v1i1.8.

Swilling, Mark. 1988. "The United Democratic Front and Township Revolt." In *Popular Struggles in South Africa*, ed. William Cobbett and Robin Cohen, 90–113. London: James Currey.

Wafawarowa, Brian. 2007. "The Business of Book Publishing in Africa." Paper presented at the WIPO International Conference on Intellectual Property and the Creative Industries, October 29–30, Geneva.

Worth, Robert R. 1996. "The US College Textbook: A Learning Tool without Rival, If Values Are Maintained." *Logos: The Journal of the World Book Community* 7 (1): 93–101.

Young, Jeffrey R. 2013. "The Object Formerly Known as the Textbook." *The Chronicle of Higher Education*, January 27, 2013. http://www.chronicle.com/article/Dont-Call-Them-Textbooks/136835/.

Yu, S. 2012. "College Students' Justification for Digital Piracy: A Mixed Methods Study." *Journal of Mixed Methods Research* 6:364–378. doi:10.1177/1558689812451790.

6   Poland: Where the State Ends, the Hamster Begins

Mirosław Filiciak and Alek Tarkowski

In Poland, student and faculty strategies for getting the books and other materials they need have been shaped by the transformation of the academic system since 1989 and by the broader political, economic, and linguistic legacies that shape post-communist Polish society. They have also been largely absent from academic and educational policy discussions—neither a subject of mainstream debate nor addressed in the numerous governmental reforms of the system. Even significant institutional developments, such as the introduction of digital, online libraries and the promotion of open access models, have been marginal forces in a process of structural change driven by the rapid expansion of higher education, integration with Europe, and competition for students and research funds. For these reasons, and unlike in some of the other countries examined in this book, there have been no grassroots initiatives focused on the provision of academic content. Academic publishing has never been seen as a political issue, or tied to such values as freedom of expression. Instead, it has been treated as a primarily technical aspect of the higher education system.

For the same reasons, academic shadow libraries have never been the subject of public debate, which over the years has nonetheless given considerable attention to broader issues of content "piracy." The informal collection and circulation of academic content has operated in a gray zone, partly due to the unclear legal status of such activities (which potentially fall under copyright exceptions) and partly due to the lack of sufficient legal awareness among key academic stakeholders. These informal practices nonetheless play a significant role in Polish higher education—albeit in ways that are often hard to distinguish from the broader informal circulation of audio, visual, and other media content.

The Higher Education System in Poland after 1989

Among many other changes, the end of communist rule in Poland led to a boom in Polish higher education. A system that until 1989 terminated in vocational training for most Poles shifted, both institutionally and aspirationally, toward college and university degrees. Student enrollment exploded over the next two decades, rising from 500,000 in 1990–1991 to over two million by 2011, in a period of overall slight population decline.

Some of this growth was accommodated by expansion of the public system, which grew from 500,000 enrolled students to 1.2 million in 2011–2012 (GUS 2012)—the year of the demographic peak—and currently enrolls around 75 percent of all students. At the same time, however, the private university sector boomed, with the number of private colleges and universities rising from 18 in 1991 to 338 in 2011 (Jakubowski 2015). Similar private expansion occurred at the primary and secondary levels, diversifying the educational system and creating pressure for modernization and consolidation of state educational policy. When these reforms emerged in 1999, they focused on primary and secondary education, with the goal of expanding pathways to higher education. Over the next decade, this was broadly achieved. Net enrollment rates in higher education rose from 9.8 percent in 1990–1991 to 30.6 percent in 2000–2001, before stabilizing in the high 30s in the 2010s (GUS 2015). Poland also has the highest share in Europe of adults with a master's degree or equivalent.

Admission to the European Union in 2004 brought a different set of challenges. Traditionally insular Polish institutions found themselves under pressure to work in an increasingly international academic environment, marked by greater student mobility, a research culture in which English was the lingua franca, and competition for research funding. In 2010, the Ministry of Science and Higher Education introduced a set of policy reforms designed to align the Polish system with these international norms. The new policies targeted many of the core features of Polish academic life, from the rules governing student stipends to the structure of degree programs, faculty employment, and funding of scientific institutions. Although the basic principles of free public and subsidized private education were reaffirmed, the reforms broke up entrenched faculty and student prerogatives that were viewed as obstacles to institutional change and burdens on limited budgets.

The 2010 reforms also coincided with the demographic peak of Polish enrollment, as the baby boom of the 1980s passed through the system (Groves 2014). At the end of this period of institutional expansion, concerns began to be raised that the project had favored growth over quality, both with regard to student achievement and research.

The 2010 reforms addressed what the government viewed as underlying issues of employment and funding that impacted quality. But the reforms sidelined other issues, among them scholarly communication and related questions about the provision of educational resources to students.

The Ministry of Science and Higher Education recognized faculty concerns with scholarly communication during deliberation on the 2010 reforms, but deferred consideration of them. Academic proposals for further change soon consolidated around the "Pact for Academia," a document prepared by a civic movement of academics fighting for a general reform of the academic and research system. The pact included recommendations for implementing formal open access requirements for publicly supported work—a measure that, given the very high level of Polish research publication subsidies, had the potential to push the scholarly publishing ecosystem decisively in that direction.[1] In 2015, the Ministry formally recommended such a move but made it nonbinding and authorized no funding to enable the transition. By 2016, there were still no visible effects of this commitment.[2] Copyright reform also passed in 2015. It clarified how educational exceptions to copyright were to be applied in some contexts, but did little to change the status quo for libraries, faculty, and students. Academic stakeholders, for the most part, were not involved in the reform process.

In 2016, a new Polish government returned to the question of educational reform, taking up the familiar goal of improving the international competitiveness of Polish universities and Polish science (Kwiek et al. 2016).[3] Among other things, the new policy places increased emphasis on foreign publication as a performance metric. While such goals are widely criticized by the research and academic community, they remain a constant in education policy discussions, even across major changes of government.

Language and Publishing

With 98.5 percent of Poland's 38.5 million inhabitants identifying as ethnic Poles, Polish is the overwhelmingly dominant language both in and outside the university system. As in other Eastern European countries, English has largely replaced Russian as the secondary language of choice, especially among younger Poles. In 2013, 18.8 percent of Poles overall claimed competence in English, rising to 37.7 percent among students. Despite this growth, the language of instruction remains Polish, with foreign materials used almost exclusively in translation—when they are available.

The local publishing market is correspondingly small and in a sense "inbred"—Polish authors write and publish mainly in Polish. Although scholarly publishing fell sharply after the post-1989 economic shock, the sector has grown steadily since 2004 with respect to the production of new academic titles (if not the overall size of the market, which does not appear to have appreciably grown). The publishing branches of educational and research institutions have led this boom, outpacing private publishers by around 6,500 new titles to 4,800 in the post-1989 period (Strycharz and Golik 2012).

This growth in the number of titles closely tracked the reform of higher education and research. As the Polish system changed to align with European norms, it adopted emerging European practices of evaluation in which the quantity of publishing became an important proxy for intellectual productivity. As these measures began to play a role in funding and promotion, academic and research institutions responded by publishing more journals and monographs. The result was something close to a two-tiered system, separated partly by language but also by subject. Polish scholars with strong international connections, research themes, and English-language skills gravitated toward international journals, which afforded more recognition in the globalizing culture of research and reputation. Scholars whose work emphasized local topics or who could not write easily in English gained little traction in the international research community. The expansion of Polish scholarly publishing was partly a response to this asymmetry as the (imported) demand for publication as a professional marker met the structural disadvantages that Polish academics (and non-native English-speaking academics in other countries) faced in working within the international tier. These asymmetries have created significant tensions within the Polish academic community, as well as more practical problems and distortions with respect to access to materials. Books from foreign publishers are in high demand, but also expensive and accordingly poorly represented in Polish libraries. Limited library resources go disproportionately to buying access to the high-prestige international journals and research databases that are perceived to be a necessary condition of working at the international level.

Public subsidies have played a key role in the expansion of this ecosystem: the vast majority of academic publication in Poland—we estimate around 86 percent—is funded or co-funded with resources obtained, directly or indirectly, from Polish or European Union public sources. For most academics, it has become relatively easy to obtain grants to support publication. It is also a common practice among publishers to issue very small print runs when grant-based funding is available—largely independent of intellectual and market rationales.

As publication has become more closely connected to professional requirements, however, it has grown more distant from the concept of readership. This problem is more acute among the university presses, which have little in the way of marketing or distribution infrastructure. Although private publishers produce fewer texts than academic and research institutions, they are much more effective in marketing and, consequently, monetizing their work: 73 percent of the stock of the largest Polish academic bookstore consists of titles produced by private publishers. This closer engagement with the market translates into larger print runs and greater sales. The two largest Polish universities—Jagiellonian University (UJ) and Warsaw University (UW)—accounted for only 0.24 percent of all copies of academic monographs released in 2011. The two largest private publishers account for 17.4 percent (Strycharz and Golik 2012).

Libraries and Databases

University libraries play a complicated role in this environment. Since the introduction of digital technologies into academia in the late 1990s, research libraries have led efforts to expand access to scholarly and instructional materials—including through the creation of digital collections. The Federation of Digital Libraries (Federacja Bibliotek Cyfrowych), an online aggregator service, has 131 data sources that make available more than 4.3 million objects—of which more than three million are available on an open access basis. While these statistics are impressive, more than half of these objects are scans of nonacademic journals. There are only 200,000 books and 150,000 academic articles in the system. Traditionally, the library community has been a strong proponent of open access publication models.

At the same time, libraries devote a growing portion of their resources to sustaining the existing hierarchical relationships in publishing—notably through the licensing of commercial scientific databases and journals. State policies have explicitly supported this role. All Polish academic and research institutions have access to some of the prominent academic databases such as EBSCO, ScienceDirect, SpringerLink, and Web of Knowledge, facilitated by a "national license" paid by the Ministry of Science and Higher Education under the Virtual Science Library program (Wirtualna Biblioteka Nauki). Subscriptions to many other databases are purchased through "consortium licenses" funded by partnering institutions and partially supported by the Ministry.

Data on the financial aspects of these licenses is hard to obtain. The national license costs the Ministry approximately 130 million Polish złoty per year (about USD$35 million), for access to major full-text databases such as Science Direct, SpringerLink, and Wiley-Blackwell, as well as other publishers (such as ACS, AIP, Emerald, IEEE, LWW, IOP, OUP, and CUP).[4] The consortium licenses, however, are bound by nondisclosure agreements with the providers, making costs much more difficult to estimate. One library told us that the annual cost of accessing the databases within the consortium amounts to $50,000, with the libraries paying a third of subscription fees and the balance covered by the Ministry.[5] Outside the consortia, pricing for Polish institutions is calibrated to perceived ability to pay, with lack of access to some of the major databases reflecting unsuccessful negotiations of those boundaries.

We had an opportunity to witness negotiations between a Polish academic institution and Sage Publishing for access to one of Sage's major databases, the Humanities and Social Science (HSS) Package. The annual cost for the university in question was around $11,000—a large sum by Polish library standards and one that the library ultimately chose not to pay. According to one of our informants, the main stake of the negotiations for Sage, however, was not maximizing payment from the university, but rather pushing adoption of the Sage database across the threshold for inclusion among the consortium licenses subsidized by the state—a step that apparently required eight subscribed schools. In the absence of such licensing, Polish students and researchers generally relied on the annual Sage "special offer," which makes access to databases free for a month.[6] As we will see in chapter 7, this creates its own boundary problems and workarounds, as Sage tries to be both an essential resource and a mostly unavailable one for students and faculty.

Polish alternatives to the major international databases suffer from perceptions of second-tier status with regard to content and—more practically—from the persistence of complex terms of access imposed by publishers, even within university library settings. Particularly with regard to monographs, most participating publishers place restrictions on the number of simultaneous copies that can be accessed. These are enforced through the online platforms, which often lack the option of downloading the publication, or through the digital rights management systems at file level. The Academica Project, an electronic interlibrary loan system organized by the Polish National Library, is notable (but not exceptional) in permitting the use of only a single copy at a time across the participating libraries. iBuk, an academic database owned by the large educational publisher Polskie Wydawnictwo Naukowe, is viewed as relatively progressive since a single institutional subscription allows up to five simultaneous copies to circulate. iBuk pays a price for this prodigality, however, by containing only older books and materials—so constrained because of publisher fear of losing control of digital content. Strict analogies between digital and print copies are still the norm.

Poland is hardly unique in this respect: although journal access has moved almost fully toward site licenses that provide complete access to authorized users, norms for books remain unsettled. The commercial e-book market is immature, representing only 3–5 percent of a Polish market estimated at around €640 million in 2014. Although neighboring Scandinavian countries provide a strong model for library-based access to e-books,[7] Polish publishers have been conservative and both public and academic libraries have been reluctant to test the legal boundaries around this issue. Although Polish copyright law permits a relatively wide range of "permitted uses" for individual educational purposes (similar to fair use or fair dealing exceptions in the United States and UK), the rights of institutions to copy and circulate materials are more limited and remain in a state of considerable uncertainty. One university librarian described how a recent effort to digitize and make available materials on course syllabi foundered on the question of whether the library had the right to make sufficient copies for a class and whether it could allow those copies to be downloaded.[8] When Polish copyright reform in 2015 failed to significantly clarify these issues, the syllabus project was abandoned. Library support for open access models is based largely on the desire to break this kind of bottleneck.

Open Access and Educational Exceptions to Copyright Law

Despite the prominent role that open access requirements play in academic reform discourse, support is far from universal—indeed the issue often meets with faculty and staff suspicion. Our interviews with academics broadly confirmed this view. With many faculty members in situations of economic precariousness, reluctance to "give anything away for free" is common.[9] There are nonetheless important differences within the academic community: awareness of open access is relatively high in fields such as cultural studies, which is unusually reflexive about academic practice, and in some of the natural sciences, where open access models are an international norm. There are also generational differences: younger authors are generally more favorable toward open access, arguably due to the fact that they search for digital content themselves and, more than their older colleagues, participate in the academic "rat race" in which widespread dissemination has important benefits for one's reputation. Finally there are extreme cases of authors who oppose any copying of their books.

The latter views align with and are often informed by publisher efforts to cloud the status of copying in Poland. Legal notices often can be found in academic texts, in particular law books, that warn against any copying of book content. These notices are notable for being false: Polish law allows for individual copying in educational and research contexts. But such notices do exercise a chilling effect on individuals and especially libraries, which are often reluctant to photocopy books, and increase the perception of risk for libraries or universities that want to test new models of access.

In the last several years, some publishers have adopted a more lenient approach. The Polish Book Publishers Chamber (Polska Izba Książki) now recommends the use of a copyright notice that explains the rights of users and their limits in a more balanced manner. This is an important shift from previous campaigns. Nevertheless, the attitude of most publishers toward the copying of content remains distrustful or negative. One telling example involves the deposit copies that publishers are required to send to about a dozen Polish libraries, including the National Library. Recent proposals to make these copies digital have met sharp opposition from Polish publishers, who fear losing control of their content.

Student Practices

Contemporary student practices reflect patterns of informal copying and sharing that emerged in the 1990s, as much of the legacy material of the communist era became obsolete. The familiar drivers of a large-scale copy culture were all in place in the period: a poorly functioning legal market, increased access to cheap copying technologies, and the entry of large numbers of poorer students into a system that made few material accommodations to their needs. Although these copying practices shared a lineage with communist-era underground publishing (samizdat; in Polish, *bibuła*), much of this academic copy culture was a new phenomenon, driven by a student population for whom communist-era intellectual repression was a relatively marginal influence. It had more in common with—and in later years, more explicit connections to—the culture of copying and downloading music, movies and TV shows, and software. For a generation of young people, cultural and educational integration into the West passed to a large degree through this process of informal acquisition of media.

As we documented in a 2012 study (Filiciak, Hofmokl, and Tarkowski 2012), these informal practices are commonplace in Poland and nearly ubiquitous among the young and among Internet users. Eighty-eight percent of young respondents acknowledged consuming music and film via downloading, streaming, or other informal channels. Among Internet users, the number was 78 percent. However, this is still a small-scale phenomenon with regard to books. A 2012 World Internet Project study indicated that only 2 percent of Polish Internet users bought e-books in 2011; only 4 percent downloaded them for free. Students aged 20–24 were the category most likely to download books for free, but even among this group the activity is relatively rare: only 9 percent admitted to downloading books. While informal circulation itself is widespread in Poland, e-books have remained an object of relatively low interest, tracking the comparatively slow adoption of readers and the underdeveloped legal market, and possibly the more general decline of reading, in which Poland regularly ranks among the lowest in Europe.[10]

This was the context in which we conducted a more detailed study of student practices. A large part of the study was quantitative. In June 2013, we surveyed 648 first-, second-, and third-year students at four universities—two public and two private, in one of the largest Polish cities—on a range of issues surrounding their acquisition and management of course materials. Respondents came from the faculties of law, cultural studies, and media studies. In addition, we surveyed twenty-five doctoral students.[11]

As with most of the survey-based work in this book, the sample does not provide a representative sample of Polish students in general.[12] But it does closely track some of the major demographic features of the larger student population, including the high percentage of women students (70 percent in our survey; 59 percent overall) (Dziewczyny na politechniki 2012); and general access to personal computers and the Internet, which is nearly universal (98.5 percent and 98 percent in our survey; 99 percent and 98.5 percent in the *Social Diagnosis 2013* report (Czapiński and Panek 2014).[13] In contrast to these very high levels of access, tablets and e-book readers showed significant but lower levels of adoption: 31.7 percent of those surveyed own one or both (compared to 9.3 percent in the general population for tablets and 3.8 percent for e-book readers).[14] Overall, we take the results as illustrative and confirmatory of many of the trends identified through the wider range of methods used in this study. In some instances, we think they provide a valid picture of the conditions and practices of Polish undergraduates. We've tried to signal when and why we make such generalizations from the data.

As other studies in this collection have amply shown, student practices are often shaped by prosaic efforts to pass exams and finish courses, rather than more intellectual investments in acquiring material or building personal libraries.[15] For a significant number of students, this implies no acquisition of materials at all: around 10 percent of students in our survey possessed no course materials—new, used, photocopied, or otherwise. Instead, these students generally relied on course and lecture notes, which are commonly—and perhaps accurately—viewed as sufficient to passing certain classes. Buying materials is an infrequent practice overall: around 14 percent never bought materials. Only 19 percent reported buying more than 60 percent of their materials new. The used market, for its part, remains relatively disorganized and plays only a small role at the margins of student practices.

Disciplinary differences were quite pronounced in responses to this question: the nature of the law curriculum clearly disposed law students to own new materials: 36 percent cited a need to own a current edition, compared to 6 percent of other students. In contrast, only 3 percent of law students mention the need to own content for a longer time or because they find it interesting, compared to 27 percent of other

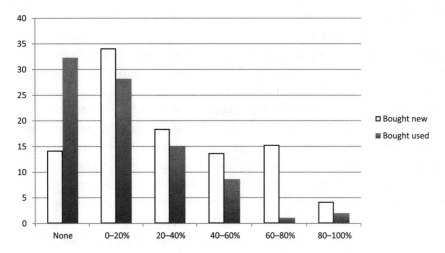

Figure 6.1
What percentage of your materials is bought new and used?

students. As we've seen in preceding chapters, fields such as law and medicine have significantly stronger connections to formal channels of acquisition because the core materials either need to be frequently updated (law) or serve as longer-term references (medicine).

Photocopying plays an important role in access to materials among nearly all students and the primary role (accounting for over 60 percent of materials) for around a quarter of them. These results varied significantly among disciplines. Only 5 percent of lawyers made such extensive use of photocopying, versus 38 percent of students in other fields.[16]

Two-thirds of students photocopy outside of their academic institutions, generally in the copy shops set up near most Polish universities. The copy shops located within their institutions play a less significant role (17 percent). In these cases, institutions often enforce limitations on the number of copies that can be made. Such limitations are not established by law, but are more the result of interpretations of the scope of exceptions accepted by both educational institutions and collecting societies.

Much of our survey focused on how students obtain content online from authorized and unauthorized sources. Our respondents fall into two groups of similar sizes: those that regularly obtain content from "unauthorized" sources and those that rarely or never do. Among those who use unauthorized sites, practices are broad: students use them to access a variety of different types of content (not just academic), with habits

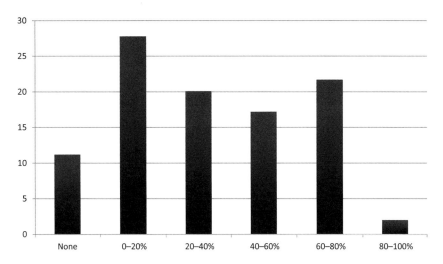

Figure 6.2
What percentage of the content that you use is photocopied?

commonly formed before starting their studies. The transition from looking for movies to looking for articles or books on these sites is an easy one.

Our results also suggest relatively widespread confusion about the legal status of different sources of content—here confirming results from a study of attitudes toward copyright law that we conducted in 2013.[17] Poles have a generally weak understanding of copyright law, consistent with low awareness and understanding of law in general. Students did not differ significantly from the rest of the society in this regard. Asked about twelve typical content-use scenarios, respondents on average properly identified the legality of only five scenarios. In general, copyright law is viewed as more restrictive than it actually is, with legal activities such as showing films in class for the purpose of illustrating teaching routinely deemed illegal by respondents. Practices associated with physical media tend to be better understood than their digital counterparts. For example, 51 percent of respondents indicated that using copyrighted content in school is illegal (in nearly all cases, it falls within the bounds of the educational exception in force in Poland). In contrast, 35 percent thought that making copyrighted content publicly available on file locker sites was legal (it is illegal under Polish law). With regard to photocopying for individual educational use, which Polish law permits (the scope of the distinction is disputed by lawyers, but a common interpretation is that even whole books can be legally copied), only 10 percent of respondents were aware of exceptions covering such use.

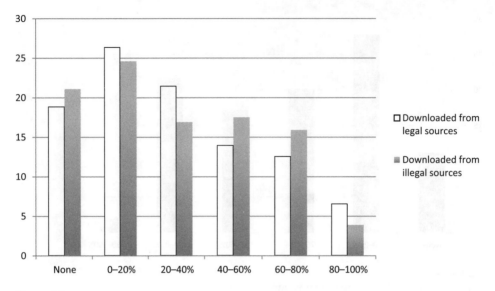

Figure 6.3
What percentage of your content is from legal and illegal sources?

Despite confusion about the letter of the law, a significant percentage of Polish students engage in downloading of educational materials that they believe to be *illegal*. Seventy-nine percent acknowledged such practices and 22 percent indicate that they download at least 60 percent of their materials this way. At the same time, 21 percent have never downloaded illegal content and 24 percent own less than 20 percent of content obtained from such sources. A large majority signaled downloading from both legal and illegal sources. In short, the level of ignorance with regard to legalities suggests a broader lack of interest in the subject and the larger pragmatism with regard to acquisition that we have seen throughout this study.

Answers to a question about the legal services students use testifies to some of the confusion on this point—the enormously popular Polish file sharing site Chomikuj was widely cited among both the legal and illegal services. At the same time, the answers suggest that university strategies for providing legal access to online resources have had some success. By far the most popular resource is eBUW—the electronic system of the University of Warsaw Library that provides access to a range of digital journals, books, and databases.[18] The next most cited is iBuk, discussed earlier, the commercial database that provides access to 70,000 book titles from all major Polish publishers (to which most academic institutions subscribe). Among other popular results are EBSCO, JSTOR, and the legal database Legalis (owned by publisher C. H. Beck), which are part

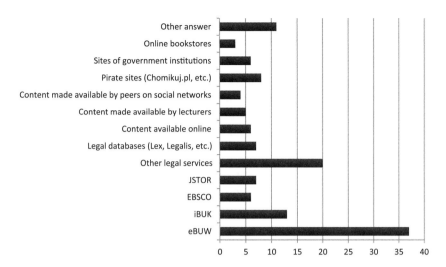

Figure 6.4
From what legal or authorized sources do you obtain materials?

of the consortia access agreements subsidized by the state and to which most campuses provide access.

When asked about the services through which they engaged in "illegal" or "unauthorized" downloading, the overwhelming favorite was Chomikuj.pl (449 students). The now defunct file locker service Rapidshare placed a distant second with seventy-three students. There was practically no third site on students' lists. Chomikuj.pl is used by 95 percent of those who indicate that they have used unauthorized sources to obtain content (70 percent of our sample).

These questions were designed to elicit student perceptions about their own actions with respect to particular sites and services. When applied more generally, however, these descriptors become somewhat inapt: Chomikuj.pl, for example, operates legally under Polish law, even if many of the actions of its users constitute copyright infringement.

Owned by the Interia.pl web portal, Chomikuj has been a source of domestic and even international controversy. Commonly called "chomik" (i.e., hamster), the site is the most popular of its kind in Poland. According to Megapanel/PBI Gemius monthly Internet-usage statistics, Chomikuj.pl was the fifteenth most popular site overall in the country in October 2013, reaching 6.8 million or 32 percent of Polish Internet users (Kępka 2014).

Chomikuj has walked a complicated line with respect to Polish copyright law. It is a commercial service with a variety of pay models that provide users access to uploaded content—much of which, it is widely understood, is unauthorized content uploaded by users. But the service also complies with notice and takedown requirements in Polish law, removing files targeted by copyright infringement complaints (thereby allowing it to argue for "safe harbor protection" with respect to infringing behavior by users). Polish publishers have generally discounted these steps. In July 2012, members of the Polish Book Chamber brought the service to court on copyright infringement charges. By early 2017, the case had been through several rounds of motions and appeals, and is currently awaiting the outcome of a publisher-filed complaint to the European Commission. A parallel lawsuit by the Polish Filmmakers Association did result in a judgment of contributory infringement against the service, leading to a requirement that Chomikuj.pl actively monitor its service for infringing materials (Dynowski and Baczykowska 2015).

The popularity of the service is clearly fading—peak traffic was in 2012 and 2013, when the site was visited by more than 30 percent of Polish Internet users. But it is still a primary means of accessing media content for many Poles: in February 2016, the site was visited by more than three million people, or 14 percent of Polish Internet users (Wirtualne Media 2016). Nor has enforcement pressure let up. In 2015, Google Search received more than seven million takedown requests for links on Chomikuj.

In educational contexts, chomikuj.pl remains especially significant because it operates as a digital library specializing in Polish-language content. For foreign publications and other media, Polish students have many other options among the top-tier international file sharing sites. But for academic purposes, the linguistic focus is paramount and other services play no significant role.

In contrast to findings in other countries, the sharing of materials among students (either electronically or face to face) is widespread but by no means a dominant practice. For 60 percent of the students, sharing is a marginal activity, representing less than 20 percent of their acquired content. These results suggest relatively little organized circulation of content within student groups, with a correspondingly greater reliance on more centralized sources. The near-monopoly of Chomikuj.pl on unauthorized Polish-language distribution may make the more cumbersome coordination of sharing through student networks less important.

Sharing among students is grounded in the (accurate) perception of the legality of these practices: 60 percent of students indicated that copying from other students was legal, 22 percent that it was sometimes legal, and 19 percent that it was simply illegal. Polish copyright law has clear exceptions for private use that allow copying

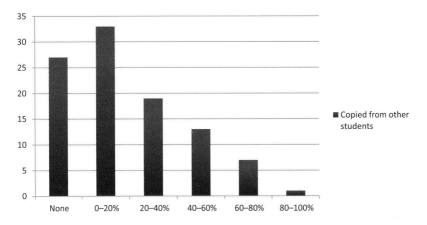

Figure 6.5
What part of the content that you own is copied from other students?

and sharing content within groups of friends or acquaintances. While the percentage of respondents who got this right is relatively high, it also implies that 40 percent of students misunderstand their rights on this point (a result in line with the results of our study "Copyright Law in Transition"). Of those who answered "sometimes legal," nearly half believed that it depends on permission from the author of the work; 23 percent believed that legal copying is limited to notes from classes or lectures; 9 percent indicated that copying for personal use or scientific purpose without monetary gain is legal (which is a pretty accurate description of Polish law), and 9 percent indicated that it's legal when they "know that copyright is not being broken in the process."

Ultimately, fewer than half of students surveyed indicate that they own PDF files of scientific articles, with a median size of twenty titles. Only 25 percent have collections of digital books, and in the case of those who do, the median size of the collection is again twenty titles. This is relatively high, taking into account that students in their early years of studies do not have significant incentives to collect academic material. The large number of students without collections suggests that they read relatively little, perhaps reflective of the general decline of reading culture in Poland, or of the widely held belief that students can, in principle, complete their degrees relying on study notes rather than books and articles.

Field Differences between Law and Communications

Consistently, students in communication studies have a higher rate of "unauthorized" access to materials than their law student counterparts, both in regard to instructional

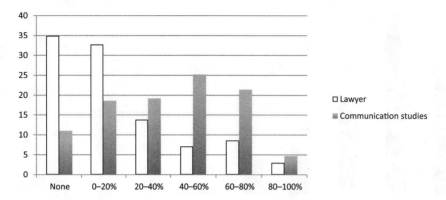

Figure 6.6
What percentage of the content that you own is obtained from illegal sources?

materials and the downloading of other media such as movies and music. Differences in the structure of the curriculum clearly plays a large role with respect to educational materials: the teaching of law generally requires up-to-date and sometimes customized materials, whereas the media and communications curriculum is organized primarily around monographs and articles, and changes slowly from year to year.[19]

Among law students, 68 percent indicated that they rarely or never downloaded academic materials from illegal sources; 12 percent indicated that they got more than 60 percent of their materials this way. Among communication studies students, the corresponding numbers are 30 percent and 60 percent. These field differences hold up—albeit less dramatically—in questions about unauthorized downloading of other media such as music and movies, where communications students again lead.

Clearly there are other contributing factors, such as spillover effects from the greater exposure of law students to efforts by legal publishers to circulate inaccurate claims about copying, or the tendency of law faculty to attract students from wealthier families, which changes the relative cost of materials, or simply differences in particular faculties or universities. We do not have a full explanation, but note that this result holds up across the country studies.

Libraries and Databases

Library availability and use appear to be relatively high compared to the other university contexts explored in this book. Seventy-five percent of students indicate that they can find the texts that they require for courses in the institutional library (15 percent

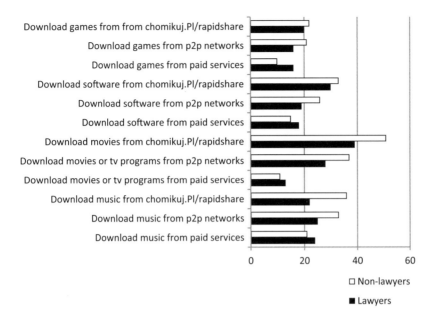

Figure 6.7
From which authorized and unauthorized sources do you download nonacademic content?

don't know, 10 percent declare they cannot). Fifty-three percent say that the library maintains course-related content for students (vs. 15 percent who say it does not; 32 percent don't know). At the same time, only 29 percent say that they borrow frequently from the library. Fifty-one percent do so sometimes; and 20 percent never borrow from the library.

Fifty-four percent of the students indicate that they use online "databases" to prepare for courses, though in most cases this referred to general resources like Wikipedia, the results of Google searches, and even Chomikuj rather than scholarly databases. Among the latter, only law databases cracked 10 percent—a predictable outcome among the law students. Once again, general lack of awareness about the status of the different services was striking.

We also asked about students' preferred means of reading. Consistent with the other studies in this collection, digital reading fared poorly: 79 percent of students prefer paper to screen as their main reading medium. Only 9 percent indicated that they do most of their reading on tablets; 9 percent on e-book readers; and 4 percent on mobile phones. Also consistent with other findings in this report, many students print out the materials they acquire digitally. The all-digital curriculum is still some way off.

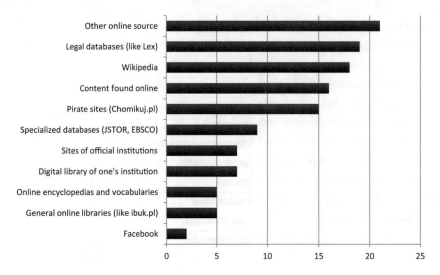

Figure 6.8
Which online databases do you use?

Content Sharing by Course Instructors and Students

As in the other contributions, our survey results found a wide range of digital tools and platforms in classroom use. The official learning management systems (LMS) deployed by universities only partly capture this diverse array of activity. All of the universities included in the survey offer e-learning services to students, but only 50 percent of students were sure about this and nearly a quarter said they did not.

Over two-thirds of students (69 percent) indicated that instructors use online tools other than the LMS for content sharing. Of these, two-thirds mentioned email (67 percent), one-third file locker sites such as Chomikuj and Rapidshare (31 percent), comparable numbers for publishing tools like Google Docs or Scribd (29 percent), and lower numbers for social networks like Facebook (16 percent) and blogs (12 percent). As in other countries in this study, university-supported systems emerged only recently and have clearly not displaced the range of other strategies and tools that faculty use for classroom support. The high rate of use of sites like Chomikuj is especially interesting as it suggests the extent to which they have become core infrastructure for an array of archiving and sharing needs.

Sharing of materials among students through these channels is also very common: 77 percent of students indicate that they share texts digitally with their peers.[20] Fifty percent specified email or mailing lists as a primary means; 41 percent mentioned

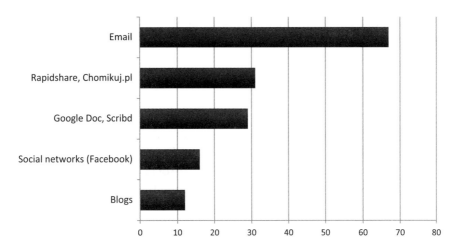

Figure 6.9
How do instructors share content online with students?

social networks (in Poland, that's probably Facebook). For both students and instructors, email clearly continues to play a large role in the circulation of materials.[21]

Conclusion

As in other countries, Polish students and faculty use an array of informal and formal means of acquiring the materials they need for their research and studies. Although the informal strategies are often called or equated with "piracy," Polish law—like that of many European countries—affords a wide margin for personal and educational copying and sharing. Moreover, there is no legal consensus about the status of some of the practices publishers fear most, such as downloading educational materials from file hosting sites. The final resolution of the Chomikuj case and emerging European law on the "intermediary liability" of Internet services will play roles in defining these boundaries.

Student opinion on all of these issues is poorly formed. As our survey shows, students do not easily distinguish between legal and unauthorized sources of materials and copying practices. In the day-to-day life of most students, pragmatic challenges of getting the materials they need for classes trump the parsing of legal and ethical gray zones. For most, the question is rarely raised.

That said, recourse to unauthorized methods is not ubiquitous. Ten percent of students in our survey have no materials at all. Among the rest, 21 percent of our respondents use only formal, market-based sources (this figure is higher in law than in media and communications studies). Around 25 percent make very limited use of unauthorized sites and own less than 20 percent of content from such sources. Around 54 percent use regularly informal channels. Among these, around half download only from sites like Chomikuj, while the remainder also copy and share content with other students.

Widespread familiarity with archives like Chomikuj, developed via music or movie downloading, makes it a logical solution for instructional materials, which in turn reinforces its status as a universal archive for Poles. For students, such use is clearly driven by continued obstacles to the cheap, easy, legal availability of instructional and research material. Despite (publicly subsidized) access to some of the large research article databases, much of the rest of the material ecosystem is more sharply constrained. There are no comparable solutions for the world of monographs that shape humanities and social scientific fields; nor is there support for textbooks and other core instructional materials. Open source initiatives in Poland have made some headway with regard to publicly funded research but will probably have to wait on European action for strong mandates.

The Polish language itself remains the most important structural feature of this ecosystem, supporting a parallel world of publishing and access models that operates at a disadvantage in an English-language dominated educational and research culture. As other institutional norms and expectations are imported from Europe and elsewhere into the Polish system, these parallel institutions come under growing pressure. Poland is hardly alone in this respect. Most of the European countries face similar challenges with regard to local language instruction and research cultures. But as a mid-sized linguistic community large enough to support institutional parallelism, Poland faces choices that smaller linguistic communities in Europe do not. The question, for policymakers, is whether existing publishing models and policies empower Polish institutions and students or entrench the disadvantages of the two-tiered model. The question for students, as always, is where to find the materials they need at the lowest possible cost and inconvenience. As usual, there are competing answers, with one set consolidating around open access models, another around commercial databases, and the third, default solution in the complex array of informal sharing and copying among students and faculty themselves.

Notes

The authors thank Michał Kotnarowski and Piotr Toczyski for their collaboration.

1. For more information on the pact, see http://obywatelenauki.pl/the-pact-for-academia/ (accessed August 1, 2017).

2. Like other EU countries, Poland will probably adopt open access requirements as part of a wider EU shift toward open access, announced in May 2016 (Enserink 2016).

3. This popular case for this reform was buttressed in part by concern that the two highest-ranking Polish institutions, University of Warsaw and the Jagiellonian University, had fallen below the 400 mark in the Center for World University Rankings (CWUR) index.

4. See https://wbn.icm.edu.pl/ (accessed August 1, 2017).

5. Given this level of public support, the case for secrecy is quite weak and challengeable.

6. Sage did not agree to provide information about the number of people who used the service in this period.

7. In Sweden, a reported 70 percent of the e-book market in 2013 was controlled by libraries (Wischenbart 2015, 79).

8. The premise of the project was that when a lecturer submits a syllabus, the library would scan it and identify the assigned texts and make them available in electronic form to course participants, via the university's student management system. In the end, the library's director did not feel sufficiently confident about the scope of Polish educational exceptions to copyright to move forward, particularly regarding the potential harm to the interests of the publisher, which can be invoked if the university crosses some undetermined threshold of issuing too many copies or allows them to circulate too widely. Such uncertainties have produced very conservative interpretations of access at many libraries, notably in the form of enforced one-to-one correspondence between paper and digital copies. The video lending library at this university operates in the same way—no longer lending movies, but providing only a specific room in which movies from the university's DVD collection can be watched.

9. These views are based on interviews with faculty, librarians, and administrative staff, and on the experience of one of the authors, who has also been involved in advocacy for open access policies at the University of Warsaw and as part of the Citizens for Science movement.

10. In the study conducted on the subject in 2012, only 39 percent of Poles claimed to have read at least one book within the past twelve months (including both traditional, published books and e-books, encyclopedias, and dictionaries). Only 7 percent of respondents stated that they read e-books. Thirty-four percent of Poles with higher education read no books over the previous year; 17 percent did not recall having read any newspaper over the previous year (Chymkowski 2013). Students' reading habits were not separately analyzed.

11. The sample included 276 law students and 343 students from schools of media or cultural studies or both. The small number of PhD respondents did not permit a statistical analysis, but it enabled us to crosscheck opinions regarding differences between these two types of student. We also extended the survey to lecturers but only obtained eighteen responses.

12. The subject matter also presented challenges in some contexts as universities or departments were at times uneasy answering questions about unauthorized access to and copying of content. In the case of law students in particular, a number of permits were required to distribute the sur-

veys. The number of universities that offer such specializations is quite limited, making (re)iden-
tification feasible. For some academic staff, the topic was a sensitive one.

13. We did find a much higher percentage with smartphones: 85.5 percent in our survey vs. 51.4
percent in the more comprehensive *Social Diagnosis 2013* study by Czapiński and Panek (2014).

14. Among the other notable demographic features: 315 were first-year students; 212 were in
their second year; and 110 in their third year—a 50/33/17 breakdown. Fifty-two percent of the
students will obtain bachelor's degrees (two-year programs); 48 percent of them master's degrees
(five-year programs under the Bologna system of education, which has recently appeared in
Poland and generated controversy). 73.4 percent are full-time students; 26.1 percent are extramural students; the remaining 0.5 percent are both full-time and extramural students. 52.8 percent
(of the valid responses) of those surveyed did not have a job, 27 percent of them worked irregular
hours, and 14 percent of the students claimed that they worked more often, but did not have a
full-time job. 6.2 percent of respondents stated that they worked full time.

15. Student reasons for buying new content varied, from lack of other forms of access (26 percent), to the need to own the latest content or current edition (26 percent), to the desire to collect
or particular interest in a given work (23 percent). Fourteen percent simply wanted new books.

16. Similarly, 23 percent of lawyers and only 3 percent of nonlawyers declare that they never
photocopy content.

17. Danielewicz and Tarkowski 2013.

18. The popularity of eBUW is almost certainly due to sample selection: many of our respondents studied at the University of Warsaw.

19. To better understand some of these curricular practices, we collected and examined patterns
of change in 364 syllabi drawn from a communication studies department over a period of five
years. Broadly speaking, we found that the content of most repeated classes changed very little
year to year, with occasional textual substitutions as prominent new work is translated into
Polish and as instructors incorporate their own new publications into classes.

20. A similar question earlier in the survey, however, found lower numbers.

21. The small number of doctoral students we surveyed had very similar profiles to the undergraduates with respect to purchasing, copying, and downloading. They differed appreciably (and
predictably, given their professional investments) only in their commitment to personal collections of digital texts. Fourteen out of twenty-four respondents had a digital library. Four stated
that they had more than one hundred texts. Nineteen out of twenty-five respondents had mentioned such websites as Chomikuj.pl; a few admitted to using Avaxhome.ws and aaaaarg.org.
Sharing of texts with each other was a marginal practice among these students.

References

Chymkowski, Roman. 2013. "Społeczny zasięg książki w Polsce w 2012 r" [Social Reach of Books in Poland in 2012]. *Biblioteka Narodowa*. http://www.bn.org.pl/download/document/1362741578 .pdf (accessed May 26, 2016).

Czapiński, Janusz, and Tomasz Panek, eds. 2014. *Social Diagnosis 2013: The Objective and Subjective Quality of Life in Poland*. Warsaw: The Council for Social Monitoring. http://www.diagnoza.com/ data/report/report_2013.pdf (accessed August 1, 2017).

Danielewicz, Michał, and Alek Tarkowski. 2013. "Copyright Law in Transition." Warsaw: Centrum Cyfrowe. https://centrumcyfrowe.pl/wp-content/uploads/2015/12/Copyright-Law-in-Transi tion.pdf (accessed August 1, 2017).

Dynowski, Piotr, and Aleksandra Baczykowska. 2015. "Polish Filmmakers' Association Sues Chomikuj.pl for Contributory IP Infringement." *Lexology*, October 16. http://www.lexology.com/ library/detail.aspx?g=2264dca1-2722-47fa-a7bb-fe081d4ff933 (accessed May 26, 2016).

Dziewczyny na politechniki. 2012. *Dziewczyny na politechniki: Raport 2012* [Girls at Technical Schools: 2012 Report]. http://dziewczynynapolitechniki.pl/2015/pdfy/raport2012.pdf (accessed May 26, 2016).

Enserink, Martin. 2016. "In Dramatic Statement, European Leaders Call for 'Immediate' Open Access to All Scientific Papers by 2020." *Science*, May 27, 2016. http://www.sciencemag.org/ news/2016/05/dramatic-statement-european-leaders-call-immediate-open-access-all-scientific-papers (accessed May 31, 2016).

Filiciak, Mirosław, Justyna Hofmokl, and Alek Tarkowski. 2012. "The Circulations of Culture. On Social Distribution of Content (Obiegi Kultury)." *SSRN Electronic Journal*. http://obiegikultury .centrumcyfrowe.pl/ (accessed May 26, 2016).

Groves, Jack. 2014. "Shrinking Enrollments in Poland." *Inside Higher Ed*, March 6. https:// www.insidehighered.com/news/2014/03/06/universities-poland-struggle-shrinking-enrollments (accessed May 26, 2016).

GUS. 2012. *Higher Education Institutions and Their Finances in 2011*. http://stat.gov.pl/cps/rde/ xbcr/gus/E_szkoly_wyzsze_2011.pdf (accessed May 26, 2016).

GUS. 2015. *Higher Education Institutions and Their Finances in 2015*. http://stat.gov.pl/download/ gfx/portalinformacyjny/pl/defaultaktualnosci/5488/2/12/1/szkoly_wyzsze_i_ich_finanse_w _2015_r.pdf (accessed May 26, 2016).

Jakubowski, Maciej. 2015. *Opening up Opportunities: Education Reforms in Poland*. IBS Policy Paper. World Bank. http://ibs.org.pl/app/uploads/2015/02/IBS_Policy_Paper_01_2015.pdf (accessed May 26, 2016).

Kępka, Maciej. 2014. "Wyniki Megapanel PBI/Gemius za październik 2013" [Megapanel PBI/ Gemius results for October 2013]. *Internet Standard*, March 18. http://www.internetstandard.pl/ news/395443/Wyniki.Megapanel.PBI.Gemius.za.pazdziernik.2013.html (accessed May 26, 2016).

Kwiek, Marek, D. Antonowicz, J. Brdulak, M. Hulicka, T. Jędrzejewski, R. Kowalski, E. Kulczycki, K. Szadkowski, A. Szot, and J. Wolszczak-Derlacz. 2016. "Projekt założeń do nowej ustawy prawo o szkolnictwie wyższym." [Draft concept of the new Law on Higher Education.] http://ustawa20 .amu.edu.pl/wp-content/uploads/2016/11/Projekt_zalozen_Kwiek_et_al.pdf (accessed February 5, 2016).

Strycharz, Jan, and Katarzyna Golik. 2012. "Academic Content in Poland: National Statistics, Market Data and Business Models." Centrum Cyfrowe, Warsaw (manuscript).

Wirtualne Media. 2016. "Wirtualna Polska przed Onetem, Grupa Gazeta.pl bliżej Grupy Interia. pl" [Wirtualna Polska before Onet, Gazeta.pl group closer to Interia.pl group]. *Wirtualnemedia*, March 9. http://www.wirtualnemedia.pl/artykul/wirtualna-polska-przed-onetem-grupa-gazeta-pl -blizej-grupy-interia-pl-top50-serwisow (accessed May 26, 2016).

Wischenbart, Rüdiger 2015. *Global E-Book 2015: A Report on Market Trends and Developments.* Vienna: Rüdiger Wischenbart Content and Consulting.

7   India: The Knowledge Thief

Lawrence Liang

Hindi popular cinema has always been a barometer of the social, political, and economic concerns affecting India. It is therefore not surprising that movie pirates have had a fruitful presence in Hindi films, reflecting both the prominent place and contested status of movie piracy in the country. But it wasn't until 2011's *Shor in the City* (Krishna D.K. and Nidimoru 2011) that a book pirate became a central character in a Bollywood film. *Shor in the City* narrates the intertwined lives of three characters in Mumbai from very different class backgrounds. The film opens with one of them, Tilak, planning to kidnap a prominent author from a party. Unlike traditional kidnappers, Tilak is not after ransom but the electronic files of the author's latest novel, which he plans to publish and sell. Tilak, it turns out, is a book pirate—and a barely literate one. His method is to strike up conversations with customers at bookstores to find out which books are popular. He then buys these books, copies them, and wholesales them to children who sell them on the streets of Mumbai.

One of the books that Tilak picks up from the bookstore is *The Alchemist* by the Brazilian author Paulo Coelho. *The Alchemist* takes on an important role in the film, serving as Tilak's method of educating himself and as the means through which he and his newly wedded wife get to know each other better. Stumped by many of the words in the book, Tilak begins to read with an English-Hindi dictionary, educating himself while also developing a relationship to the book beyond its value to his trade. Coelho's *The Alchemist* is not an accidental choice in the film. The book was widely pirated in India and remains very popular, both in mainstream bookshops as well as among pirate sellers on the street.[1] When Coelho was alerted to the fact that *The Alchemist* was being sold by teenagers on the streets of India, he said that he was honored that his book was being sold in "the smallest bookstore in the world" (Bazzle 2015).

Coelho's position on Indian piracy was informed by his experience in Russia. Reportedly, the initial sales of *The Alchemist* in Russia were not encouraging. Sales picked up after he posted a digital Russian copy on his website, however, and within two years he had sold 100,000 copies. Coelho has since uploaded others of his books to file sharing networks.

The juxtaposition of Tilak and Coelho in the film provides a brief sketch of one of the characteristic forms of Indian book piracy, marked by the small-scale organization of acquisition, copying, and street vending, and focused primarily on the biggest best-sellers. This is the type of piracy that has attracted the most attention from publishers, business groups, and the authorities. For example, a 2014 report issued by FICCI (Federation of Indian Chambers of Commerce), the largest business advocacy group in India, urged authors and publishers to "stand united and fight against the menace of piracy in publishing that was threatening the growth of the sector."[2] In collaboration with Ernst and Young, FICCI has also sought to link intellectual property piracy with national security.[3]

Practices like those shown in the film *Shor in the City* have played an important role in the development of literacy and book culture in India, serving publics for whom the commercial market and the library system have failed to significantly expand access to literary works. As we will see, the intellectual biographies of many Indians pass through such networks. As we will also see, these forms of street and commercial piracy are distinct from the needs and forms of access associated with student life. Higher education creates a different set of challenges, structured by demand for more specialized materials and met by a different constellation of legal, illegal, and contested forms of access. Here, supply and demand relate primarily to the specialized textbooks, monographs, and journal articles required for participation in increasingly globalized fields of knowledge. This chapter explores both sides of this ecosystem— the popular and the academic—and their diverse points of contact in intellectual biographies and institutions that mediate the two spheres, such as public libraries. As in the other chapters in this book, we take a close look at how these issues play out in the lives of students in the social sciences, law, and medicine at several major universities.

As in other countries, this account of India is complicated by complex trajectories of policymaking and institution building, especially regarding libraries and copyright law, and by the rapidly changing environment around publishing and digitization. This chapter tries to distill some of the key histories, developments, and relationships that shape the larger problem of educational access and literacy in India, and the narrower question of how students get what they need.

Academic Libraries Real and Imagined

Let's stay with film references for a moment to look at another exemplary scene of piracy—here with respect to university journals. In 2013, as part of an effort to popularize its academic journal databases in India, Sage Publishing offered a week of unlimited access to students at a leading university in a south Indian city. This was a promotional arrangement intended to encourage the university to subscribe to the service. This taste of access, however, led to an unexpected gulp. Anticipating that the university might reject Sage's subscription costs, a group of students, led by a PhD candidate in literature, downloaded all of the important Sage journals into an offline archive. They called themselves "Pradeep's Eleven"—a reference to the U.S. heist film *Ocean's Eleven*. Within days, the university received a warning and free access was withdrawn. By then, however, the students had assembled a very large archive. This new archive, in turn, was combined with a still-larger unofficial library assembled from other clandestine copying, including material brought by students returning from abroad. This combined library now circulates widely within the university on portable hard drives and flash drives. As students acquire new materials, the collection slowly grows and new versions become canonical. As new students enter the university, the collection is passed on.

There are many ways to unpack this story: as an immature act of theft, as a noble act of sharing and resistance, as a response to a problem of inequitable access, or as a manifestation of a will to collect. Let's put the first two possibilities aside for now. Neither theft nor resistance helps much in understanding the context that produced Pradeep's Eleven or its many less ambitious (and occasionally more ambitious) analogs across the university system. The third and fourth possibilities, however, go to deeper issues that structure the intellectual lives of students. The immediate context for Pradeep's Eleven is the lack of database access at the university: few Indian universities can afford subscriptions to the major academic databases, even with the negotiated discounts that many publishers provide.[4]

Access to Databases in University Libraries

The potential of digital technologies to address the chronic lack of materials in university libraries was recognized early on in India. In 1991, the University Grants commission established INFLIBNET (Information and Library Network), a computer network for linking libraries and information centers in roughly two hundred fifty universities, colleges, and research institutions (Chand et al. 2007). INFLIBNET served as a framework for the creation of a national library catalog (IndCat), whose main purpose is to make consortia-based access to electronic databases and journals available to research-ers and students. Currently INFLIBNET provides electronic access to more than forty-five hundred full text electronic journals at a discounted price, including from leading databases such as JSTOR.

Yet such numbers do not yet begin to approach the scale of the need: in 2014, there were more than 677 universities, 37,204 colleges, and 11,443 other standalone educa-tional institutions in India.[5] INFLIBNET reaches fewer than 15 percent of the universi-ties and a much smaller proportion of the other types of institution. And even these institutions are sorely oversubscribed.

Even among elite institutions, access remains a serious challenge. Arunachalam and Muthu (2011) noted that, in 2002, the largest academic library in India—the Indian Institute of Science (IISc)—subscribed to only 1,381 print journals (of which 200 were accessible online). The situation improved with the launch of the Indian National Digi-tal Library in Engineering Sciences and Technology or "INDEST" launched in 2003, which enabled consortia-based access to electronic databases, and by 2009 the IISc subscription had access to more than nine thousand journals. While this is an undeni-able improvement, in practice it still represents a small fraction of the number of jour-nals typically received by U.S. universities. Columbia University, for example, received 133,831 serials (journal titles and book series) in 2007; Johns Hopkins University received 105,453 and Pennsylvania State University received 88,668. Even a smaller university like the University of Delaware received 29,246 serials. Such discrepancies mark what Padmanabhan Balaram, the director of the IISc, has described as the prob-lem of asymmetry in publishing, which excludes poorer countries from participation in the circuits of global knowledge.[6] India, in this context, is far from the worst posi-tioned. Citing an example from the World Health Organization, Arunachalam notes that in the seventy-five countries with a GNP per-capita per year of less than $1,000, fewer than half of medical institutions had *any* journal subscriptions. In countries with a GNP between $1,000 and $3,000, 34 percent had no subscriptions; a further 34 per-cent had an average of two subscriptions per year.

With electronic databases making universal access possible in principle, disparities of this kind are maintained through pricing. This is not the place for a deep dive into the political economy of journal and database publishing, which has seen the emer-gence of very large aggregators such as Reed-Elsevier and Springer. As in other countries, vendors negotiate prices with universities, leading to wide variation in pricing depend-ing on ability to pay and nondisclosure agreements with regard to terms that preserve the opacity of these practices. Yet some institutional information escapes this secretive process. At the Institute of Mathematical Sciences in Chennai (IMSc), for example, the total annual budget is around $2 million, of which $400,000 is spent on subscriptions to academic journals. Fifty-five percent of this amount is paid to Reed-Elsevier and Springer. In other words, these publishers account for more than 10 percent of the total budget of the school—and more than the entire budget for faculty salaries.[7]

Although this arrangement seems penurious, it is in fact highly privileged compared to the majority of Indian universities. Both the IISc and the IMSc are leading research institutions that benefit from grants from the government as well as private foundations. As V. S. Sunder of IMSc puts it, "barring a miniscule number of institutions (such as IMSc and Tata Institute of Fundamental Research), the majority of universities in India (and even some good research institutes …) simply cannot afford to access many journals as they are priced today."

This situation is not new, of course, but the increasing global connectedness of research and educational communities make disparities in access more visible and sharply felt. Indian students and faculty in particular, as peripheral participants in the dominant Anglophone research community, are routinely forced to find other ways to access materials that allow them to participate in global research conversations. Since the 1990s, one of the main imports of Indian students returning from abroad has been the digital archive, downloaded or copied while at U.S. or UK institutions. To a large extent, the Indian research world is still dependent on such trafficking. When Sage opened the gates to its journal database as a way of convincing the university to devote a large part of its budget to journal access, Pradeep's Eleven was a logical outcome.

The Universal Library

Intellectual constraints of this kind are a fact of life in most Indian universities, and extend to other material conditions such as wireless access and data plans, which limit the use of online archives and favor downloading and local storage. Yet there are other, less material motivations for the types of archiving visible in such cases. What happens if we see Pradeep's Eleven not in terms of stealing or even the expansion of access, but as a part of the longer history of bibliophilia that shapes libraries—a desire met by institutions in large parts of the West but left to individuals in many Indian contexts. This is the library as a more personal world of knowledge—as a collection shaped more by aspirations for participation in a wider culture than by immediate needs.

The imaginative leap from the personal to the universal archive is very much a part of the cultural history of the technology of books. Most of the important technological changes in publishing—from movable type to offset printing to paperbacks—have been aspirational in this sense. They all enabled more affordable and accessible books, disseminating not only knowledge but also the desire for access to knowledge. As print grew cheaper, personal libraries became attainable—from bibles in every home to the prototypical "Everyman's Classics," which envisioned a 1,000-volume library of world literature "affordable for … every kind of person, from students to the working classes to the cultural elite."[8]

How should we think about the relationship between these personal collections and the more institutional history of libraries? This question gains significance in an era in which digital collections can grow far beyond the hundreds or thousands of books that until recently constituted the practical horizon of personal libraries—and that once marked a practical distinction between two types of collection. For students who perceive themselves at the periphery of a richer global system of higher education, the building of large personal libraries slides easily from the personal imaginary, marked by desire for participation in wider communities of knowledge, to a public imaginary shaped by solidarity with other students. The line between private archive and public library becomes very thin in this context, and easily crossed.

This effect is reinforced by the erosion of distinctions between the labor of learning or research and the creation of large archives. Unlike the print-era distinction between the formal archive of the library and the private labor of building personal archives by way of notebooks, private papers, and selected purchases, the rise of digital research blurs the two practices. Every researcher is simultaneously a librarian and archivist as they conduct their work. In India, this is often manifested in a physical process of translation, as researchers circulate in archives and libraries with digital cameras, hand-held scanners, pen drives, and computers drawing in media and texts. In other contexts, it is primarily digital, as the process of research becomes inseparable from the accumulation and management of large corpuses of digital work.

From Alexandria to Shadow Libraries

The idea of a universal library containing all the knowledge of the world has always been a powerful Utopian myth, running from Babel to Alexandria to the Google books project. Less prominent but arguably equally powerful is the idea of the failure of the library—its breakup and, in diminished form, the survival of its fragments. The story of the Library of Alexandria provides one of the most powerful examples of this dualism. No one knows what the Library looked like, or even what it contained. The process of building it began with King Ptolemy I, who sent letters "to all the sovereigns and governors on earth" beseeching them to send to him texts by "poets and prose-writers, rhetoricians and sophists, doctors and soothsayers, historians, and all others too." Going a step further, the king also decreed that any scrolls on ships passing through the port at Alexandria be turned over so that copies could be made. The king's scholars calculated that five hundred thousand scrolls would be required if they were to collect "all the books of all the peoples of the world" (Manguel 2011, 22).

What made the Library of Alexandria more than just a storehouse of knowledge was its relative accessibility to scholars and visitors—a degree of access that anchored an unprecedented concept of the reading public. Until that time, the libraries of the ancient world had no such public ambitions. They were either private collections or government archives where legal and literary documents were kept for official reference. By imagining a space where outsiders could have access to all the knowledge of the world, the library expressed a new idea of human culture.

While the Library of Alexandria is rightfully celebrated, it comes down to us primarily through the story of its loss. The destruction of the library was most likely the result of several disasters spread out over several centuries. But the most famous was the (possibly unintentional) burning of the building by Caesar in 48 BCE, during the Siege of Alexandria—a disaster that lives on as perhaps the iconic act of cultural destruction.

What is often forgotten in this story is that there was a "daughter" library whose location ensured that it survived Caesar's flames. According to the Sicilian historian Diodorus Siculus, writing in the first century BCE, this second library was intended for the use of scholars not affiliated with the Museion (the research institute that housed the main library). It was situated in a different part of Alexandria, close to the temple of Serapis, and was stocked with duplicate copies of the library's holdings. The daughter library survived the fire with its materials intact, though it never acquired the same renown as its larger "parent." The two libraries were built on the copying of text at several stages—some offered as gifts or tribute, some acquired through practices that at times resembled maritime (not copyright) piracy. The main library was the symbol of universal knowledge, and of the sovereign authority that built it; the daughter library acted primarily to disseminate and preserve. Many of the digital libraries discussed in this report—Pradeep's Eleven, or BiblioFyL, or LibGen—can be understood in this second register. As the archive circulates, students can claim some slight ownership of and place in wider traditions of knowledge and culture. When the Sage Publishing bills can no longer be paid, the shadow library survives. Reflecting on these shifting purposes and the affective investments they entail, the Argentine essayist Alberto Manguel (2011) writes:

Two monuments that, it could be said, stand for everything we are. The first, erected to reach the unreachable heavens, rose from our desire to conquer space, a desire punished by the plurality of tongues that even today lays daily obstacles against our attempts at making ourselves known to one another. The second, built to assemble, from all over the world, what those tongues had tried to record, sprang from our hope to vanquish time, and ended in a legendary fire that consumed even the present. The Tower of Babel in space and the Library of Alexandria in time are the twin symbols of these ambitions. In their shadow, my small library is a reminder of both impossible yearnings—the desire to contain all the tongues of Babel and the longing to possess all the volumes of Alexandria.

Ekalavya

An Indian lineage for the shadow library would almost certainly pass through the story of Ekalavya, a minor character in the Mahabharata, the Indian epic with origins in the eighth or ninth century BCE. In the story, Ekalavya is a lower-caste tribal boy who wants to become the greatest archer in the world. In pursuit of this goal, he approaches Dronacharya, the famous warrior (and teacher of the Panadava princes whose story forms the center of the epic) for instruction. Dronacharya, however, refuses Ekalavya: his lower caste status excludes him from martial training. Ekalavya retreats to the jungle but does not give up his dream. Instead, he makes a clay statue of Dronacharya to guide his training. Months later, the princes are out hunting in the jungle. They hear a dog bark, then fall silent. When they find the dog, they discover that its mouth is held closed against a tree by arrows, shot so precisely that they left it uninjured. Of course the archer is Ekalavya. Amazed by this feat, the princes ask Ekalavya to name his teacher. Ekalavya replies that it is Dronacharya. This news is unwelcome because Dronacharya has promised one of the princes, Arjuna, that he would make him the best archer in the world. When Dronacharya confronts Ekalavya, the boy shows him the statue. Although touched by Ekalavya's devotion, Dronacharya feels bound by his promise to Arjuna. He tells Ekalavya that if he truly considers him a teacher, he must offer a *guru dakshina*—an offering that a student makes to a teacher. When Ekalavya agrees, Dronacharya demands the thumb from his bow hand. Ekalavya complies.

This cruel parable provides an interesting point of entry into the contemporary ecology of knowledge. Ekalavya is one of the first knowledge pirates, having created an unauthorized version of Dronacharya as a means of educating himself and establishing, in the process, an unofficial shadow library. He also joins the list of mythical figures punished for stealing knowledge or transgressing the boundaries set around it, from Eve to Prometheus to Pandora. One of the most violent avatars of this injunction can be found in the ancient Hindu text which dictates that "if a *shudra* [the lowest caste] intentionally listens to the vedas [hymns] in order to commit them to memory, then his ears should be filled with (molten) lead and lac; if he utters the veda, then his

tongue should be cut off; if he has mastered the veda his body should be cut to pieces."
(Manusmrithi n.d., XII.4)[5]

The Social and Political Life of Books

These kinds of injunctions are still with us, if in less gruesome form, and they continue
to produce tragic avatars. The story of Aaron Swartz, a young man hounded to suicide by government prosecutors for the crime of downloading thousands of academic
articles should remind us of their continuing force. Such punishments point to one
of the major conflicts described in this study: law and interdiction on the side of the
gatekeepers of knowledge, and the power of human curiosity and auto-didacticism
among those outside the gates. In places where there are ample resources to mediate
between the two, these relationships become very complex, passing through libraries, markets, and other formalized patterns of buying, lending, exchange, and access.
Where resources are scarce, such curiosity is fulfilled haphazardly through a range of
less formal channels and occasionally violent interdictions. Arul Mani—a teacher, ama-
teur quiz hobbyist, and bibliophile in Bangalore—describes a typical path of discovery
through this haphazard landscape:

Sometime in 1985, I was told about fabulous places in the Majestic neighborhood where you
could get books really cheap. A relative took me to Upparpet where I saw books hanging like
clothes from a clothes line. Looking back, I guess that was my first encounter with pirated books.
This man also had second-hand books. I came across an author I'd encountered already by the
simple accident of going to the local library. This was *A Bend in the Ganges* by Manohar Mal-
gonkar, a partition-era narrative. It sounded completely thrilling. I looked around and I didn't
recognize any of the other authors. Then it started raining. That was a tragedy because I could see
shop after shop of books. That was my first encounter with Bangalore's second-hand bookshops.

The other way to encounter books was the Bangalore City Central Library. My father got me a
life membership for fifteen rupees. It was subsidized by the government and they put energy and
enthusiasm into it. They got new books regularly and there was a reference section, a magazine
section, and a borrowers' section which had books in English, Kannada, Tamil, Malayalam, Hindi
and Telugu. Many of my discoveries as a young reader happened by accident simply because of
this subsidized government service. I discovered Graham Greene and George Orwell and many
guys I wouldn't want to read now. But you read everything you got your hands on. The City
Central Library was easily one of the kick-starters for the reading that I did at the time. You didn't
really read at that time by way of recommendations. I think that the way that most people read
was in a sort of police state where children had to show their parents the sort of books they read
and you listened to elders on what to borrow and what to read. My parents were quite busy with
their own stuff so they didn't really care about this. I read a whole bunch of authors much before
I was supposed to.

The collecting thing started because of the Upparpet trip. Every time I had money I would go back and spend it there. The only things I could afford to buy were paperbacks. There was one place known as the Five Buck Joint. It had no signboard of any kind. It was in some basement. The owner sold remaindered books. Publishers would remainder books by splitting them into three and then they would mix all these sections up and sell them to second hand bookstores. So some enterprising soul thought that if you bought one lot and painstakingly found separate triplets and sewed them back together and then put newspaper wrapping them, you could sell them for five Rupees.

My father told me I must always bargain. Every time I went home with a book he asked me what I'd done to beat the price down. So this was part of the routine. I said I'll give you ten and we haggled and haggled. I walked away and then he called me back and gave it to me for twelve. At twelve rupees I could go home with three. Through my university years and to the present day, the Shivajinagar guy is one of the people I buy from. He is full of sorrow and indignation at how the trade has been taken over by Blossoms [a bookstore], which effectively dredged the bottom out of the business. All the small players, the ones who had stalls outside Cauvery Bhavan, or the City Civil Court, all these guys got out knocked out of business. Plus, in Upparpet those places began to be rebuilt in a big way. So all these holes in the walls where people did business disappeared.

In the '90s, Bangalore was full of bookshops. There was Fountainhead, Premier, Gangaram's, and Higginbothams. Strand came to Bangalore. They closed shop last year but when they came they were a big thing. On Ulsoor road there was a place called R 'n B which stood for Restaurant and Books. You could drink coffee there and look at the books, you could read them if you didn't smudge them. It was an experiment that lasted a year before they folded. It was replaced by another shop called the Bookery which lasted for about two years. The only ones still running are Higginbothams and Blossoms.

I began hearing about ebooks way back in '88 or '89. My first e-book actually was some Jasper Ford novel that someone mailed me a copy of. I had to download some software to read it on my computer. I found I quite liked it. I didn't really object to the experience. Then at some point my sister gave me a Kindle and I became a devotee. At one point I went slightly crazy—I remember when I saw the first episode of *Game of Thrones*. There was a moment where the zombies emerge from the snow and hunt some people down. I decided to read the books. But they were not available. Blossoms didn't have a copy. So I looked online and The Pirate Bay had all of them. I downloaded them onto my Kindle and went through five novels in about two weeks.

When you move from an economy of deficit to an economy of surplus, your energies go into stockpiling rather than reading. You're building surpluses with more energy than you're actually doing anything about it. In that sense, the physical book and the electronic book are roughly the same for me. At home I have very little space because I'm constantly piling up books that I think I will read at some point of time. There was a moment in my life, I think going back to the time when I was 28–29 when I could say I read about half the books I had. And with a little effort, that half became 60–75 percent. Then I lost control. The availability of books changed dramatically and I was buying more than I could read. The same happened with the e-books as well.

There's a purity to knowing with some certainty that you're never going to get to the end of the pile. You see a book, you see a possibility, you see a version of yourself and that version is so pleasing to the eye that you buy the book. It's your way of being that person for those 3–4 seconds, and then you never return to it. The surplus confronts you in different ways, a room full of books that you haven't read is harder to ignore than a hard drive that you can just put away.

The Unfulfilled Public Library

Mani's story suggests the range of other infrastructures and forms of circulation that shape the world of the book in India, in relation to and sometimes in tension with the traditional library. Libraries are a complicated topic in India—a vessel for the hopes of reformers and educators but never one that enjoyed the sustained support that would allow them to meet Indian needs.

The history of modern libraries in India can be traced back to the colonial period with the establishment of the first public libraries in Calcutta, Bombay, and Madras (Kalia 1974). The use of the word "public" in this context was largely a misnomer. These early institutions were subscription libraries that charged fees for the use of books. Many were run as adjuncts to commercial enterprises by officers of the East India Company. The development of libraries within institutions of higher learning occurred in fits and starts, hindered by the fact that universities in India remained primarily "affiliating universities"[9] in the colonial period, with no research role for many decades after their establishment. In 1902, a Universities Commission established by the colonial administration observed that "of the present University libraries, there is not much to be said. … The library at Madras appears to be entirely neglected; Bombay has a good collection of oriental and other books; but the library is little used by graduates and hardly at all by students."[10]

In an effort to remedy this neglect, the Universities Commission recommended making an accessible library a prerequisite for granting colleges university affiliations. For the most part, however, improvements in both the public and university-based library infrastructure were modest, with a few notable exceptions at the state level, such as the state of Baroda, where the Maharaja Sayajirao Gaekwad III pioneered the creation of a network of public libraries that collected in local languages and reached into rarely-served rural areas. Broader action on libraries did not emerge for several more decades. When it did, it was due largely to the work of S. R. Ranganathan, a mathematician-turned-librarian whose vision and advocacy on behalf of libraries helped define the institution in the post-Independence era. Ranganathan's Model Library Bill, passed in 1930, and Model Public Library Bill, passed in 1942, supported the establishment of public libraries and created a framework of public financing that went some way toward addressing the chronic weakness of the system. Both efforts were organized around Ranganathan's "five laws" of library science, articulated in 1931, which committed the library to a democratic, open, and evolving mission:

1. Books are for use.
2. Books are for all.
3. To every book its reader.
4. Save the time of the reader.
5. The library is a growing organism.

The first law challenged the fetishized preservation of books that dominated the work of many Indian libraries. Instead, Ranganathan argued that the primary purpose of the library was to facilitate access—a broad concept that encompassed everything from location, to hours, to building architecture, to the skills of library staff. The second law laid out an egalitarian vision in which the library serves all users regardless of age, gender, class, location, or disability. The third law referenced the role of librarians to make connections between users and books. The fourth law reiterated the primacy of the library users in relation to forms of access, such as maintaining open shelves for browsing (in contrast to the common practice of making available only catalogs of books for order). The fifth law insisted that the library is an evolving institution that should change to accommodate new uses. For Ranganathan, this included fundamental matters such as the organization of the physical plant, classification systems, and administration. Above all, Ranganathan's "laws" placed positive obligations on librarians to maximize access at the level of reader services and in the curation of materials.

Post-Independence education policy strongly emphasized the role of public libraries. Many Indian independence activists were convinced that a strong library system was a prerequisite of mass literacy, which in turn was a foundation for national development. As the historians Sandhu and Sandhu characterized this view: "India could not make any progress with its plans of development … unless the illiterate rural masses were given a certain amount of literacy. That created a new need for the village libraries, which could serve as centers of adult education and information" (Sandhu and Sandhu 1979, 269).[11]

The post-Independence tone for university libraries was very similar. As the 1948–1949 Radhakrishnan Commission put it: "the library is the heart of all the university's work, directly so, as regards its research work and indirectly as regards its educational work, which derives its life from research." The current state of these institutions, however, was woeful: "ill housed, ill stocked and ill staffed."[12] Despite the strong rhetoric, plans for stronger official support continued to stall in the face of financial and political constraints. In 1948, Ranganathan drafted national legislation for libraries (the Union

Library Bill), but the bill was never introduced. Subsequent national-level attention to the issue was intermittent and generally attached to broader discussions about educational reform. These efforts produced some modest progress on the critical funding questions, but no large-scale campaigns or investments. In 1957, Ranganathan was called back to evaluate progress on university libraries. The resulting report led to new funding mechanisms based on the size of the student and faculty population served.[13] A few years later, the Kothari Commission (1964–1966) made further recommendations, including a requirement that before establishing a new university, college, or department, provisions had to be made for an adequate library—a significant decision given the rapidly growing student population.

The stream of commissions, reports, and other official actions played a powerful role in shaping the public imagination regarding the role and importance of libraries. But significant national programs never emerged. After the failure of the Union Library Bill in 1948, library legislation was left to the states. Few made them a priority. As of 2006, only ten of India's twenty-nine states had enacted Public Libraries Acts, and these of varying quality. Among them, the Mysore Public Libraries Act of 1965 is generally viewed as "the most progressive and forward-looking of all the Library Acts," insofar as it established separate Library Authorities for every city with a population of 100,000 or more, levied a new tax (on the preexisting vehicle tax) to fund libraries, and declared library employees to be state employees, which allowed their salaries to be paid out of state funds instead of through civic or district authorities.[14] Despite these efforts, some observers put India "a century behind in matters of library legislation," compared to Great Britain and the United States (Heitzman and Asundi 2000, 142–143).

The reliance on state-level policy for public libraries resulted, predictably, in haphazard development, a lack of entrenched political support, and broad scope for caprice and corruption at local levels. An illustrative example is the state of Karnataka's central library, which is one of the oldest public libraries in the country. In the 1960s, Karnataka passed what was widely viewed as a model Public Libraries Act (drafted by Ranganathan), under which the municipality of Bangalore was tasked with collecting a 6 percent surcharge on property taxes for improving its libraries—a step usually reserved in India for extraordinary expenses and emergencies. The infusion of funds successfully expanded the Bangalore library system, which was arguably India's best in the 1970s. But this support was not sustained. Bangalore's City Central Library abandoned public borrowing in 1985. Its card catalog was destroyed during a renovation project in the early 2000s, but officials waited for five years before starting work on a digital replacement. This catalog remains unfinished, making it very difficult to actually find books. The physical plant of the library is also in a shambles.

In the last few years the library has found itself stuck between various disputing local bodies. Approximately $2 million is owed to the library by the local municipal body, which is suffering its own financial crisis.[15] According to the deputy director of the City Central Library, the budgets for Bangalore's 120 public branches were cut by close to 50 percent in a single year (2012) even as the amount of money raised in the name of libraries increases as a result of the growth in real estate transactions.[16]

Stories like that of the Bangalore central library mark the decline of the public library in India as both a civic ideal and public infrastructure. Although the Internet has only barely begun to impact the book ecosystem in India, it has had a much faster and more powerful effect on other information services that were once among the library's primary functions, such as access to newspapers,[17] which formerly drove a large portion of patron traffic. This larger challenge to the core purposes of the library as an institution is not unique to India: all libraries confront the question of the value they add beyond the expanding range of online information services. But it has given rise to a line of official Indian thinking on the subject.

In 2012, the Government of India established a National Mission on Libraries based on the recommendations of the National Knowledge Commission (NKC)—a group set up to advise the government on measures needed to make India competitive in the knowledge economy.[18] The aim of the National Mission is to digitize and link the collections of the 9,000 public libraries in India. The significance of the Mission is that it is the first major public intervention in rethinking libraries since the mid-1980s.

The National Mission is complemented by semi-private efforts such as the Digital Empowerment Foundation (DEF) and the Developing Library Network (DELNET), which are supported by the Bill & Melinda Gates Foundation to upgrade public libraries in India. Currently, most of the public libraries are focused on digitizing collections. None of them provide access to electronic databases and journals.

Publishing Politics

By most accounts, there is no consistent or reliable data on the size and scale of the publishing industry in India.[19] According to the Federation of Indian Publishers, however, there are more than sixteen thousand companies (some sources say 19,000),[20] responsible for around ninety thousand new titles a year in twenty-four languages. English and Hindi language titles account for around 50 percent of the market, with roughly equal shares for each language. All such estimates are complicated by the fact that perhaps as many as a third of these publishers do not register their titles with the national ISBN agency. According to the New Delhi-based German Book Office, total revenues in the sector were around $2 billion[21] in 2012 with a growth rate of 15 percent per annum.[22] Of this, the academic market is estimated to represent 40 percent, which would place its value at around $800 million. Academic publishing is a heterogeneous market dominated by state publishers in the area of widely used textbooks and by foreign publishing firms (or their offices in India) for more specialized materials and monographs. Independent Indian publishers fill the wide range of niche markets, especially for non-English and non-Hindi materials.

Nationalization of the Textbook Market

Together with library advocacy, the establishment of a large government role in text-book publishing was one of the pillars of post-Independence educational policy. Compared to library advocacy, it was much more effectively implemented. Some of this change responded to (and was enabled by) the disruption in commercial publishing after Indian independence in 1947. Dominated for decades by UK publishers, these firms temporarily retreated from the market, creating an opening for indigenous firms. These grew in an ad hoc manner to meet the expanding demand. Because there were very few domestic publishing companies, many branched out from bookselling, wholesaling, and importing. The first major Indian publishing firm was the Asia Publishing House, which was also the first to implement editorial and production standards comparable to those of the international firms. But the overall quality of indigenous publishing during this period was low, resulting in a growing import market for textbooks, literature, and more specialized materials, initially from the United Kingdom and then the United States. The turning point in the consolidation of the import market was the U.S. Wheat Loan program.

Books for Wheat

In the early 1950s, the most pressing problem in India was not books but food shortages. To support the newly independent country, the United States passed a bill in 1951 to loan India $19 million to buy two million tons of U.S. wheat. The repayment terms reflected a mix of altruism, interest group lobbying, and Cold War diplomacy: interest payments on the loan were directed to U.S. publishers for the purchase of American books, periodicals, and equipment for Indian libraries. Part of the money was also spent on the exchange of scholars and librarians between the two countries. Altogether, Indian libraries received around $1.4 million in American books, $160,000 in equipment, and $115,000 on travel and study grants.[23] The backdrop to such assistance was the Cold War competition between the United States and the USSR over ideas and culture—especially in the newly decolonized, "nonaligned" countries. This effort took many forms and involved many U.S. government agencies, including the United States Information Service, which was quite open about its goals:

The Agency promotes the translation and distribution abroad of American books which illustrate important aspects of American life and culture or which contribute significantly to the exposure of communist theory and practice. Most of these books are sold through existing or newly developed commercial channels. Many are used in schools or universities or are made available for supplementary reading.[24]

The 1950s and early 1960s were the heyday of American Cold War book politics, resulting in the publication of roughly 80 million copies of 9,000 titles in fifty-one languages—almost all distributed in the Third World. In India, such programs accounted for around fifteen hundred titles in English and Indian languages between 1951 and 1972.[25]

By the mid-1950s, this ideological competition had entered into Indian political conversations about the need for cultural and educational independence from the Cold War powers. By the late 1950s, the Ministry of Education was expressing concern that Indian textbooks should reflect a "national" approach and that the use of "irrelevant" foreign books should be ended. These arguments aligned with the interests of the emerging Indian publishers, who viewed the books for wheat program as putting them at a competitive disadvantage.[26] The main outcome of these debates was the creation of large, new publishing organizations at the national level, complemented by a wide array of parallel organizations and policies at the state level. The NCERT (National Council of Educational Research and Training) was the first of these national bodies, established in 1961 to develop "model" textbooks that would lend themselves to easy translation and printing. The national government also founded the National Book Trust,[27] the Publication and Information Directorate, Sahitya Akademi, Lalit Kala Akademi, the Children's Book Trust, and publication wings of research institutions like the Indian Council of Social Science Research (ICSSR).[28]

Many of these new organizations had complementary and sometimes overlapping missions. The National Book Trust (NBT), for example, was charged with encouraging the production of quality reading materials at moderate prices, and promoting vernacular editions. The Ministry of Education and Social Welfare established a separate division to promote books published by Indian publishers. A National Book Development Board was set up in 1967 to create guidelines for the development of Indian book publishing in the context of the development needs of the country. This period also saw a number of vernacular-language publishers enter English-language publishing.[29]

Throughout, there were private publishers involved in the production of textbooks, guides, and supplementary materials, but they remained marginal compared to the role of the state.[30] Currently, the government is estimated to be responsible for 20 percent of the books produced in India.

As a result of these measures, secondary education and lower levels of higher education have been served mostly by standardized, publicly subsidized textbooks since the 1960s. In most states, the government is also the major purchaser of textbooks. Although the quality of these editions relative to imported materials has been regularly debated, government subsidies and lower domestic royalties introduce clear cost advantages, even relative to the lower-priced Indian editions of foreign textbooks.

The price of textbooks remains a highly political issue in India, with national-level efforts complemented by diverse state-level subsidies to ensure that prices do not rise.[31] The price and availability of textbooks are also highly politicized at the local level. Kerala—the only state with a 100 percent literacy rate—saw riots in 2015 over delays in the printing of school textbooks.[32] The controversy started with a decision by the state government to outsource the printing—a role traditionally reserved for the state-owned Kerala Books and Publications Society (KBPS).[33] According to the protestors, the new publishers delivered fewer than half the needed textbooks by the start of school (with a shortfall of around twelve million). Opposition parties argued that privatization would make textbooks much more expensive. In July, activists from the communist parties took to the streets in protest. The demonstration turned violent and the police resorted to tear gas shells and water cannons to disperse the protestors. After the riots, the chief minister launched a high-level investigation of the delay. The opposition, in turn, demanded the resignation of the education minister and a judicial probe.

Higher Education Publishing

The market for more specialized texts in higher education is organized differently than that for elementary and secondary school textbooks. Although basic and introductory university textbooks often remain subject to state subsidies and provision, public support plays little to no role in the market for professional or research materials. In these areas, private publishers and importers play the dominant role. This was not for lack of effort to expand the state model into these areas. For a period during the 1970s, the government attempted to replicate a nationalizing strategy that would curb the importation of foreign books. In 1973, the central government instructed university libraries to order imported books only via the State Trading Corporation (STC), which was responsible for imports and exports more generally. Critics denounced this measure as a limitation on the freedom of information, since the STC could restrict books coming into the country. Libraries opposed the plan as well, based on pressure from publishers and because they feared that obtaining imported books would become more difficult. The initiative was abandoned before it was ever fully implemented, partially due to opposition from the publishing community, but also because the Indian Government was not adequately prepared for the complexity of managing book importation.

The influence of U.S.-sponsored book programs was also critical in this early period of contestation of the market. The American "Standard Textbook Program" placed 1,000 "low-cost" textbook titles on the market in India in fields where suitable Indian books were unavailable.[34] The U.S. Information Service also subsidized the production of hundreds of titles aimed at the general book market. These included biographies of Presidents Abraham Lincoln and Richard Nixon, accounts of the Vietcong, and other generally pro-American and/or anti-communist titles offered to Indian publishers, with production subsidies of up to 80 percent.[35] Although successful on its own terms, the book program made it difficult for Indian publishers to compete in unsubsidized areas, including in the high-value professional markets where Indian books were either available or could have been quickly produced. Because some Indian publishers benefitted handsomely from the program, the initiative remained a source of considerable controversy.

This environment began to change in the 1970s. U.S. library and book subsidy programs waned and were ultimately defunded under the Reagan administration: formal ties between U.S. publishers and the U.S. Information Agency ended in 1980.[36] Indian efforts to replicate the foreign licensing model for textbooks in more specialized markets, moreover, proved challenging. As Mohan Primlani, managing director of Oxford-India Book House in the 1970s put it, foreign publishers were reluctant to lease out rights as "they would rather sell 100 copies of their own copy rather than 1,000 Indian copies."[37] Even when reprinted, the price of foreign works without the subsidies was often exorbitant and unaffordable for Indian students.[38] According to Primlani, this is what motivated him to chase Indian authors "and gear them to write for the student market."

Through this process of publisher-led market development, historian Ramachandra Guha argues, the Indian social sciences and humanities came of age in this period.[39] Scholars like M. N. Srinivas, Romila Thapar, Kaushik Basu, and Ashis Nandywere, who all went on to become distinguished global scholars, published their early works overseas—with Cambridge University Press, the University of Chicago Press, Blackwell, and other presses. But Indian editors, especially Ravi Dayal, then with the independent Oxford University Press–India,[40] had growing success in persuading them to publish their subsequent books with Indian presses. By the end of 1970s, Dayal and Oxford University Press had shifted the locus of scholarly publishing on South Asian subjects out of the West.

Despite this process of local development, the academic publishing market remained a highly uneven one. Overall, Indian authors remained a small part of the market for specialized academic work in India. Publishing was, in effect, a "two-speed economy"[41] with a small but highly developed foreign-owned or foreign-operated publishing sector running alongside a large but underdeveloped local sector—particularly in regard to journals. As Eric Antony Brotchie put it:

In the upper speed of this economy, the neo-colonial infrastructure for the production of English journals and monographs by foreign conglomerates dominates the visible output in papers, theses and monographs. As in many Western nations, the best and brightest scholars in large research institutes and universities usually approach, or are (rarely) approached by, these conglomerates seeking submissions for journals. Failing this, researchers simply publish through their research institute, a process usually funded by the Indian government.[42]

With the emergence of digital technologies and the Internet, this market structure has come under further pressure—though to what eventual extent remains unclear. Smaller publishers, freed from the worst constraints of physical distribution and marketing across a large and diverse country, have made inroads into the secondary tier of the academic publishing market. Some of this growth is driven by the formalization of publishing requirements for academic promotion, which creates much greater publishing demand from Indian academics than the top academic journals can accommodate. Some of these publishers use open access models, simultaneously addressing the issues of cost and distribution that have been the first-order problems for the domestic market.

Book Piracy

Book piracy is widespread in India but has tended to remain confined to a narrow segment of bestsellers due to the small scale on which distribution is typically organized. The most visible form of this trade is carried out by street vendors, often children, who sell books at traffic signals.[43] Distribution also extends into more organized bookselling in street markets—sometimes indistinguishable from or mixed in with legitimate trade. As reproduction and printing technologies have grown more sophisticated, the organizational scale of this activity has tended to diminish rather than grow—no longer requiring large capital investments in printing presses or large print runs, and passing instead through figures like Tilak from *Shor in the City*.

Unlike DVD piracy in India, where limited legal availability and very low costs of reproduction resulted in a great diversification of the materials available on the market, the smaller-scale distribution structure of book piracy imposes tighter market discipline. As Nilanjana Roy argues, "The book pirates always get it right: they anoint a few (and only a few) literary writers (Amitav Ghosh, Jhumpa Lahiri, Vikram Seth), they know when the market shifts from an obsession with *The Secret* to books by Indian authors on diets" (Roy 2014). Such selection practices make commercial book piracy a particularly poor fit with the academic market, where mass appeal is rarely a factor. It is almost impossible, consequently, to find academic titles pirated and distributed in a mass scale. Copying in the academic market is ubiquitous, but passes primarily through copy shops located near university campuses, which cater to the on-demand, small runs required by classes and individual students and faculty.

How Students Get What They Need

As usual, students find ways to circumvent the limitations of the main institutional forms of access, from the weakness of the library system to the relatively high-cost commercial publishing market. Our exploration of these practices involved a survey of approximately three hundred students at Delhi University, Maulana Azad Medical College, and the national law schools (Kolkatta, Bhopal, Hyderabad, and New Delhi)[44] within three disciplines—law, medicine, and social sciences—in 2013. We also held six focus group discussions with approximately eight students in each.

As in the other country studies in this volume, we found relatively little student purchasing of new materials—though these results differed sharply by field. Nearly all of the medical students (91 percent) bought new editions of the major text and reference books—motivated, many reported, by the value of updates and the importance of high-quality color diagrams, which are expensive and difficult to reproduce.[45]

Even within medicine, however, practices appear to vary significantly. Nearly all of the one hundred medical students in our survey were undergraduates. Several highlighted the difference between the undergraduate and postgraduate tracks with respect to the type and availability of materials. As one student put it: "Postgraduates use xeroxed copies of books much more frequently because the costs of the specialized books go up quite steeply and also because as postgraduates we have to read a variety of books, not just one or two books per subject, as is the case in undergrad. Otherwise, an average student would spend $500 on just reading material."

Law and humanities students, in contrast, who bought new materials much less frequently—28 percent and 27 percent, respectively, reported doing so for their

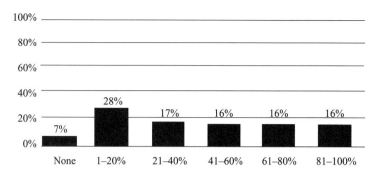

Figure 7.1
How much of your material is purchased new?

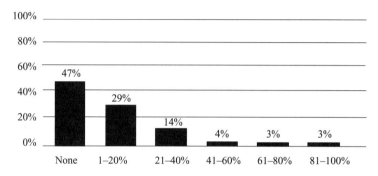

Figure 7.2
How much of your material is purchased used?

coursework. Among the law students, textbooks or statute books useful after graduation were among the most frequently cited "new" purchases. Sharing used textbooks
within the student body is common, with significant numbers of respondents describ-
ing practices of borrowing from older students. But there is no well-organized market
for used materials in India. Unlike the United States, which has an organized second-
hand book market that works through commercial websites like Amazon and Chegg,
the second-hand market in India is primarily a street-level operation within the book-
buying neighborhoods.[46] Half of students had never purchased used materials. Only
around 10 percent had purchased the majority of their materials used.

Photocopying is ubiquitous and, for many students, provides the majority or entirety
of their access to materials. Among Delhi University students, 55 percent copied at least
40 percent of their materials; only 7 percent copied none of them.

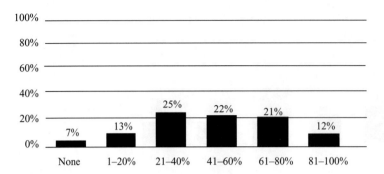

Figure 7.3
How much of your material is photocopied?

Students in the humanities and social sciences led the way in this category by a wide margin: over 50 percent reported copying at least 60 percent of their materials. Among law students, 29 percent did so. Medical students, in contrast, were far less reliant on photocopied material: none crossed the 60 percent threshold in the survey. A bit over half reported lower levels of copying, ranging between 20 percent and 60 percent of materials.

Differences in the types of materials used in the three curricula explain much of this difference. In the case of the social sciences and humanities, much of the curriculum—especially at the graduate level—consists of expensive theoretical or philosophical texts.[47] Because India is a common-law country that relies heavily on English and American precedents, many of the more analytical textbooks used by Indian law students are foreign books,[48] and these are absolutely unaffordable. Often students only need a few pages or, in some cases, chapters of the books.

Consistent with the stronger demand for new materials, the average spent on materials for medical school was significantly higher than in other fields. On average, medical students spent just over $100 per semester on new materials. Law students reported spending around $20 per semester; humanities and social science students about $22. Reported expenses on photocopies were much lower and show less variation, averaging $8–$15 per semester in the three cohorts.

Differences in reported spending on new materials also closely track ability to pay across the three fields. Students in medicine come from wealthier families by a large margin. Seventy-three percent reported family incomes over $1,200 per month—a level that places them in the 0.11 percent percentile in Indian family income.[49] None reported income under $600 per month. Among law students, 54 percent met or surpassed the $1,200 threshold. Among humanities and social science students, only 25 percent did. Humanities and social sciences also had the highest percentage of low-income students by a wide margin, with 32 percent reporting family income under $600 month (vs. 18 percent in law and none in medicine).

Much of the motivation for photocopying over buying new has a clear economic basis. Materials are expensive and student (and family) resources are often highly constrained. It is worth noting, however, the social dimension of copying and text sharing identified by some of the students. As one observed, "texts prescribed in our class were not available for all students, so we had to photocopy and exchange texts amongst ourselves. I think, in hindsight, it was probably one of the major reasons why we as students of the same class hung out much more with each other, discussed the texts (among other things), and eventually became friends." In this and many other examples throughout this study, the building of shadow libraries is a community practice.

Digital Access

Digital access has been slow to emerge in India, both in the commercial sector, where major vendors like Flipkart and Amazon have developed substantial e-book storefronts only in the past four years,[50] and in the library sector, where the pace of development has been glacial. This is true of scholarship in general, but particularly in regard to domestically authored work.

Although there have been periodic efforts to computerize libraries—generally in reference to creating catalogs and providing Internet access[51]—efforts to develop digital collections have been scarce and efforts to address the legal and market issues impeding digitization are nonexistent.[52] Despite the obvious transition toward digital modalities of discovery and reading, and the chronic failures of the library system, there are no successful large-scale digitization efforts.[53] In contrast to intense independence-era advocacy for libraries, the challenge of expanding access in the digital era has fallen off political agendas. Local efforts remain small and lack coordination or even communication among them. As a result, the same lessons are learned, forgotten, and relearned. The same failures are experienced repeatedly.

Uneven economic growth has exacerbated this fragmentation. As Banerjee notes, "[at] one end of the spectrum the country can boast of a highly specialized information retrieval system"; at the other, many in the Indian populace lack access "even to basic reading material or advice," much less to the databases or information networks available to better-funded libraries.

In our survey, students in both law and social sciences reported widespread use of online resources for their classes; in both cases over three quarters reported doing the majority of their work this way. Law students, in particular, have become dependent on online access to case law. The majority of this access passes through subscription-based access provided by the university, including the legal databases Manupatra (100 percent), LexisNexis (71 percent), and HeinOnline (43 percent). Lower but still significant numbers of students also reported using databases to which the university *did not subscribe*, including Westlaw, Walter Kluwer Online, Halsbury's Laws of India, and Encyclopedia Britannica (14.28 percent). Survey responses and faculty interviews suggested that, in these cases, access was based primarily on passwords shared by members of other institutions. Even this level of access is limited to India's roughly ten elite law schools. The average law college across the country has no such access.

In the school of humanities and socials sciences, curricular and research needs are organized differently and still highly dependent on books and articles. As we have discussed, there are no affordable legal frameworks for acquiring either outside the contested arena of photocopying. The digital book ecosystem for academic work is very poorly developed and the terms of access to many of the large scholarly databases, such as Sage, have yet to be worked out—even in universities as relatively well off as Delhi. The use of online resources for studies and research is high, but with much higher representation of illegal services. Over 30 percent of social science and humanities students indicated downloading most of their material from pirate sites, with nearly a quarter citing the defunct pirate Library.nu archive as a major source (compared to around 20 percent overall).

These practices are complemented across all three disciplines by copying and sharing among students. Over 80 percent of students shared digital files, though infrequently in large quantities. Students at the National Law School described an online electronic archive (an informal intranet) available at the student hostels, composed of articles downloaded from the major legal databases as well as sources like Library.nu, to which students would add from year to year. This includes a "First-Year Folder" of materials passed down to incoming classes, as well as a database of old projects written by senior students.

This is not a well-organized effort, but rather a matter of custom among upper classes. It is also typical of the lack of institutional support for managing learning materials at the university. None of the three schools surveyed used learning management systems or similar tools to manage access to class materials. Students and faculty provide their own such services, relying heavily on email, followed by Facebook and Google Docs.

A large majority of students, accordingly, are shadow librarians by necessity if not choice. Students bear primary responsibility for managing their own libraries of PDFs of articles or other research. Such collections are very common, ranging from 73 percent

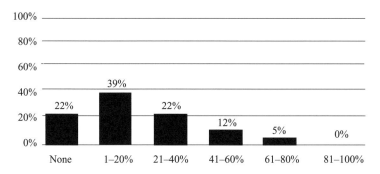

Figure 7.4
How much of your material is copied (digitally) from other students

of medical students to 80 percent of law students. Despite these overall similarities, the humanities and social science students tended to have the largest collections by a wide margin. Where law student collections averaged one hundred articles, collections in the humanities and social sciences often ran much higher, with 10 percent of respondents estimating their collections at one thousand or more articles. Here, as in other areas, we see the combined effects of an expensive curriculum, comparatively low incomes, and weak legal digital access. Here we see the origin story for Pradeep's Eleven, BiblioFyL, and many other shadow archives

Predictably, reading habits also track disciplinary differences in the use of materials—particularly online databases, photocopies, and textbooks. Sixty percent of law students indicated that they do most of their reading for classes on a computer screen. For humanities and social sciences, the number was 44 percent; for medicine, only 6 percent. Tablet and e-reader use was minimal in all groups.

These are relatively high rates for digital reading compared to other country findings, where students demonstrate a strong preference for print. The practice also appears to extend well beyond classroom materials. In spite of the low penetration of tablets and e-reading devices, nearly 50 percent of respondents possess e-book collections, strongly implying habits of acquisition that predate the launch of the major book portals. Consistent with the problems of pricing and availability in the legal digital market, few of the respondents buy e-books. Across the surveys, there was only one individual who read e-books and *did not also* download them via P2P services or file locker sites. Such common use of file sharing sites for e-book acquisition was corroborated in questions about music and movies. Among the 82 percent of students that share course materials digitally, three quarters also shared other types of media—particularly music and film. Only a small percentage (5 percent) acknowledged using pay sites like iTunes. Although legal digital markets are emerging in India, they have not yet provided compelling alternatives for students.

Enforcement and the Delhi University Photocopy Case

In most university libraries across India, most books are available in only a single copy, which has to be shared among all the students. This scarcity has a direct effect on library policies. At the major law schools, for instance, books can be borrowed only for a day, which means that a book is often borrowed not to read but to photocopy. By the same token, there is often only a single photocopying machine in the library, which in turn gives rise to networks of copy shops around universities that provide cheap reproduction services. Near Delhi University, for example, where we conducted part of our survey work, there is an entire neighborhood comprised of such shops. This network plays the dominant role in providing access to materials, serving (according to our survey) 85 percent of those who photocopy, including nearly all of the students in law and social sciences. Although publishers have often complained about the photocopying of academic materials, these complaints had never translated into legal action. The ubiquity of the practice made enforcement controversial and, indeed, potentially destabilizing in a country where rising textbook prices could lead to riots. At a minimum, it guaranteed bad press for publishers who needed to retain students as customers. The Delhi University photocopy case (as it has become known) ended this policy of toleration. In 2011, three publishers—Oxford University Press, Cambridge University Press, and Taylor & Francis—sued Delhi University and a photocopy shop on its premises for unauthorized distribution of coursepacks to students—with a claimed $100,000 (six million rupees) in damages.

The details of the case were unusual. The shop, Rameshwari Photocopiers, was given space on the campus of the School of Economics following an open tender, with a later agreement that it would copy 3,000 pages per student free of cost in lieu of payment for an operating license. Faculty, in turn, could assign course materials that could be taken from the library (or other sources) by students and submitted to the photocopy shop. The shop would then circulate the combined photocopied materials to the students at a rate of Rs 0.40 ($.01) per page.

In their complaint, the publishers argued that Rameshwari Photocopiers was reproducing and issuing unauthorized copies of their publications for a commercial purpose and that such circulation did not amount to "fair dealing" under Indian law. Unlike U.S. law, where "fair use" involves a process of triangulating among different factors such as the "purpose and character" of the use (e.g., parody or educational use), the substantiality of the reproduction, and the effect on the commercial market for the original, Indian fair dealing follows the UK tradition in requiring specific statutory language for exceptions. The case quickly became a litmus test for what constituted fair dealing when it came to photocopying academic materials.

The case turned largely on interpretation of two provisions in the Indian Copyright Act. The first is the fairly wide educational exception provided under Section 52(1)(i) which allows for "the reproduction of any work by a teacher or a pupil in the course of instruction or as a part of questions or answers to questions." The second is Sec. 52(1)(a), which allows for fair dealing with any work (except computer programs) for the purposes of private or personal use, including research. The two provisions anchored the university's argument that it was within its rights (and students were, accordingly within their rights) to photocopy academic texts and articles and to create coursepacks in the course of instruction.

The devil, of course, is in the details. The Indian Copyright Act does not prescribe a limit to the extent of reproduction available under the education and personal exceptions—either in terms of the substantiality or number of the copies. In theory, the complete photocopying of an academic work is permissible under the fair dealing provisions. Yet, Indian courts have, on several occasions, introduced substantiality and quantity tests, drawing on the English case of *Hubbard v. Vosper*, which pitted the Church of Scientology against one of its critics in regard to a book that drew extensively on the work of L. Ron Hubbard.[54] The Delhi case thus turned on the question of whether the copy shop reproductions were too substantial and/or too numerous to be considered "fair," where substantiality can refer not just to the percentage of use of the work, but also to the copying of the key parts of the work.

Because the case dealt with specific instances of copying particular texts,[55] it was relatively easy to determine whether the copying involved a large percentage of the works in question. In most cases, the page counts represented under 10 percent of the work—though in a few this number climbed to between 20 percent and 30 percent. The overall average was 12.5 percent. If the accepted U.S. "fair use" threshold of 10 percent is used, eleven out of the nineteen books fell within the limit.

In the absence of statutory guidelines, the question for the Indian court was whether a fair-minded person would consider 12.5 percent of a book to be "substantial." There is of course no right answer to this.[56] But it is worth emphasizing the irrelevance of the counterfactual, in which students actually buy all of the books in the offending coursepack—some seventeen with a total retail price of around $1,700. This is a sum slightly larger than average GDP per capita in India. The Delhi case is not about getting the students to buy physical copies of the book so much as creating pressure on the university to impose a reprographic fee for photocopying excerpts as well to clarify quantitative restrictions on the amount that can be legally copied from a book.[57] The problem with this proposal is that the envisaged license fee roughly triples the price of photocopying from its current level (40 paisa or around 0.5 cents) to a rupee per page (currently around 1.5 cents).

The publishers have argued that this is a relatively small amount that will not affect the students—the license fee, in an often-repeated argument, amounts to around one expensive meal. However, this assumes the perspective of the richest students, not the poorest students who are the real beneficiaries of photocopying. Rather than measuring the fee against imaginary meals, it may be more useful to compare this to the average fees paid at Delhi University. At the master's level a student pays approximately $150 (Rs. 10,000) per semester (depending on the college that they are enrolled at). At one rupee per page, the cost of photocopying materials just for coursepacks would amount to around a 10 percent increase in fees.

The Decision

In September 2016, Justice Rajiv Endlaw on the Delhi high court dismissed the 2012 copyright infringement petition. His ruling is, in the Indian context, a remarkable defense of the public purposes of copyright limitations, informed in part by his own obvious identification with the difficulties of the students. Where the petitioners had argued for a narrow reading of fair dealing, claiming that the section allows only for the provision of materials in the course of a lecture and in the classroom, the judge arrived at a broader answer to the question (para. 62): "when does the imparting of instruction begin and when does it end?" The answer is as follows: "The meaning of Section 52(1)(i) supra would include reproduction of any work while the process of imparting instruction by the teacher and receiving instruction by the pupil continues i.e. during the entire academic session for which the pupil is under the tutelage of the teacher … not limited to personal interface between teacher and pupil" (para. 72).

Justice Endlaw then drew on his own experience as a law student to describe the significance of the changing technological environment to interpretation of the law. In short, the salient issue for fair dealing is the purpose of the activity—teaching—not the technologies that facilitate it. His ruling states:

When an action, if onerously done is not an offence, it cannot become an offence when, owing to advancement in technology doing thereof has been simplified. That is what has happened in the present case. In the times when I was studying law, the facility available [for] photocopying was limited, time consuming and costly. The students then, used to take turns to sit in the library and copy by hand pages after pages of chapters in the books suggested for reading and subsequently either make carbon copies thereof or having the same photocopied. The photocopying machines then in vogue did not permit photocopying of voluminous books without dismembering the same. However with the advancement of technology the voluminous books also can be photocopied and at a very low cost. Thus the students are now not required to spend day after day sitting in the library and copying pages after pages of the relevant chapter of the syllabus books. When the effect of the action is the same, the difference in the mode of action cannot make a difference so as to make one an offence.

The publishers were understandably unenthusiastic about the judgment and filed an appeal before a division bench (consisting of two judges) of the Delhi high court. In December 2016, the division bench upheld most of Justice Endlaw's orders while making a few further distinctions. Aware that nonlawyers might get lost within the thicket of technical legal arguments, toward the end of the judgment the high court provided an analogy between music and the complexity of law that summarizes the jurisprudential backbone of the judgment.

A melody is the outcome of the sounds created when different instruments, such as a lute, flute, timbale, harp and drums are played in harmony. The notes of the instruments which are loud and resonating have to be controlled so that the sound of the delicate instruments can be heard. But it has to be kept in mind that at proper times the sound of the drums drowns out the sound of all other instruments under a deafening thunder of the brilliant beating of the drums. Thus, it is possible that the melody of a statute may at times require a particular Section, in a limited circumstance, to so outstretch itself that, within the confines of the limited circumstance, another Section or Sections may be muted.

Translated back into the Copyright Act, the judges are making clear that if the predominant purpose of the law is to provide exclusive rights to owners of copyright, this right sometimes has to be muted to serve other equally important purposes such as education. Echoing the policy intentions of the legislature, the judges chose to ignore the technical distinctions between education and instruction, and between textbooks and coursepacks and held that:

education alone is the foundation on which a progressive and prosperous society can be built. Teaching is an essential part of education, at least in the formative years, and perhaps till postgraduate level. It would be difficult for a human to educate herself without somebody: a teacher, helping. It is thus necessary, by whatever nomenclature we may call them, that development of knowledge modules, having the right content, to take care of the needs of the learner is encouraged. We may loosely call them textbooks. We may loosely call them guide books. We may loosely call them reference books. We may loosely call them coursepacks. So fundamental is education to a society—it warrants the promotion of equitable access to knowledge to all segments of the society, irrespective of their caste, creed and financial position. Of course, the more indigent the learner, the greater the responsibility to ensure equitable access. (para. 30)

The judges specify that fairness is an essential aspect of the statute especially when there it impacts a person's legal rights, such as those of a copyright holder. But what is fairness? In a crucial paragraph the court states that "the utilization of the copyrighted work would be a fair use to the extent justified for purpose of education. It would have no concern with the extent of the material used, both qualitative or quantitative."

The significance of this ruling's interpretation is that it rejects the adoption of American standards (the four-factor test) into Indian copyright law and grounds the principle of fairness within a philosophy of education. No arbitrary restrictions in terms of quantity or substantiality are to be applied.[58]

However, the case is not completely over. One crucial difference between Justice Endlaw's judgment and the division bench ruling is that while Endlaw found no fact that was worthy of being tried since there was no prima facie infringement, the division bench held that the specific question of whether the reproduction of full works is valid in the course of instruction is a matter that should be determined in trial. The division bench consequently remanded that issue back to a trial judge. The larger significance of the ruling is that while it arose out of a seemingly narrow question of whether the photocopying of coursepacks was allowed in copyright law, the judges chose to answer by returning copyright to its normative foundations—in Justice Endlaw's words "to increase and not to impede the harvest of knowledge" (para. 80). This is a powerful and potentially portable argument with implications beyond India.

Toward a Better Legal Framework for Access to Educational Materials

The contrast between the provisions for access to primary/secondary school learning materials and higher education materials in India is a sharp one. While there are many challenges facing quality primary and secondary schooling in India, on the one hand, state policies have ensured that relatively equitable access to learning materials is not prominent among them. For higher education, on the other hand, the state has largely eschewed a role in provision or regulation of the market and—at the same time—failed to create a well-financed, sustainable library system, either for students or the general public. Although the publishing industry has expanded in the face of growing demand, most student access relies on large-scale practices of informality, embedded in a confusing, contested system of rights.

Although it would be comforting to think that this failure will be addressed by the transformation of the publishing sector in the digital era and the growth of legal services, it is worth noting that none of the major institutional initiatives described in this chapter—whether the expansion of database subscriptions or the imposition of photo-copy licensing—show much prospect of lowering the costs of access to knowledge for students. The informality of much of the present ecosystem is inefficient but also, and above all else, cheap. With large numbers of Indian students and Indian institutions operating in precarious financial situations, the impact of even small changes in forms of access can be large.

In the absence of a larger state role in the provisioning of materials, policy debates around the terms of access have tended to focus on the scope of fair dealing provisions in Indian copyright law—of what can be done, in short, with privately provisioned materials. But while important, the copyright-fair dealing pair is not the only legal framework that has potential to change the day-to-day conditions of access. India also has a right to education, copyright limitations for libraries, and a growing open access movement. To date, these have been relatively marginal factors in the ecosystem, but they could have large impacts in the coming years.

The Right to Education

While the focus of most poverty alleviation strategies has been on primary education, there is convincing development case for emphasizing education at all levels. India has the highest youth population in the world, with 600 million people under the age of 25. There is no problem of primary education, in short, that does not quickly become a problem at the secondary and higher levels on a truly massive scale. The National Knowledge Commission has argued that India will need at least fifteen hundred new universities to cope with the demand for education in the coming years.[59] Here the influence of Amartya Sen has been profound. In Sen's analysis, the extension of education from primary to higher education has significant impacts on a wide range of development challenges, including health, gender equity, and awareness of political rights. Sen himself connected these concerns to the Delhi University case in a letter to Oxford University Press, which asked the press to refrain from using the force of the law against the students.

A "Right to Education" for children below the age of fourteen is expressly guaranteed under Article 21-A of the Indian Constitution. By most accounts, universal primary and middle schooling in India has achieved a minimal application of that right. But courts have repeatedly pushed for more expansive interpretations of the article. In 1992, in *Mohini Jain (Miss) v. State of Karnataka & Others* India's Supreme Court characterized the right to education as a component of the broader right to life under Article 21, arguing that "the dignity of an individual cannot be assured unless it is accompanied by the

right to education. The State Government is under an obligation to endeavor to provide educational facilities at all levels to its citizens."

The legal development of this right in recent years has generally involved its expansion beyond a basic notion of the availability of education toward a broader understanding of social and economic obstacles.[60] There is clearly an opportunity for stronger
integration of the constitutional right to education with policies governing access to
learning materials and, accordingly, with copyright reform. In India, the main precedents for such integration are in the area of patents, where access to medicines has
been read into the right to life in Art. 21.[61]

While there is a long history of student agitation over the privatization of education in India, we have not seen the same political energies directed toward questions
of copyright and access to knowledge. If the Delhi University photocopy case is any
indication, however, increased enforcement measures and pressures on costs and access
could change this dynamic, producing stronger linkages between debates about copyright, access to knowledge, and broader constitutional rights.

The Library Exception

Stronger interpretations of existing limitations and exceptions to copyright offer
another approach to expanding access to books and educational materials in India,
in large part by regularizing some of the informal practices that already shape student practices. One virtue of such an approach—and part of its attraction to Indian
education advocates—is that it could improve access without requiring substantial
new policy initiatives, investments by the state, or, arguably, significant changes to
publisher revenue streams, which as we have seen are concentrated around must-
have reference texts rather than the range of materials used in most coursework.
A generous interpretation of the fair dealing exception for educational uses in the
Delhi University photocopy case would provide one such lever, but there are others.
Sec. 52 of the Copyright Act contains a range of exceptions for personal use, research,
and libraries.

Libraries, for example, benefit from an exception under Section 52(1)(o), which
allows for the making of additional copies for general use—specifically, "the making of
not more than three copies of a book (including a pamphlet, sheet of music, map, chart
or plan) by or under the direction of the person in charge of a public library for the use
of the library if such book is not available for sale in India." The ability of libraries to
make ample use of the exception could significantly expand and—where necessary—
legalize collections.

The case for a broader interpretation of the exception draws primarily on the ambiguity surrounding a number of the key terms in the Copyright Act. Legal scholar Prashant Iyengar argues that the lack of definition of the terms "public library," "book," and "use of the library" opens space for more contextual readings that could bring the normative vision of Ranganathan's laws of library science more strongly into play.[62] Iyengar argues, in short, for a library clause for *users*, as opposed to a library clause for *lawyers*.

The definition of a "book," for example, varies widely across the different states with Public Library enactments. The Maharashtra Public Libraries Act 1967, for instance, clearly encompasses non-print and digital media that go well beyond the relatively restrictive norms commonly attributed to the Copyright Act. According to the Maharashtra act: "A 'book' includes every volume, part or division of a volume and pamphlet in any language, and every sheet of music, map, chart or plan separately printed or lithographed, newspapers, periodicals, paintings, films, slides discs, or tapes used for audiovisual information and such other materials. (emphasis added)

The right to make a limited number of digital copies would represent an important expansion of library capacities. Still more important is the phrase "available for sale in India," which limits library copying to unavailable texts. The most literal interpretation of this phrase would essentially void this possibility in the digital era, insofar as Amazon and other online book stores can make all books at least notionally available. But there is also a basis for understanding availability in terms of accessibility, reflecting a determination of whether a book had been made adequately available. As right to education cases identify cost as an important factor in the exercise of rights, it is easy to see how such reasoning could be applied to library exceptions. Section 6 of the Copyright Act already leads in this direction when it stipulates that the Copyright Board may deny a work status as a "publication" if it is communicated to the public in an insignificant manner. There is ample reason, in other words, to think that the framers of the Copyright Act did not view "publication," "communication," "issuance of copies," and "availability" in narrow or purely technical terms. If building a robust library system to meet India's information needs remains an important goal, nor should we.

Open Access

The spread of open access models for scholarly publication could also become a significant factor as research released under open access policies gradually accumulates into large bodies of work. The principle that publicly funded research should be open access had been discussed for some time in India, with selective adoption by Indian journals in the early 2000s,[63] endorsement by the 2005 National Knowledge Commission, and adoption by several leading scientific funding bodies in 2014.[64] Open access models in other fields gained traction more slowly. Several major law schools have now formed a consortium to bring materials, modules, and conference proceedings through the Legal Information Institute, an Indian open access law portal. None of these initiatives addresses the vast history of work available only on expensive commercial terms or the database access that increasingly defines equal participation in the global research community. None of them individually go far enough to significantly impact the shadow library practices that shape research, education, and even formal librarianship in many settings in India. But they are a start and, in combination with other measures, could shift the conditions of access to knowledge in India toward a more open regime that does not so gratuitously deny modern-day Ekalavyas their opportunities to learn.

Notes

1. This pattern has not changed significantly since the 1970s, when photocopying machines began to be widely available in Indian cities. An article on book piracy in the popular Indian magazine *India Today* from 1976 described the pirate market this way: "The business flourishes during the second half of the year, as new titles are issued in the West to catch the Christmas sales. Pirates in India average 18 books a year. A popular Western novelist like Alistair Maclean has a market of 25,000 copies. His latest novel, *Circus*, was out in the West only a month ago, but is already available in India. The same was the case with Arthur Hailey's *Money Changers* a few months ago" (Depthnews 1976).

2. See http://www.ficci.com/pressrelease/1541/ficci-press-feb21-publishing.pdf (accessed February 25, 2017).

3. See http://www.ficci.com/spdocument/20307/FICCI-Anti-piracy-paper.pdf (accessed February 25, 2017). While FICCI has worked closely with the film industry for a long time, its 2014 conference signaled the closer role FICCI intends to play in the arena of book publishing.

4. See Arunachalam and Muthu 2011.

5. Standalone institutions include polytechnics, semi-skilled education schools, and diploma-granting institutions. See *All India Survey on Higher Education (2010–2011)*, 2013. http://mhrd .gov.in/sites/upload_files/mhrd/files/statistics/AISHE201011_0.pdf(accessed February 25, 2017).

6. See http://www.scidev.net/global/communication/feature/q-a-open-archives-the-alternative-to -open-access.html (accessed February 25, 2017).

7. See http://infochangeindia.org/component/content/article/121-technology/features/7173-knowl edge-for-all (accessed February 25, 2017).

8. On this point, see the marvelous work of Nicholas Basbanes (2001, 2012).

9. The role of an affiliating university is to provide accreditation to colleges that do the actual teaching while the university merely provides the degree.

10. Quoted in Bose 1965.

11. For a detailed account, see Bhatt 1995 and Bhatt 2009.

12. Bhatt 1995.

13. The Ranganathan Committee recommended that state funds for libraries be rationed at Rs. 15 per enrolled student and Rs. 200 per teacher and research fellow. It also advocated the establishment of initial library grants and development grants from the University Grants Commission. See ibid., 61.

14. Das and Lal 2006.

15. Cohen 2013.

16. For a contrasting account of spending on libraries in India, see "Public Libraries Are Doing Well in India, Thank You," February 28, 2014, http://www.indiaspend.com/special-reports/public-libraries-are-doing-well-in-india-thank-you-49780(accessedFebruary25,2017). This article tracks the overall rise in library budgets based on Ministry of Culture finances but does not go into an examination of the actual spending on or condition of public libraries.

17. For a representative account, see Singh 2012.

18. The NKC focused on reforms to the education sector and intellectual property, and on the future role of libraries.

19. This may begin to be remedied with the anticipated introduction of Nielsen's BookScan. See John 2015; also http://www.nielsenbookscan.co.uk/uploads/7695_Nielsen_BOSSIndia_Sell_sheets _2_D1.pdf. For an account by an independent publisher, see http://www.tarabooks.com/blog/profiting-by-managing-a-propensity-for-chaos/ (accessed February 25, 2017). See also Wolf 2013.

20. German Book Office New Delhi, "India" [fact sheet]. Frankfurt Buchmesse (2012). http://www.buchmesse.de/bilder/buchmesse/book_market_india__2012.pdf (accessed February 25, 2017).

21. One report places the number at $2.5 billion but begins by stating that there are no accurate numbers. See http://www.pik.org.pl/upload/files/Global_Trends_in_Publishing_2014.pdf (accessed February 25, 2017).

22. German Book Office New Delhi, "India" [fact sheet].

23. See Bhatt 2009 and Konnur 1990. More generally, for a history of education policy see essays by Philip Altbach in Agarwal 2012.

24. Agarwal 2012.

25. Ibid.

26. Altbach quotes Peter Jayasinghe: "The PL 480 [books for wheat] programme delivers a crippling blow to the Indian publisher who refuses to be tempted by the blandishments of foreign governments and publishers to become a mere reprint house for their books and who insists on

performing a more exalted task—that of presenting and promoting the finest in Indian thought and scholarship. He has to compete on grossly unequal terms with the foreign publisher whose vast resources are more than amply augmented by generous subsidies from his own government" (Altbach 1975, 331).

27. For an example of the subsidized book publishing of NBT see http://www.nbtindia.gov.in/scheme__13__subsidized-books-publications.nbt (accessed February 25, 2017).

28. Thakur, Thakur, and Khan 1998.

29. Ibid. Some of these include publishers that went on to become significant players, such as Jaico.

30. For an interesting account of the nascent publishing industry in the 1970s, see http://indiatoday.intoday.in/story/indian-authors-have-the-advantage-of-possessing-a-wider-choice-of-publishers/1/436988.html (accessed February 25, 2017).

31. Sen 2002.

32. On the riots, see Deccan Chronicle 2015 and O'Brien 2015.

33. See http://www.printpackipama.com/controversy-over-kerala-govts-decision-to-outsource-textbook-printing/ (accessed February 25, 2017).

34. See Agarwal 2012, 330.

35. Altbach: "In the Near East and South Asia alone, a total of 2,000,000 copies of 511 books were published in the year ending June 30, 1969. The books selected are simply given to various Indian publishers by the U.S. Information Service, with no screening by any Indian agency, and are subsidized by as much as 80 percent of the cost of publication. The Indian publisher is free to sell the books as he sees fit, or even to throw them away. There is no indication in these books that they are subsidized by the United States Government." Quoted in ibid., 94.

36. Arndt 2005, 159.

37. Ibid.

38. "Interviews with Publisher." *India Today*, February 15, 1976. See http://indiatoday.intoday.in/story/indian-authors-have-the-advantage-of-possessing-a-wider-choice-of-publishers/1/436988.html (accessed February 25, 2017).

39. Guha 2012.

40. See http://www.theguardian.com/news/2006/jul/04/obituaries.mainsection (accessed February 25, 2017).

41. Brotchie 2014.

42. Ibid., 118.

43. For an insightful account of street-level piracy, see Faleiro 2013.

44. Delhi University is a central university and one of the largest in India with 65 associated colleges and over 130,000 students. Maulana Azad Medical College is a government medical school attached to one of the leading government hospitals. The national law schools are statutory universities established in different states and are considered to be the elite law colleges of the country. Of the three, Delhi University has the widest demographic representation.

45. It will be interesting to see whether this practice changes with the advent of cheap hand-held scanners, smart phones, and tablets with software that permits high-quality reproduction. It is not uncommon now to see students taking pictures of books in libraries.

46. College Street in Calcutta, Darya Ganj in Delhi, and Avenue Road in Bangalore are some examples.

47. For example: In the sociological theory course at Delhi University, of the thirty-two books on the suggested readings list, almost all of them are published by foreign publishers and very expensive to buy in the market.

48. A few representative examples including standard legal commentaries such as Chitty on contracts, Nimmer on copyright.

49. For an income calculator, see http://timesofindia.indiatimes.com/calculator.cms (accessed February 25, 2017).

50. Flipkart started in 2007 while Amazon India started only in 2013.

51. The recommendations of the Chattopadhaya Committee on National Policy for Library and Information Systems (of 1986), for example, received inadequate attention and were ultimately abandoned. At universities, the UGC's Information and Library Network (Inflibnet) program has focused on acquiring "computers and other related infrastructure."

52. Bhattacharya (2004), for example, condemns the "sporadic and partial" attempts at digitization of Indian library resources, limited to "getting a few databases on CD-ROM," "subscribing to a few e-journals," "scanning a few documents," or "creating Adobe Acrobat files and installing them on an intranet."

53. The Inflibnet program among university libraries has been the partial exception to this rule. The National Mission on Libraries—a digitization effort launched in 2014—is not yet sufficiently operational to affect this assessment.

54. *Hubbard v Vosper* [1972] 2 Q.B. 84. This case laid out the parameters of fair dealing in the UK. The judgment of Lord Denning held that "no fair dealing with a literary, dramatic or musical work shall constitute an infringement of the copyright in the work if it is for purposes of criticism or review, whether of that work or of another work, and is accompanied by a sufficient acknowledgment."

55. Including numerous works on the history of India by Oxford University Press, as well as some more general "classics" such as Foucault's *The Order of Things*.

56. As one law librarian put it, "Yes, the library has certain internal rules about photocopying restrictions, and these rules have been put up in the photocopy room. The copying of an entire book is not allowed. Typically, we allow only 10–15 percent of a resource to be photocopied but since the number of pages which can be copied under fair dealing are not clear under Section 52 of the Indian Copyright Act, this is not an entirely inflexible percentage. But yes, it is the usual standard." Interview with the authors, 2012.

57. After the initial hearing, an email from the lawyers representing the publishers was leaked online in which it was clearly asserted that this is a test case to establish stronger enforcement of reprographic rights and fees in India.

58. The court used similar logic to reject the publishers' contention that Section 52 allows for reproduction of a work, but that if made available via photocopies it is no longer a reproduction but a publication.

59. See http://knowledgecommissionarchive.nic.in/reports/report09.asp.

60. In *Kumari Surya Shukla and Anr. v. State of U.P. and Ors.* (2007), for example, the court linked the availability of education to educational expenses and the cost of books in particular, arguing—in a case about the extent of financial and other obligations that may be imposed on students—that "Books or curriculum should not be changed at short span of time as it imposes additional burden on the family budget of lower strata of the society. ... [S]uch action affects the quality of life of the citizens, hence violative of Article 21."

61. The judgment of the courts in the 1998 Novartis case regarding the scope of patent protection for pharmaceuticals, for instance, explicitly located the discussion of Section 3(d) of the Patent Act within the terms of the right to life in Article 21.

62. Iyengar 2010.

63. Notably *The Indian Journal of Postgraduate Medicine*.

64. Priyadarshini 2014.

References

Agarwal, Pawan, ed. 2012. *A Half-Century of Indian Higher Education: Essays by Philip G. Altbach*. Delhi: SAGE Publications India.

Altbach, Philip. 1975. *Publishing in India: An Analysis*. Delhi: Oxford University Press.

Arndt, Richard. 2005. *The First Resort of Kings: American Cultural Diplomacy in the Twentieth Century*. Lincoln: Potomac Books.

Arunachalam, Subbiah, and Madhan Muthu. 2011. *Open Access to Scholarly Literature in India: A Status Report*. Center for Internet and Society. http://cis-india.org/openness/publications/open-access-scholarly-literature.pdf (accessed February 25, 2017).

Basbanes, Nicholas. 2012. *A Gentle Madness: Bibliophiles, Bibliomanes, and the Eternal Passion for Books*. Chapel Hill, NC: Fine Books Press.

Basbanes, Nicholas. 2001. *Patience & Fortitude: A Roving Chronicle of Book People, Book Places, and Book Culture*. New York: HarperCollins.

Bazzle, Steph. 2015. "Author Paulo Coelho Caught a Kid Selling Pirated Copies of His Book—He's Not Even Mad." *The Inquisitr News*. March 14. http://www.inquisitr.com/1924634/author-paulo-coelho-caught-a-kid-selling-pirated-copies-of-his-book-hes-not-even-mad/.

Bhatt, R. K. 1995. *History and Development of Libraries in India*. Delhi: Mittal Publications.

Bhatt, R. K. 2009. "Academic Libraries in India: A Historical Study." *International Conference on Academic Libaries*. http://crl.du.ac.in/ical09/papers/index_files/ical-10_180_494_2_RV.pdf.

Bhattacharya, P. 2004. "Advances in Digital Library Initiatives: A Developing Country Perspective." *The International Information & Library Review* 36 (3): 165–175.

Bose, Pamil Chandra. 1965. "School and College Libraries in the Evolution of Education in Modern India." *Indian Library Association Bulletin* 1:20.

Brotchie, Eric Antony. 2014. "Academic Publishing in India: Sites of Reform and Resistance." *Publishing Research Quarterly* 30:115–134.

Chand, Prem, K. Prakash, Thiyam Satyabati, and Suresh Chauhan. 2007. "Access to Scholarly Literature in Higher Education Institutions under Inflibnet Consortium." Presented at the 5th International CALIBER, Panjab University.

Cohen, Margot. 2013. "Shelved Hopes." *Talk*. March 29. http://www.talkmag.in/cms/mauled/22-news/city/184-shelved-hopes (accessed February 25, 2017).

Das, Anup Kumar, and Banwari Lal. 2006. "Information Literacy and Public Libraries in India." Manuscript. http://eprints.rclis.org/7247/1/Information_Literacy_Public_Libraries_India.pdf (accessed February 25, 2017).

Deccan Chronicle. 2015. "Textbook Talks Fail to Clinch Consensus in Kerala," July 10. http://www.deccanchronicle.com/150710/nation-current-affairs/article/textbook-talks-fail-clinch-consensus-kerala.

Depthnews. 1976. "Book Fakers Hit Big Biz." February 15. *India Times*. http://indiatoday.intoday.in/story/government-plans-to-plug-book-piracy-under-new-copyright-law/1/436989.html (accessed September 7, 2017).

Faleiro, Sonia. 2013. "The Book Boys of Mumbai." *The New York Times*, January 4. http://www.nytimes.com/2013/01/06/books/review/the-book-boys-of-mumbai.html.

Guha, Ramachandra. 2012. "Shelf Life: A Personal History of the Oxford University Press India at 100." *The Caravan,* February 1. http://www.caravanmagazine.in/essay/shelf-life.

Heitzman, James, and A. Y. Asundi. 2000. "Evaluation of Public Libraries in India: The Case of Karnataka." *Information Development* 16 (3): 142–154.

Iyengar, Prashant. 2010. "The Library Exception under the Indian Copyright Act 1957." http://papers.ssrn.com/sol3/papers.cfm?abstract_id=1555718.

John, Binoo K. 2015. "How Big Is Indian Publishing, Really? Coming: A Survey with the Answers." February 24. http://scroll.in/article/709035/how-big-is-indian-publishing-really-coming-a-survey-with-the-answers (accessed February 25, 2017).

Kalia, D. A. 1974. "A Review of Public Library Development in India." *International Library Review* 6 (29): 29–33.

Konnur, Madhukar Bhimrao. 1990. *Transnational Library Relations: The Indo-American Experience.* Delhi: Concept Publishing.

Krishna D.K., and Raj Nidimoru, dir. *Shor in the City.* 2011. India: ALT Entertainment and Balaji Motion Pictures.

Manguel, Alberto. 2011. *The Library at Night.* Toronto: Knopf Canada.

"Manusmriti in Sanskrit with English Translation." n.d. https://archive.org/details/ManuSmriti_201601.

O'Brien, Liam. 2015. "What's Causing India's Textbook Crisis?" *Melville House Books.* http://www.mhpbooks.com/whats-causing-indias-textbook-crisis/ (accessed October 30, 2016).

Priyadarshini, Subhra. "India Unveils New Open Access Policy." *Nature India*, December 26. http://blogs.nature.com/indigenus/2014/12/india-unveils-new-open-access-policy.html (accessed February 25, 2017).

Roy, Nilanjana. 2014. "Nilanjana S Roy: The Pirate Wars." March 17. http://www.business-standard.com/article/opinion/nilanjana-s-roy-the-pirate-wars-114031700592_1.htm l.

Sandhu, R. K., and H. S. Sandhu. 1979. "Villages with and without Libraries in India." *International Library Review* 11 (2): 269.

Sen, J. M. 2002. *History and Development of Elementary Education in India.* New Delhi: Sarup & Sons.

Singh, Nagen. 2012. "Declining Popularity of Libraries." *Deccan Herald*, January 30. http://www.deccanherald.com/content/223203/declining-popularity-libraries.html (accessed February 25, 2017).

Thakur, K. S., D. S. Thakur, and S. D. Khan. 1998. "Scenario of Book Publishing and Trade in India." http://www.nuepa.org/libdoc/e-library/articles/1998dst.pdf (accessed February 25, 2017).

Wolf, Arun. 2013. "India: Profiting by Managing a Propensity for Chaos." *Frankfurt Academy Quarterly* (Spring): 10–11. http://www.book-fair.com/pdf/faq_spring_2013__februar_deutsch_englisch.pdf.

8 Brazil: The Copy Shop and the Cloud

Pedro Mizukami and Jhessica Reia

In Brazil, debates about access to educational materials in higher education have been dominated for years by disputes about the legal and moral implications surrounding photocopying. Until 1998, Brazilian copyright law permitted anyone to make full, single copies of protected works for personal, not-for-profit use.[1] This limitation on copyright protection anchored a complex web of curricular and student practices that developed in the course of the 1970s and 1980s as photocopiers came into widespread use. When that permission was withdrawn in the copyright reform act of 1998 (Law 9610/98), publishers tried to recapture that part of the market—first by trying to persuade universities to negotiate licenses and later opting for police raids to break the copy culture on university campuses. For the most part, these efforts failed, leaving university copy culture largely unaffected and creating a stalemate on copyright reform that continues to this day. In the meantime, parts of the photocopying ecosystem have shifted online—though publisher enforcement efforts have undercut the emergence of any large-scale shadow libraries to rival the Russian examples from chapter 1.

While parts of the publishing ecosystem have moved toward open access models (in which Brazil has been a leading international force), undergraduate students' needs are still mostly served by conventionally licensed content and university life continues to rely heavily on infringement as a means for access. Attempts at collective management have failed, and business models for paid online access have—so far—offered debatable value for universities. As students and institutions move toward digital materials and models of access, Brazil is in a transitional period. Copyright law is clearly broken, but the balance of forces between publishers, universities, and state has not yet been able to consolidate around a new regime. The dominant role played by the Brazilian state in educational and scholarly publishing means that access to materials—more than in many other countries—is a question for public policy. This role has provided scope for experiments with open access, proposals for alternative compensation models, and other strategies for navigating the transition from print to digital. It also means that, in a period of political instability and ascendency of large business interests, those experiments are unusually vulnerable.

This chapter divides this story into three sections. The first chronicles the disputes surrounding photocopy culture in Brazilian universities, focusing on the legal controversies and enforcement actions that have led Brazil to the current impasse over copying in educational contexts.

The second section explores efforts to expand online access to educational materials in Brazil, including through general-purpose online services, publisher-backed platforms, open access and licensing projects, and of course, shadow libraries.[2]

The third section explores student practices, based primarily on a survey and focus groups conducted among undergraduate students in medicine, communication studies, and law in the city of Rio de Janeiro.[3] The data offers a snapshot of this transitional period in which students and faculty use a mix of old and new strategies—print and digital, infringing and legal—to access materials.

Universities, Publishers, and the Battle over Copying

Xerox opened a Brazilian branch in 1965 (Rosa 2007, 73), but the photocopying era really began in the early 1970s, backed by a copyright reform in 1973 that introduced a broad, private copy exception that permitted full, single copies of protected works for personal, not-for-profit use. By the early 1980s, widespread access to photocopiers had turned this right into a foundation of university curricular practices.

Within most universities, photocopying came to be organized by the student unions for the different schools, by library staff, or by third-party contractors setting up shop within campuses. The State University of Rio de Janeiro (UERJ), for example, has around eleven copy shops in its main building, all operating under the supervision of the student union.[4] The Pontifical Catholic University of São Paulo (PUC-SP) has a similar arrangement in which the law, literature, psychology, social sciences, economics, and social work schools all have a copy shop at their respective student centers, with the university library providing additional machines.

These shops act as distribution centers for class materials. Generally, faculty put folders containing class readings and handouts on file with the university copy shops. Students can request any professor's folder and copy the available materials. The copy shops do enforce university copying policies in some instances, but the ecosystem is large and complex enough to permit determined students to copy what they want. What they can't copy inside, they can copy in the shops located outside the universities.

The Brazilian Reprographic Rights Association (ABDR)

The main intermediary between publishers and universities is the Brazilian Reprographic Rights Association (ABDR, Associação Brasileira de Direitos Reprográficos). The ABDR was established in 1992 to negotiate collective licensing agreements with universities, which would permit the collection of royalties on works copied through university channels.[5] As a means of encouraging universities to sign and enforce these agreements, the association also became a frequent filer of lawsuits against universities for what it believed to be illegal copying.

One of the association's first targets was the engineering students' union at São Paulo's Mackenzie University, which it sued in 1993 for distributing unlicensed reproductions of a book called *Exercícios de Topografia* (*Exercises in Topography*). Despite the private copy exception in the 1973 law, the judge characterized the reproductions as works for sale and ruled in favor of the publishers.[6] Legal incentives to sign licensing deals, nonetheless, remained relatively weak. The issue of commercial sales and profits could be argued away by drawing a distinction between acts of lawful copying by students and the actions of the copy shop operators hired to perform them. Only a few universities, such as São Paulo's Federal University of São Carlos (UFSCar), signed agreements with the ABDR.[7]

It was with these interpretative quirks in mind that publishers successfully campaigned for modifications in the private copy exception in 1998, when Brazil amended its copyright law. Article 46, II, of the 1998 law outlawed integral private copies of protected works and added additional, vague requirements for a copy to be determined lawful. With weaker legal cover for copy shop activity, the ABDR's hand was significantly strengthened. According to ABDR data, just one month after the new law came into force, ten universities had signed licensing agreements and fifty more were about to do the same. The terms for copy shops involved the payment of a monthly R$100 (around USD$32)[8] fee, and an additional R$10 ($3.20) per one thousand copies.[9] By March 1999, 126 institutions had made agreements with the ABDR.[10] By 2004, that number had reached around two thousand. The agreements allowed for only 10 percent of any given item to be copied.[11]

Not all of the publishers were satisfied with this outcome. In 1999, a faction within the ABDR concluded that the association was not successful enough in enforcing its licensing agreements, and that collective management for reprographic rights in Brazil had largely failed. These publishers established a dissident association, the Brazilian Association for the Protection of Editorial and Authors' Rights (ABPDEA, Associação Brasileira para a Proteção dos Direitos Editoriais e Autorais).[12]

The ABPDEA approached unauthorized copying strictly through the lens of copyright enforcement. In 2001, ABPDEA launched fifteen raids against universities, followed by at least thirty the next year.[13] In 2003, it reported ninety ongoing lawsuits to a congressional investigation on piracy that had been launched that year in response to demands from the IP industries (Câmara dos Deputados 2004, 113). In the publishing community, the enforcement approach gradually prevailed. In 2004, the ABDR ceased to grant further licenses, and the ABPDEA dissident group was reincorporated into the association (ABDR n.d).[14]

In many respects, this was a sign of the times. CD and DVD piracy had become ubiquitous in recent years, and international copyright lobbying was at the apogee of its influence in Brazil and many other countries (Mizukami et al. 2011). When the congressional investigation completed its work, it recommended the creation of a National Council on Combating Piracy (CNCP, Conselho Nacional de Combate à Pirataria). The CNCP, in turn, authored and led a National Antipiracy Plan focused on increased enforcement—implementing domestically an agenda promoted by the content industry around the world.

For years, the ABDR approach defined the extreme wing of copyright politics in Brazil, both in terms of its direct actions against universities and its inflexible interpretations of educational limitations and exceptions, which played an obvious and critical role in Brazilian higher education. It is worth spending a moment on the latter issue. Broadly, ABDR argued (and still argues) that the only legal form of access is to buy a book or borrow one from a library. Any copying must follow the letter of the 1998 statute,[15] which allows for a "single copy" of a "small excerpt" of a protected work, for the "private use of the copyist," "made by the copyist," "with no intent to profit." A "small excerpt," according to the ABDR, can never be defined in terms of a percentage of a work (as happens under U.S. fair use provisions, among others). Instead, it is limited to a "fragment of a work that does not represent its substance" (ABDR n.d.). Needless to say, this reading makes the limitation all but useless for educational purposes. It was a recipe for conflict in a country with a growing and mostly low-income student population, insufficient libraries, weak or nonexistent infrastructure for the book business outside the major cities, and several decades of reliance on photocopying for student needs.

Not all publishers remained on board. José Castilho, who ran Editora UNESP—one of the most important Brazilian university presses—expressed the press's reasons for withdrawing membership from the association: "we left, not because we're pro-piracy, but because [the ABDR] totally changed its philosophy. What was preventive and educational became punitive action. And from the moment we heard, in an ABDR meeting, that university professors should be handcuffed, we decided to leave."[16]

The 2004–2005 Crackdowns

Between late 2004 and October 2005, the association launched twenty lawsuits and initiated 150 police raids against copy shops and several flagship universities in São Paulo.[17] On March 2005 alone, twenty-one universities were targeted. The police, acting on the ABDR's request, confiscated course material folders from professors at the University of São Paulo (USP), Pontifical Catholic University of São Paulo (PUC-SP), Universidade Presbiteriana Mackenzie, Fundação Getulio Vargas (FGV), Universidades Metropolitanas Unidas (UniFMU), Universidade Paulista (Unip), Fundação Armando Álvares Penteado (FAAP), and the Escola Superior de Propaganda e Marketing (ESPM), among others.[18]

Universities initially attempted to negotiate. PUC-SP proposed to manage an intranet-based system to control on-campus copying, with the collection of royalties to be transferred to publishers. ABDR refused the proposal[19] and instead offered universities a 40 percent discount on its members' books for library acquisitions—provided the institutions monitored and enforced copyright on their premises. The universities rejected this proposal.[20]

An alternative ABDR proposal involved university purchases of large number of copies of customized, preselected books, which they could then sell back to students at lower prices. This model was not compatible with how most institutions operated, but it found a major adopter in Anhanguera Educacional, part of Kroton, Brazil's largest educational company, and its main competitor Estácio. Anhanguera had the scale and discretionary authority to implement a large-scale book-buying program—the Programa Livro-Texto—in 2005.[21]

Because the new enforcement-focused ABDR was built on publisher frustration with the earlier licensing models, the new round of negotiations emphasized book purchasing rather than licensing. This model had few takers, but two more years would pass before the ABDR tried licensing again through a system ironically called Pasta do Professor—"the Professor's Folder." Initially, Pasta do Professor allowed students to select from a list of previously licensed texts and order copies through copy shops located in participating universities. Copies came watermarked with students' names and ID numbers to dissuade further copying.[22] That model has changed over the years and is now managed by the online platform Minha Biblioteca (My Library), owned by a publisher consortium. As described by Minha Biblioteca's CEO:

Pasta do Professor ... was created around eight years ago as an alternative to copy shops, to curb piracy. A device was installed on printers, so that ... information was sent to the ABDR that content was being printed, and royalties could be paid. This project ceased to operate on a retail model and became institutional, so that the university pays for the content. ... [Our] biggest client today is [the education group] Estácio, whose entire pedagogical concept is based around Pasta do Professor. So Estácio buys the content and makes it available to students, in print or digitally.[23]

The more prestigious institutions targeted by the ABDR in 2004–2005, however, were in a position to resist ABDR pressure. In response, USP, PUC-SP, and FGV passed internal resolutions that established a common understanding of the permissible scope of photocopying in those institutions.[24] In 2010, after another ABDR-instigated police raid, they were joined by the Federal University of Rio de Janeiro (UFRJ).

The resolutions are very similar but diverge somewhat in the range of rights defined and justifications offered. All authorize the reproduction of chapters, articles, and other substantial portions of works for personal use—as well as copies of full works that have been out of print for at least a decade. All authorize the "professor's folder" as means of distributing materials via the copy shops. All require the library to tag work that can be fully copied. Most authorized the copying of foreign works not available in the domestic market. Broadly, USP and PUC-SP were relatively generous in their interpretation of constitutional and copyright law, while FGV opted for a more conservative approach.

Publishers, predictably, were not happy with this outcome. The resolutions became one of the recurring complaints of the ABDR in domestic debates and formed the basis of its reporting to U.S. rights holder groups for inclusion in the U.S. Trade Representative's annual intellectual property enforcement report—the "Special 301" process.[25] As the U.S.-based International Intellectual Property Association stated, in its 2005 submission to the USTR:

The most immediate concern of academic publishers in Brazil is the continued influence of Resolution No. 5213/2005, an administrative rule implemented by the State of São Paulo University (USP) almost four years ago. ... ABDR presented a formal request for revocation of this rule to USP, receiving a refusal on the basis that the rule is "constitutional" and grants access to education and knowledge. Thus the ruling still stands, so forming a terrible precedent for others to follow. At least two private universities—Fundação Getúlio Vargas of São Paulo (FGV-SP) and Pontificia Universidade Católica de São Paulo (PUC-SP)—have implemented similar rules. This phenomenon contributes to an overall climate of disrespect for copyright in the academic context among universities in particular, and among government authorities more generally. (IIPA 2009, 158–159)

The ABDR's continued pressure and threats against the universities did not have the intended dissuasive effect. Instead, it led to the emergence of a more aggressive position among the student unions at USP, PUC-SP, FGV, Mackenzie, Ibmec-RJ, and Universidade São Judas Tadeu, which released a manifesto entitled "Copiar Livro É

Direito" (To Copy Books Is a Right). In the words of main representative of the group, they were fighting for "something that is already legal, that is, the right of access to information."[26]

2007–2017: A Stalled Copyright Reform

Copyright reform in Brazil has never been a simple or fast process. Before 1973, copyright was mainly regulated by provisions from the 1916 Civil Code (under the rubric of "literary, scientific and artistic property") and by other sparse pieces of legislation. Between 1955 and 1973, the Federal Senate and Chamber of Deputies considered at least twenty different reform proposals, but none succeeded. The 1973 reform took place only after the military government sent a bill to Congress with the requirement that it be voted on within forty days.[27]

The debate surrounding the 1973 bill took up proposals to outlaw the photocopying of texts without prior authorization from the rights holder, as exemplified by an amendment proposed by Senator Lourival Baptista:

The [proposed] provision seeks to incorporate into Brazilian law a principle that is already being considered by many other countries, with the goal of curtailing the abuse of non-authorized reproductions of the texts through photocopying, Xerox, etc.

We recognize that it is difficult to establish a practical means of monitoring and control of the fraudulent use of these modern machines, but, on the other hand, it is also true that it is necessary to impose the maximum possible number of obstacles, by every means, on this abusive procedure.

In that sense, under express legal prohibition, those who wish to transgress it—and we believe that accounts for most people—will abstain from such acts, unless they can locate the rights holder and obtain a license.[28]

The 1973 legislators decided otherwise, however—recognizing even at that early date the importance of copying in Brazilian university life. Twenty-five years of student and faculty practices developed around that clause in the law. When the legislature took up copyright again in 1989—in a discussion that eventually stretched out for almost a decade—the outcome was different. Late in the process, ABDR succeeded in introducing an amendment that specified that copies would be lawful only if they consisted of "small excerpts" made "by the copyist."[29] The justification for the amendment referred to the "enormous losses" incurred by publishers due to an alleged "1 billion" copies of entire books made each year.[30]

The 1998 law opened the door to the more aggressive approach to enforcement described earlier, and more broadly signaled the alignment of Brazil with the larger international copyright enforcement agenda promoted by the United States (and U.S.-based movie, music, and software industries in particular). The election of a new president, Inácio Lula da Silva, in 2002, however, introduced a major hitch in this rollout. The newly appointed Minister of Culture, the musician Gilberto Gil (and his successor Juca Ferreira) was heavily invested in the emancipatory promise of "digital culture" and the potential of a "creative economy" organized around free software, open licensing, and access to tools for cultural production and diffusion (Costa 2011; Dibbel 2004).

Within this framework, copyright became one of the main cultural policy issues of the new Ministry of Culture. The ministry's internal copyright department was restructured and expanded, and the Intellectual Rights Directorship (DDI, Diretoria de Direitos Intelectuais) was created. Marcos Souza, a career public servant with a background in anthropology, was put in charge of the department, and a new copyright reform process began to take shape.

Procedurally, the Ministry of Culture's main stated concern was that there was almost no participation by the public sector in important matters of copyright policy—leading to unbalanced policy that did not adequately account for the interests of the public. Substantively, it argued that the 1998 law was already outdated given the transformations brought about by the Internet and digitization. The Ministry of Culture noted in particular that the limitations and exceptions to copyright in the 1998 law were "out of alignment with the socioeconomic reality of the country" (Ministry of Culture n.d., a, 22–23).

Overall, the ministry placed a great deal of hope in collective rights management. The 1973 law had established a system of rights management unified under the Central Office of Collection and Distribution (ECAD, Escritório Central de Arrecadação e Distribuição). All collective rights organizations for music are affiliated with ECAD, which collects royalties and relays them to its member organizations. ECAD has been a consistently controversial organization, however, plagued by accusations of mismanagement and the target, to date, of five congressional investigations. Originally supervised by the National Copyright Council (CNDA, Conselho Nacional de Direito Autoral), state oversight was terminated by the 1998 copyright law, leaving ECAD an independent and—investigations would show—less accountable organization. One of the main objectives of the new copyright reform process was to reinstate some measure of state control over ECAD's activities, and potentially to extend collective management beyond music, to all areas of cultural activity (Francisco and Valente 2016).

The new bill also significantly expanded the limitations and exceptions in Article 46. A broad general limitation was proposed that allowed the reproduction, distribution, and communication to the public of copyrighted works without previous authorization from the rights holder for "educational, didactic, informative, or research purposes, or as a creative resource" if done "in the necessary measure to achieve the pursued ends, without affecting the normal exploitation of the work, and without causing unjustified prejudice to the legitimate interests of authors"—complicated phraseology intended to keep the measure in line with the international Berne Convention for the Protection of Literary and Artistic Works. The consultation draft also altered the private copy provision in Article 46, II, to allow for "the reproduction, by any means or process, of any legitimately acquired work, provided that it is done in a single copy, by the copyist, for personal, noncommercial use."[31] After the initial consultation period, the Ministry of Culture released a report consolidating the received contributions and proposing modifications to the text (Ministry of Culture n.d., b).

Then things got messy. Progress on the bill ground to a halt when newly elected president Dilma Rousseff (who also came from the Workers Party) nominated Ana de Hollanda as her Minister of Culture. De Hollanda was a musician with ties to the recording industry and was widely seen as pro-ECAD. She dismissed Souza and effectively brought the consultation process to a standstill (Silveira, Machado, and Savazoni 2013; Silveiras and Gouvea 2016). After a year of protest from civil society groups, Rousseff replaced de Hollanda with senator Marta Suplicy (serving from 2012 to 2014), who resumed the consultation process and reinstated Souza at the Intellectual Rights Directorship. Given the turmoil and the mounting evidence of ECAD's dysfunction,[32] the Ministry of Culture decided to carry out collective management reform in a separate bill. This bill passed in 2013 as Law 12853/13, and reestablished Ministry of Culture supervision of copyright collective management.[33]

The copyright bill was not so lucky. The impeachment of President Rousseff in 2016 interrupted the consultation process once more. Michel Temer, who took office after Rousseff, abolished the Ministry of Culture in his first ministerial reform. When public outcry led him to reconsider, he appointed Marcelo Calero as minister, who fired Souza once again and stripped the Intellectual Rights Directorship of its new monitoring function—resulting in a de facto dismantling of the system created by the 2013 collective management reform bill. The policy plans of the new administration are unclear but so far have locked out the public interest groups in favor of the traditional copyright lobbies, which chafed under the demands for "balance" in the Lula and (Dilma Vana) Rousseff administrations.[34]

Photocopies and Collective Management

The Ministry of Culture expected that copyright reform would solve the controversy surrounding photocopies in the universities by subjecting it to state-supervised collective management, with some room for unlicensed reproduction through limitations to copyright. Schools would pay royalties on some portion of the total number of copies made at the university. Publishers would, hopefully, be satisfied with more recovery of campus materials costs than they had received under the existing practices.

The first draft of the Copyright Reform Bill (2010)[35] established that total or partial copies of literary, artistic, and scientific works made by photocopying or similar processes would be subject to remuneration paid to the rights holders *if carried out for commercial or for-profit purposes*. At first glance, then, it is questionable whether educational copying would be subject to compensation. Article 88-A, II, however, clearly imposes that obligation on commercial establishments providing photocopying services (i.e., copy shops) by requiring them to obtain authorization from rights holders or collective rights management organizations in order to make copies of copyrighted works. The user's intent—noncommercial, educational, or otherwise—is not taken into account.

Collection and distribution of the royalties would be carried out by collective management associations created for this purpose, and copy shops would be required to keep detailed records of the works and quantity of pages copied to allow for the proper identification of the money collected as compensation for copying. Publishers would be legally bound to give authors at least 50 percent of the proceeds.

This part of the proposal was very controversial. ABRELIVROS, which represents primary and secondary education publishers, raised concerns about the difficulty of collecting royalties.[36] The National Syndicate of Book Publishers (SNEL, Sindicato Nacional dos Editores de Livros), the most powerful book industry association in Brazil, claimed that the entire chapter on collective licensing for reprographic copies was redundant because the 1998 law already authorized such a system, and questioned the necessity of an explicit statement with regard to photocopies.[37] Free culture advocates, however, worried that the collective management system might override the proposed exceptions for private copies and education, which did not require compensation (Ministry of Culture n.d., b).

Despite the turmoil, the legal basis for a strong state role in the regulation of collective management was eventually created in 2013. The publication of Law 12853/13 provided a clear incentive for the creation of collective rights management organizations for reprographic rights. In August 2016, Brazilian book publishers announced the foundation of a new entity, the Brazilian Collective Licensing Association (ABRALC, Associação Brasileira de Licenciamento Coletivo),[38] which they explicitly advertised as an "ECAD for books" modeled after Norway's Kopinor and the U.S. Copyright Clearance Center. As of early 2017, however, its future was unclear. The gutting of the Ministry of Culture and its supervisory role appears to have put the new association on hold. A year and a half after its announcement, ABRALC doesn't have a website.

Collective Management and the Digital Environment

The Ministry of Culture pushed as hard as it did for collective management in photo-copying because it had begun to see collective management as a solution to the wider range of challenges surrounding digital distribution and remuneration. Initially, the ministry had explored the creation of a "cultural flat tax" similar to William Fisher's proposal of a "governmentally administered reward system" in which the Copyright Office would be in charge of compensating rights holders.[39] The Brazilian proposal (drafted by German researcher Volker Grassmuck, then at the University of São Paulo) involved the collection of a small fee at the ISP level, under the supervision of a new multistakeholder entity, which would then compensate rights holders for nonmarket online distribution of their works (Machado 2015). The distribution of these payments would be determined by sampling P2P traffic.

After the new collective management law was passed, however, and as unauthorized downloading habits shifted from P2P-based distribution toward harder-to-monitor streaming sites, the Ministry of Culture began to favor a collective management-based solution. Collective management offered a way to shift the debate from the punitive and sharply contested ground of copyright enforcement to the question of fair remuneration for artists and content producers. It also suggested a way to address growing concern with the power of large Internet companies to circumvent national policy on issues of transparency, remuneration, and taxation.

Domestically, the collective management approach meant transplanting the system established by Law 12853/13 into the online environment. For music, part of the plan depended on Brazilian courts extending the interpretation of a "public performance" to the online environment and streaming services, so that ECAD or similar associations would be allowed to collect and distribute royalties based on online streaming or downloading. Juca Ferreira—having already left the ministry—clearly expressed the strategy when celebrating a judicial victory at Brazil's highest appellate court, the Superior Court of Justice:

The understanding by the STJ [Superior Court of Justice] judges that transmissions over the Internet characterize public performance of musical works and constitutes an originating fact for the collection of copyrights by the ECAD promotes an equilibrium in the new environment of musical consumption, and is of extreme importance for the future of our creators, performers and musicians, which from now on will have an instrument that will allow them to negotiate, in better conditions, the uses that the new platforms, dominated mainly by Google, Facebook and Apple, make of their music. (Ferreira 2017)

Infringement, in theory, would be dealt with through by a formal takedown system to be approved in the new copyright law. Sometimes this was advertised as inspired by Canada's "notice-and-notice" system—an alternative to the American model that did not require online services to remove content—but the ministry never published a public proposal. The broader strategy involved establishing rules that subjected the distribution of content via online platforms, including services making books available online, to collective management. Following a period of public consultation, the Ministry of Culture issued these rules in May 2016.[40]

This strategy also had an important international dimension. Brazil was a leader in debates at the World Intellectual Property Organization and other venues about digital revenue flows and the challenges to national control posed by the global online music and audio-visual services. A workable online collective management regime, in particular, required much greater transparency regarding traffic and access metrics and rights management information—including authorship and ownership metadata attached to every media item.

The principle statement of these concerns was a document called the "Proposal for Analysis of Copyright Related to the Digital Environment," authored with other Latin American countries and submitted to WIPO in 2015. By raising concern shared by content creators, governments, and Internet stakeholders,[41] the document had a good chance of gaining traction at WIPO. However, Brazilian government leadership vanished with the impeachment of Rousseff. In its absence, it is unclear if these issues will be taken up at a multilateral level in the foreseeable future.[42]

The Internet as Source

Increasingly, online sources compete aggressively with print sources as a means of access to educational materials. Graduate students are expected to read foreign language works and, for English language materials, the large international shadow libraries such as LibGen, Bookzz, and Aaaarg are the destinations of choice. At the undergraduate level, demand is predominantly for Portuguese language works, which none of the major international sites collect on a significant scale. Portuguese-language shadow libraries have emerged at several points in the past fifteen years, but none have survived long enough to become definitive archives. In nearly all cases, collections remain small and local, built from ad hoc sharing of materials between students or between students and professors, and usually focused on specific courses or degrees. These collections rarely circulate to the public at large, even if sometimes they end up on the Internet as thematically organized compilations posted to file hosting services and linked from Facebook or blog posts.

The defunct website *Livros de Humanas* (Humanities Books) remains, so far, the best example of Brazilian attempt at a large-scale student-built shadow library. Livros de Humanas was a blog that collected links to texts stored on file hosting services. It was organized by Thiago Cândido, a student of literature from the University of São Paulo, based on files uploaded by his colleagues and himself, often scanned from physical copies. As in so many other cases, the initial motivation was cost. "In 2009, the copy shop that served the school—illegal, according to ABDR, but without which no one can study at USP or any other Brazilian university—raised the price for a photocopied page to R$0.15, a 50 percent increase," Cândido said in an interview. "That motivated a group of students to share the content of their courses in sites like 4shared and Mediafire. The blog functioned as an index of those links."[43]

Unfortunately for Livros de Humanas, they had to contend with the ABDR. Beginning in August 2009, the ABDR began to systematically send takedown notices to hosting and linking sites and initiate lawsuits against supposed infringers. By July 2010, around forty thousand notices had been sent, with what ABDR alleged was a takedown success rate of 90 percent.[44] In 2014, the ABDR claimed to be removing links to pirated content at a rate of around eight thousand links per month.[45]

This type of enforcement was not enough to keep infringing content offline, but has proved successful, at least so far, in deterring the emergence of large-scale, online pirate libraries. While the ABDR claims that Livros de Humanas was "just another website," and that the lawsuit against it was one of at least thirty others that had been filed until then,[46] no other student-curated collection of digital materials like it has appeared since. The site was taken down as it was becoming the main source for digital Portuguese-language academic materials in the humanities and social sciences.

The community of users served by Cândido's collection protested loudly against the lawsuit. Livros de Humanas gained support from publishers,[47] intellectuals,[48] and bestselling, pro-piracy novelist Paulo Coelho.[49] International support came from Neil Gaiman, who chimed in via Twitter that he was "Standing up for #FreeLivrosdeHumanas."[50] Milena Duchiade, the former owner of Rio de Janeiro's traditional humanities bookstore Leonardo da Vinci, wrote a letter of support, grounded on the fairness of sharing materials that are hard to find: "A few years ago, a boy at the University of São Paulo created a forum and was sued. I wrote a support letter, I got to know [about the case] from my son. I wrote him telling him that I supported making [those files] available. Why? Because Brazil has become a country of first editions, which are the first and only. Editions that have diminishing numbers of copies. How can you stop someone from having access [to those books]?"[51]

When it was taken offline, the blog provided access to 2,496 files—full-length books and academic articles—in the humanities, arts, and social sciences. Based on email requests that he received when running the blog, Cândido argued that the users of Livros de Humanas were mostly "students from Brazilian universities with terrible libraries." During the last months of activity, the site was reaching more than ten thousand page views per day.[52]

The ABDR won a favorable decision in the trial and later in the first appellate court.[53] An incomplete backup of the Livros de Humanas archive was uploaded to The Pirate Bay[54] and is still available as of January 2017, but to the best of our knowledge that archive has not been used as a seed for the construction of a new site.

As of early 2017, the website Lê Livros[55] is probably the largest shadow library for Portuguese-language content. Lê Livros differs from Livros de Humanas in part in that it is not exclusively academic. Among its 7,500 titles, Lê Livros has a wide range of literary and nonfiction content—as well as books in fields such as law, economics, and philosophy. Having learned from the experience of other sites, the developers of Lê Livros keep a low profile. The site's "about us" page[56] traces Lê Livros history back to iOS-Books, a book-sharing site taken down by the ABDR in 2012.[57] This history claims that Lê Livros is run by "a group of students living in Portugal," with the goal of "democratizing access to free reading, and consequently without any intent to profit." Public information about the service remains sparse and, judging by our survey results, its impact on the ecosystem remains low.

Online Services as Informal Digital Libraries

Livros de Humanas had a two-tiered structure common to many shadow libraries, in which the index or catalog is maintained separately from file storage. This is partly a matter of convenience—the technical requirements of managing a catalog or index are minimal—but also a matter of safety as the search, indexing, and discovery services remain a step removed from the act of downloading unauthorized content. Dedicated search and cataloguing features aid discovery, sharing, and organization of content in these contexts, but are not indispensable. Social media sites, email lists, and blogs can do an adequate job. Often, Google Search serves as the glue that holds these resources together.

Among the file storage services (or *cyberlockers*), 4shared is one of the most widely used in Brazil. Like other file storage services, it is a general-purpose service with that hosts a wide range of content. It is also well known as a destination for unauthorized media and has been included in the USTR's list of notorious markets.[58] Minhateca, where users can organize personal folders containing files and make them publicly available, is a Brazilian service that plays a similar role. Minhateca was singled out by the recording industry in the IIPA's 2017 Special 301 submission: "One local cyber-locker site, minhateca.com.br, hosted more than half a million infringing music files that were reported by the recording industry and removed in 2016" (IIPA 2017).

Given this capacity, the status and responsibilities of file hosting platforms have been the subject of intense debate—driven by content industry lobbies that see them as for-profit enablers of piracy. The publishing industry groups have tended to follow rather than lead in this debate. The ABDR's strategy for online enforcement follows broader industry practice in relying first on takedown notices sent to services when allegedly infringing material is found. This practice is not grounded in law but in the norms that have developed around the U.S. Digital Millennium Copyright Act (DMCA), which established takedown procedures for the dominant U.S.-based Internet services. Despite legislative efforts, there is no law establishing a DMCA-like regime for copyright infringement in Brazil. When the issue came up during the public debates around the Civil Rights Framework for the Internet (the Marco Civil da Internet), which became law in 2014, content industries successfully lobbied to exclude copyright issues from the framework (Souza and Schirru 2016).[59] Discussions about a takedown regime and related issues of intermediary liability for copyright infringement were moved into the ongoing discussion about copyright reform.[60]

The absence of an explicit regime did not prevent the development of an informal takedown mechanism: platforms usually comply when they receive notices. This de facto system has been backed by Brazilian courts, which have generally used a statutory damages provision conceived for pirate editions of books to determine penalties for online infringement. In cases where the number of infringing copies published is not determinable—as in most online infringement cases—Article 103 of the 1998 Copyright Law (Law 9610/98) sets damages equivalent to the price of 3,000 copies of the infringing work. This can quickly lead to absurd amounts in the context of online services, which may host or provide access to thousands of infringing works.

In general, the ABDR has tolerated services that comply with takedown requests. The meaning of acceptable compliance has been a moving target over the years, but one that even the "notorious" services like 4shared make efforts to accommodate. 4shared, for example, has a "partnership program" that offers options for content blocking and monetization, inspired by YouTube.[61] Dropbox, which is used widely in Brazilian universities, has its own system for managing takedown requests across user folders.[62]

More specialized publishing platforms such as Scribd and Issuu are also used to share books and journal articles—often with the same dual purposes. Issuu, for example, is used by major university publishers such as Saraiva[63] and Grupo Gen[64] to distribute samples of texts, and—at the same time—by students to distribute scanned or natively digital copies of books and articles. Scribd, likewise, serves as an official storefront for publishers but also contains a wide range of user-uploaded infringing content. Provided that these platforms maintain takedown systems, or collaborate with publishers offering functionality that allows for blocking, monetization, or other types of measures, they have been able to operate safely, even with the occasional lawsuit. Over time, however, those conditions have become significantly more constraining on general use.

The Brazilian services Passei Direto and Ebah represent a different sort of platform for sharing and organizing collections of materials, similar in nature to educational startups like Academia.edu and ResearchGate, but with a focus on the undergraduate market. Both are structured as social networks for students, centered on the sharing of a wide range of materials—from syllabi, class notes, and tests to full copies of textbooks.

Like Livros de Humanas, Ebah was on the receiving end of a lawsuit filed by ABDR. Unlike Livros de Humanas, Ebah managed to settle.[65] As a condition of the settlement, Ebah now has a detailed section on copyright in its website that reads as if it were written by the ABDR—as well as strict takedown compliance.[66]

Because students will always share materials, the scope available to developers of student-based services has been constantly tested by rights holders. In the words of a Passei Direto representative:

[The] materials are shared by the students themselves. So what we have is a team focused on evaluating if the materials have the correct names, if they are not in infringement of copyrights. … That's basically it, we control the materials. Students are free to upload, however. We don't curate ahead of time; we don't know how to predict what the user is going to put on the platform. But the moment he does, we have to take care of it. [When we receive a notice,] we usually have 48 hours to take down materials. Usually, we do that within the day.[67]

In 2014, however, ABDR sued Passei Direto at the request of affiliated publishers Saraiva and Método, regarding alleged infringement of two books. Passei Direto lost, and the publishers were awarded around $190,000 (R$600,000) in damages, but the case was settled as it reached the appellate court.[68] In 2016, two more plaintiffs—the publisher Editora Manole and a law professor named Dimitri Dimoulis—sued Passei Direto for copyright infringement. Both cases are pending a final decision at the time of this writing (Procedures 1005559-52.2016.8.26.0068 and 1014183-81.2016.8.26.0071, São Paulo). In February 2017, Passei Direto disabled the download function in its platforms. Files can now only be viewed within a window in the site—a change that Passei Direto claims was implemented to "protect the authorship of the materials published by students and curb their unauthorized reproduction."[69]

Publisher-backed Platforms

As elsewhere, Brazilian publishers have focused on institutional subscription-based access models. The leading example is Minha Biblioteca,[70] a platform established by Grupo A, Grupo Editorial Gen, Atlas, Manole, and Saraiva—all major publishers in the higher education market. Minha Biblioteca sells access directly to universities, which then make the service available to their students. In 2014, Minha Biblioteca took over administration of Pasta do Professor[71] from the ABDR and now also allows individual users to purchase full books or book chapters.

Pearson's Biblioteca Virtual Universitária is a similar service offering content from sixteen publishers, and boasts serving 2.5 million active users with more than four thousand titles, ranging from textbooks to monographs.[72] Whether these services effectively meet student needs is an unanswered question. In effect, institutional subscriptions became a viable business in Brazil only after 2012, when the National Evaluation System for Higher Education added access to online databases to the criteria for evaluating university libraries.[73] As explained by Mauro Koogan of Grupo Gen, one of Minha Biblioteca's founders:

We started [Minha Biblioteca] two years ago, with difficulty, and now we have almost 500,000 students with access to the library. Basically the Ministry of Education said: "Universities, we know you do not have the means to buy [books], so we'll take digital libraries into consideration in the score you get [in our evaluation]." So universities say "hey, now that interests me." But if you're going to analyze the use that students make of this library, which has almost six thousand titles now, it's very low.[74]

Open Licensing

Brazil has a very strong open access community, with public support for both traditional peer-reviewed "gold" models and pre-print-archive-based "green" models. This support passes through two main channels: IBICT (Instituto Brasileiro de Informação em Ciência e Tecnologia) and SciELO (Scientific Electronic Library Online), one of the world's most successful gold open-access projects.

IBICT was founded in 1954 with a mandate to support information science and libraries. In 1999, it started an online library that aggregated theses and dissertations made available by public and private universities.[75] Soon, the institute became a hub for capacity building and technical assistance in open access archives and journals:

Before 2003, our work was not directly related to open access, but open archives. ... The idea was disseminating theses and dissertations over the Internet without any access restrictions. ... Then, international open access gained a little more momentum, and ... IBICT started to work along these lines. First, we customized and offered training for the Open Journal Systems Software, which we translated to Portuguese. We spent a few good years doing this sort of massive dissemination [of OJS], and because of that there was a boom in the number of open access journals. Parallel to that, we started working with institutional repositories.[76]

The creation of institutional repositories received a boost through a requirement that graduate programs in Brazil make all of their students' output available online.[77] The authors of theses and dissertations can opt out—administrative rules cannot trump copyright legislation—but the rule effectively forced schools to set up their own institutional repositories.

Open access mandates for faculty and student publication, nonetheless, have not taken off. The only institution with a mandate is the Fundação Oswaldo Cruz (FIOCruz), established in 2014.[78] At the legislative level, a bill that would make open access mandatory for any work supported with public funds was proposed in 2011 and remains stalled.[79]

The second major Brazilian open access project is SciELO, a publicly funded project that has grown into one of the largest portals for open access articles in the world.[80] SciELO operates on multiple levels—cataloguing articles, but also providing a methodology for journal publishing, indexing, and archiving. As described by one of the project's founders, Abel Packer:

SciELO began as pilot project in 1997. Between 1997 and 1998, we worked with ten journals. Back then, the Internet was just beginning. It was a very innovative project, and we faced lots of resistance to online publishing. But after a year we managed to create a methodology to put journals online, and after the pilot project [...] we established SciELO as bibliographic index [that links to] the full text. It's a mixture of index, publishing model, and repository, all open access.[81]

After Google Scholar started to index SciELO journals, page access numbers increased dramatically, jumping from 25 million a year in 2005 to 103 million in 2007 (Packer et al. 2014, 100). The SciELO model was also gradually adopted by other countries:

Right after we launched SciELO in 1998, the Chilean Nacional Commission of Science and Technology started an electronic journal program and decided to adopt our methodology ... Chile helped us export [to other countries] and SciELO became a network. ... [T]oday we have 16 countries, with around 1,000 journals and more than 500 thousand published articles. So it's a large operation, and SciELO Brazil functions as kind of a network secretariat. We maintain the methodology, and we are generally the ones who introduce innovations, although everyone is free to do what they want.[82]

SciELO's success is not universal: it is strongest in the humanities, social sciences, and health sciences. Engineering and the hard sciences are comparatively underrepresented (Packer et al. 2014) because of the strong incentives for Brazilian researchers working in those areas to publish in the closed-access, international journals controlled by major publishers.

In 2011, SciELO launched SciELO Books—a platform for digital distribution of books from university presses.[83] SciELO Books is not, however, fully open access: participating publishers, who also funded the project, insisted that some of the books needed to remain closed access. As SciELO Coordinator Abel Packer put it:

> SciELO's hope, obviously, was to publish on an open access basis. But our publishers think that they should be self-sustainable, so we had to pollute SciELO by allowing commercial books. … The project is extraordinarily successful [but] the commercial books have very limited sales. I think in the future they might sell more. But SciELO still maintains that academic books from universities should be published in open access. There should be a national funding policy that would allow this.[84]

By February 2017, SciELO Books had an archive of 837 books, of which 545 could be downloaded freely. For the commercial books, SciELO provides links to Amazon, Kobo Books, and Google Play.

Brazil also has an active community involved in the development of open educational resources (OERs) such as textbooks and other instructional materials—although primarily for the primary and secondary levels and on a smaller scale than projects such as SciELO (Venturini 2014; Rossini and Castro 2016). There has been a push at the state and municipal levels for pro-OER legislation, and a bill emerged at the federal level in 2011.[85] But publisher opposition, grounded in fear that OER would undermine those lucrative markets, means there have been no major legislative successes to date. OER models will continue to play a role in educational policy conversations because of the obvious potential of open textbooks for Brazil's rapidly growing student population. But the momentum behind access-friendly policies during the Gilberto Gil/Juca Ferreira years in the Ministry of Culture has broken down in the wake of the impeachment and it is unclear how or when it will be reestablished.

The CAPES Journals Portal

The CAPES Journals Portal (Portal de Periódicos da CAPES)[86] is probably the most important source of online materials for most Brazilian researchers and graduate students. The site provides one-stop access to journals and databases for universities with graduate programs across the country.[87] In 2015, this included 37,818 full-text journals and 125 reference and abstract databases—made available to 436 university partners—from just about every major publisher, including Elsevier, Project MUSE, JSTOR, Nature, Oxford University Press, Cambridge University Press, Emerald, Taylor & Francis, SAGE, and Wiley, among others.

The CAPES portal is part of a well-established tradition of government-supported content acquisition for libraries and students. Brazil has a massive book buying programs for primary and secondary schools, the PNLD, which ensures the availability of basic textbooks for all students in public schools—at the cost of considerable market concentration in the sector.[88] Past government initiatives have, with different degrees of success, targeted higher education—the foremost example being the National Institute of the Book (INL, Instituto Nacional do Livro) in the 1970s. During that period, the INL coedited (sharing part of the costs of production), bought, and redistributed books to libraries (Hallewell 2005, 552–561; Filgueiras 2015; Vahl and Peres 2016; Bragança 2009; Tavares 2014; Peres and Vahl 2014). More recent attempts to extend these practices to the university level, however, have been unsuccessful.[89]

The CAPES portal proved, however, that journal articles were an easier proposition. The program initially focused on the acquisition of print journals for university libraries in the 1990s, and shifted to database subscriptions in 2000 after incorporating ProBE, a São Paulo state-based program initiated by a consortium of university libraries (Almeida, Guimarães, and Alves 2010). Over the following years, CAPES struck deals with a wide range of content providers and the number of full-text journals quickly increased.

As the cost of journal access has risen, the CAPES portal has become an increasingly expensive program. CAPES's journal budget went from $21.11 million in 2004

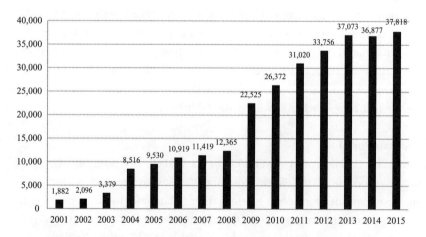

Figure 8.1
Number of full-text journals included in the CAPES portal (2001–2015)
Source: CAPES, "Relatório de Gestão," 2014, http://www.capes.gov.br/images/stories/download/Contas_Publicas/2014_Relatorio_de_Gestao_CAPES.pdf.

to $99.34 million in 2014.[90] In the current economic crisis, rumors about the demise of the program or a drastic reduction in the number of subscriptions, or both, are frequent.

Brazilian universities, in any event, remain extremely dependent on the CAPES portal. For many it is the sole source of journal access. The institutions that have the resources to license other databases often lack proper legal assistance to analyze licensing contracts. Libraries are often the weakest partner in a negotiation that involves powerful companies like Elsevier, Thomson, and Pegasus, resulting in nonnegotiable agreements surrounded by nondisclosure clauses. Another concern is the ephemeral and impermanent nature of the access to these databases, which can be easily terminated.[91]

And this, of course, is the dilemma. On the one hand, the CAPES portal is a fundamental resource for researchers in Brazil, providing free access, on a massive scale, to thousands of proprietary journals and databases. On the other hand, it also incentivizes a model of scholarly publishing that is viewed as exploitative by large portions of the academic community. This contradiction is well expressed in the words of Bianca Amaro, an open access advocate and a lawyer at IBICT: "I'm extremely in favor of the CAPES Portal. The CAPES Portal is invaluable to Brazil, and will continue to be during many years, decades, I think, unfortunately," Amaro writes. "But I think [it] should be reevaluated. What, effectively, are we buying? What sort of power do we have [in the negotiations]? I suspect we're still—and even more so after this internationalization project—hostage to these foreign publishers."[92]

The internationalization project Amaro mentioned was an effort to bring international publishers in as distribution partners for one hundred Brazilian open access journals—on the assumption that international publishers could raise the visibility of Brazilian research. In other words, CAPES would pay international publishers to take control of top-ranked Brazilian open access journals, as a means to better position these publications internationally.

The proposal was disclosed by CAPES at a meeting with sixty journal editors in 2014, and included presentations by Elsevier, Emerald, Springer, Wiley, and Taylor & Francis.[93] The project received strong pushback from SciELO and the Brazilian Association of Scientific Editors (ABEC, Associação Brasileira de Editores Científicos), who argued that Brazilian publishers had more than enough technical capacity to produce journals with international reach, and that they should be the beneficiaries of any publishing incentives.

This episode is illustrative of the ambivalence surrounding CAPES's approach to the dissemination of scholarly materials. The internationalization project was seen as a spillover from the years of proximity to and dependence on international publishers within the larger journals initiative, which is seen as both as a blessing and a curse. It reinforces the existing closed-access structures of academic journal publishing even as it grants free access to literature that would be cost prohibitive for many universities and research institutions in Brazil.

Student Practices

The preceding sections focused on institutional factors shaping print and digital access to educational materials in Brazil, from the role of photocopying and debates over copyright infringement to the expanding ecosystem of digital content providers and open licensing initiatives. As in the other country studies in this book, we also conducted focus groups and a survey to better understand how students access and share materials in the midst of this transition. As in the other surveys, we focused on fields with very different curricular requirements and, consequently, significant differences in student practices: medicine, communication studies, and law.

In our case, the survey is based on a representative sample of the population of undergraduates in the three fields in the city of Rio de Janeiro, the second largest in the country.[94] The focus on Rio means that we cannot generalize results to Brazil as whole—though we can make some informed guesses about the role of geographic differences. In general, we expect reliance on photocopying and unauthorized downloading to be stronger outside large metropolitan areas, which tend to have better infrastructure for legal access.

Means of Access

As in the other surveys, we asked students about how much of their materials were purchased new, purchased used, photocopied, and downloaded—and, in the last case, asking them to distinguish further between legal and illegal access. These percentages combine tranches from different student groups and so do not add up to one hundred. But they do offer a rough, eloquent impression of relative importance of a given means of access to materials, compared to other means. Libraries were not part of this series of questions. We address them in more detail in a later section.

Photocopies are the primary means of access to educational materials for students in medicine (38 percent) and communication studies (44 percent) students, followed by Internet downloads (24 percent and 29 percent, respectively) and purchasing new books (24 percent and 19 percent). For reasons that we will explore, law students described a very different set of practices, with new book purchases the main strategy for acquiring materials (46 percent), followed by Internet downloads (25 percent) and photocopying (17 percent). Used materials play a very limited role across all three fields. More than half of surveyed students claimed to have bought no used materials during the current semester. Only 5 percent of students described heavy reliance on used materials.

Why so little uptake of used books? One of the main reasons appears to be shipping costs. The used book market in Brazil passes mostly through small bookstores that sell over the Internet, thereby requiring students to buy online and pay for shipping costs. According to Alexandre Camargo, the operations manager of Estante Virtual, the dominant online book marketplace, these costs often exceed the price of books themselves, undermining the cost rationale for students. According to Camargo, technical and professional books for classes nonetheless represent the largest part of Estante Virtual's sales.[95]

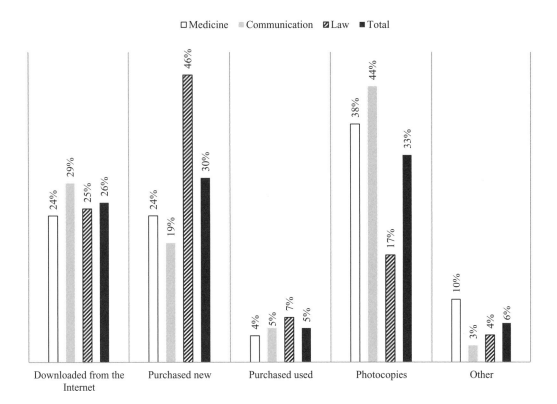

Figure 8.2
In relation to your bibliographic materials, what is your main source of access?

The major differences across fields reflect a number of factors, including the comparatively greater wealth of students in medicine and law. But the overriding one is the different curricular requirements in the different disciplines. Law and medicine students are part of textbook-heavy disciplinary cultures, with law in particular tied to rapid cycles of updated materials as legislation and jurisprudence evolves. Communication studies students are much more reliant on excerpts drawn from multiple books and monographs. None of the three groups rely heavily on journal articles at the undergraduate level and, consequently, none of the three are well served by the main open access initiatives, which have privileged scientific journal articles. SciELO Books is the notable exception for monographs, but it only has the partial participation of ten university presses and a very limited catalog of around five hundred books.

Books Despite publishers' concerns with photocopying, students do buy books. In law, just over 40 percent of respondents claim to buy most (81–100 percent) of their materials new. This investment is driven, as mentioned, by the need for current references that reflect changes in legislation and jurisprudence. But the value of building a personal practitioner's library for use after graduation also frequently appeared as a reason for the acquiring new books. This situation is flipped for students in communication studies and medicine, almost half of whom claimed to buy less than 20 percent of their materials new.

As elsewhere, students demonstrated a strong preference for printed material—including in their decisions about what to purchase. Eighty-two percent of students had purchased physical books but only 22 percent had purchased e-books—despite the nearly universal penetration of computers, phones, tablets, and other means of digital reading. "No one buys digital [books] on the Internet," a law student told us in a focus group. Clearly some of this preference also reflects pricing strategies that equate paper and digital. As one medicine student put it, "with a digital book I'll pay the same price as a paper book and if I have to pay the same price, I'd rather have the paper book."

Photocopying Photocopying is still the most important form of access to materials in Brazil—despite years of digital availability of educational materials. Over 90 percent of students get at least some of their materials by photocopying, with over 40 percent indicating that they get at least 60 percent of their materials this way. Communication studies students rely very heavily on photocopying; law students much less so, due to the disciplinary culture of book acquisition in that field.

One of the ways to understand this phenomenon is that the "pasta do professor"—the professors' folders used to distribute classroom material—tend to become small

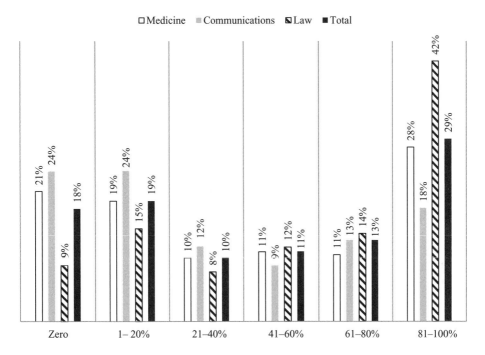

Figure 8.3
How much of your academic material is purchased new?

libraries in and of themselves. It takes time and effort to select class materials and make them available in copy shops. Once this task has been completed, folders can be used by professors from one year to the next, with small updates as necessary. As younger professors and students replace older generations, one can expect habits to change and preferences to shift in favor of digital sharing—even if many of those digital files are eventually printed. In the words of a law student, "Most professors are old, and the old ones use the copy shops the most." We are still, nonetheless, living in a transitional period where the photocopy still competes with the cloud.

The sharing of materials via professors' folders at copy shops is extremely common, with some moderate variation across fields. Overall, almost 86 percent of students in our sample indicated that they are able to copy at least some of their class materials from professors' folders in copy shops. Roughly the same percentage claimed professors shared with them digitally.

For reasons we described earlier, most copying is done on campus (76 percent), even if limitations on copying are frequently imposed by universities. In focus groups, most students indicated that they had encountered university restrictions on copying entire

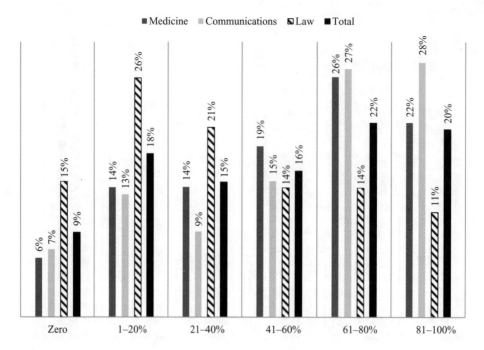

Figure 8.4
How much of your academic material is photocopied?

books, but also that such restrictions were easy to circumvent—either by making additional trips to the shops to copy different portions or by copying books outside the university campus, where restrictions are less frequently observed.

Downloading   We also asked students what proportion of materials they had acquired from online sources during the current semester. They were asked to indicate what proportion they believed to be from legal and illegal sources, and to give examples of the latter. Overall, 23 percent of respondents said that they obtain at least 60 percent of their materials from sources they perceive to be *illegal*. Given the substantial number of nonresponses to this question and the likelihood of underreporting perceived illegal behavior, we think the actual numbers are likely to be higher. When asked how much of their materials they download from sources they believe to be legal, roughly a third claimed to acquire at least 60 percent of their materials from legal sources, and the percentage for the "zero" tier dropped to 16 percent.

The usual disciplinary spread is visible in responses to this question, but the differences are not dramatic. Among law students, 18 percent said that they downloaded

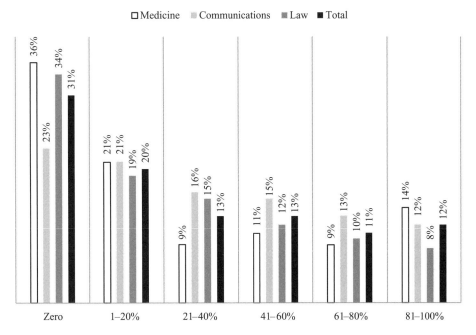

Figure 8.5
How much of your academic material is downloaded from sources believed to be illegal?

at least 60 percent of their materials from *illegal* sources. Among medical students, 23 percent did so.

As in the other country surveys in this book (and consistent with the wider literature on file sharing), students do a poor job of distinguishing legal from illegal access—and for a variety of reasons. The status of online texts can be unclear, the law is often poorly understood, and transgressions of laws and norms are routinely confused—commonly, for example, the difference between copyright infringement and plagiarism. Copyright awareness is low among the surveyed students: when asked to specify how much of a book can be legally copied under Brazilian law for educational purposes, 68 percent of respondents claimed ignorance.

When asked how students accessed material they considered "illegal" the responses ran the gamut from search engines and common file storage services like Dropbox and student social network Passei Direto to well-known hosts of infringing material such as 4shared and The Pirate Bay. Google Search—the entry point for most students to the web—ranked first by a wide margin: students mentioned the search engine 536 times, against 106 times for second ranker 4shared. As one student in the focus groups put it, "You put the name of the book and 'download' [in the search box], it's super easy."

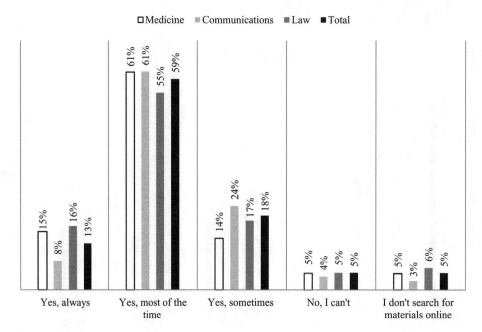

Figure 8.6
Can you usually find what you need online?

Student confusion was visible in the number of services mentioned that had no infringing content, such as medical abstracts database PubMed and legal websites Jus Brasil and Jus Navigandi. Jus Brasil aggregates legal opinions and blog posts; Jus Navigandi is a web portal for law news and articles. Wikipedia was the third most-cited source, likely due to faculty requests that students not use the site as a reference for research.[96]

As for the availability of digital materials, 59 percent of students indicated that they can find what they look for online "most of the time"; another 13 percent indicated that they could "always" do so.

Libraries   Though often described as in a state of crisis and frequently unable to meet student demand for books, libraries are a very important part of student life in Brazil. The great majority of students make use of their school's libraries—over 80 percent in our survey. This roughly correlates with data from the National Student Performance Exam survey, which suggests that roughly 45 percent of communication studies students and 63 percent of law students make use of the library at least once a week

(INEP 2012a,b). Most of those library users indicate, moreover, that they can find what they need for their classes—some 82 percent in our sample.

These results reflect the relatively strong connection between teaching and library acquisition strategies in most Brazilian universities. Libraries have access to syllabi and—when resources permit—purchase and make available required materials. Since 2004, these linkages have been built into the Ministry of Education's evaluation of undergraduate programs (SINAES), which requires that the library acquire materials from a series of model syllabi developed for each field. In practice, such acquisitions are often limited by budgetary constraints (Maia and Santos 2015) and by the frequent divergence between syllabi and actual classroom practice.

Personal Collections

Personal collections of e-books remain rare at the undergraduate level. Only around 20 percent of students claimed to have collections—closely tracking the percentage of e-book buyers. One possible explanation is the perceived adequacy of the larger online sources, which provide ad hoc access to files stored on the Internet. Another is the continued preference for print-based reading.

These numbers increase significantly when the question expands to include "papers, articles, and other materials." Around 42 percent of students have personal archives of this sort, rising to half of medical students (who make more systematic use of online article databases than others).

The most consistent explanation of these practices is that collections of digital resources are created as need dictates—tied to specific groups of students or courses and utilitarian in nature. They consist of whatever is needed to complete an assignment or pass a given test or course. This is a reflection of the ephemerality of the materials ecosystem. For most students, materials are discarded once they fulfill their function. In this respect, students approach digital materials much the same way they approach photocopies.

Sharing

Sharing of class notes, readings, and other materials among students is the norm across all three fields, ranging from 71 percent of respondents in law to 92 percent in medicine. Brazilian students sometimes bundle these materials into "apostilas," which circulate within classes and to new students. Fields differ in the degree of organization of this practice—again following distinctive curricular requirements and patterns of mentoring. Medical students consistently reported the highest degree of organization, commonly organized by individuals tasked with organizing and distributing materials.

Medical students also reported systematic sharing between older and younger students, as part of a larger structure of mentoring across levels. One student reported: "We have a different class each year, so a student from the second year will choose a student from the first year, a freshman who is just coming in, to pass on materials, tips, exams, and usual, at least in my time, paper materials. Nowadays, it's a lot more digital: a thumb drive with everything is passed on to the freshmen."

By the same token, it is only in medicine that these practices play a dominant role. Such practices clearly exist among law and communication studies students, but our results suggest that they are not as formalized or ubiquitous.

Students mostly share via email or Facebook groups—in both cases leveraging a variety of other tools such as listservs and Dropbox accounts, or workarounds such as the use of a dummy email account as a classroom message board and document archive.

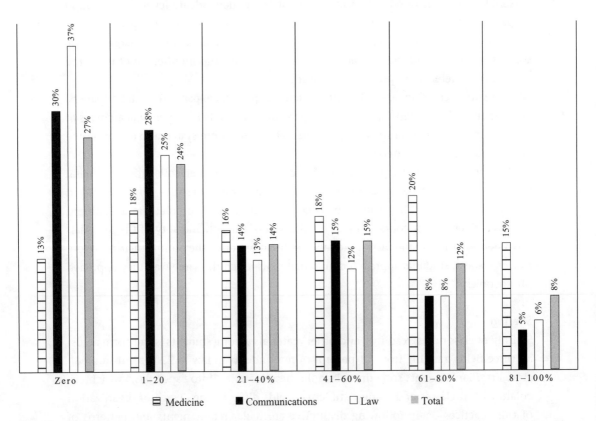

Figure 8.7
How much of your academic material is copied from fellow students?

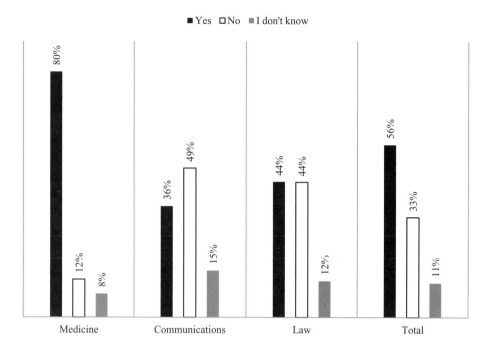

Figure 8.8

Are materials shared downstream (with newer classes)?

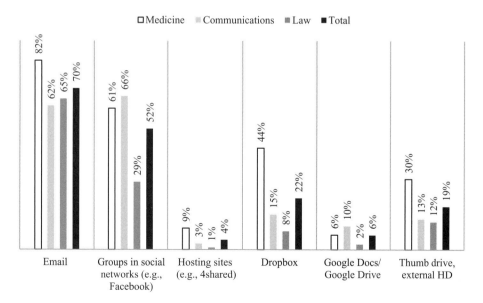

Figure 8.9

How do you share materials with your colleagues?

Dropbox—and to a lesser degree, Google Drive—are the hosting platforms of choice for document sharing, but fall considerably behind email and social networks in classroom use. Facebook is a very common tool for classroom support and, in many cases, is preferred to home institution learning management systems (when they do exist). Information about courses, discussions/forums, the organization of content, and last-minute notifications are all efficiently supported by Facebook's "group" tool.

Faculty routinely facilitate these small group exchanges, with older faculty tending to favor the pasta do professor while younger faculty rely more on the online ecosystem: "Sometimes the professor will write down the email of someone from the class, a student, and will share with this student. The student is then responsible [for sharing with the others], like an assistant."

The practice of taking photos of print materials is also very common. 60 percent of our respondents indicated that they do so; 83 percent of these said they share the photos with colleagues. This practice extends to wider documentation of classroom activities, including work presented on the blackboard, presentation slides, and class notes. Perhaps most importantly, it also represents a low-cost alternative to photocopying and means of amortizing investments in expensive devices. As one student explained, "I don't take photocopies, I use my iPad. What I don't want to spend money, I'll take a photo of the photocopy. I'll take it from someone who took the photocopies, who went there every week and paid 30, 20 reais ... and I'll patiently take photo after photo with my iPad."

The specific mix of technologies used by students is clearly a moving target, as services drop in and out of use and new resources become available. Email, Facebook, and Dropbox are at the center, surrounded by the wider social web that supports small-group communication and file storage. Cameras on cell phones and devices provide a constant stream of documentation of classroom materials and activities. Collectively, these tools define a sharing ecosystem that falls between the copy shops and the high-level shadow libraries.

Pricing

The price of materials is clearly the main driver of these copying practices, but other factors also play contributing roles. Student copying is shaped by a wide range of motivations, from the convenience of digital formats, to the utility of owning materials in the long term, to poor availability through bookstores or the library. Across all of the focus groups, however, pricing provided the main ethical framework for unauthorized copying. "In a school such as ours, in which books are absurdly expensive, it should be legal [to copy books for educational purposes]. But if, for example, books were sold on a

Table 8.1
Price estimates for a semester of materials (USD$, average, rounded up)

	Medicine	Communication studies	Law	Total average
New	101	37	96	78
Used	53	26	50	42
Photocopies	38	22	20	27

relatively affordable price for everyone, I believe you could decide that 'Really, you can only photocopy part of the books.' But only if prices were affordable."

Affordability is, of course, a relative term that depends on student resources, perceptions of value, and other costs. A study by the University of São Paulo's Research Group in Public Policy for Access to Information (GPOPAI-USP), however, found that for three-quarters of students enrolled in ten of the university's courses, the costs for a semester of materials—out-of-print books excluded—was close to or above the average monthly household income for students (Craveiro, Machado, Ortellado 2008, 35–36). Pricing studies carried out by the Brazilian Consumer Defense Institute (IDEC 2008, 2012) also concluded that high prices, out-of-print materials, and deficient libraries made piracy unavoidable to many students (IDEC 2008, 2012). In 2012, a medicine student at the University of São Paulo would have had to spend approximately $3,405 to buy all the materials for the first semester—an amount that was almost six times the average income of employed workers in São Paulo (IDEC 2012).

Answers to our question about how much students spend on new books, used books, and photocopies in a semester show a substantial difference between medicine, communication studies, and law, with materials in medicine the most expensive and communication studies the least.

Students make their own calculations each semester and understand the relative costs of different strategies for acquiring materials. When we asked what percentage of their materials they would be able to buy if copying was possible, only 25 percent of students said they would be able to purchase nearly everything (81–100 percent of their materials); 38 percent said they would be able to buy, at most, 40 percent of materials.

Conclusion: Taking Access for Granted

It is hard to talk to students, professors, librarians, publishers, and bookstore owners these days and not come away with a sense of crisis playing out across the whole ecosystem. Libraries face difficult increasing costs, decreasing budgets, and unsettled terms

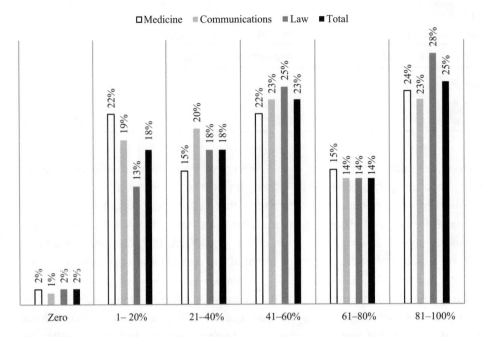

Figure 8.10
How much would you be able to purchase if you weren't able to copy?

for the shift to digital lending. Bookstores face a process of market consolidation that is driving smaller players out of business. Three of our informant booksellers closed shop since we interviewed them in 2014. The publishing business is also replete with the language of crisis.

And not a small one, we are led to believe. The Brazilian book industry is undergoing a decades-long "crisis of monumental proportions," as Earp and Kornis argued roughly a decade ago (Earp and Kornis 2005, 2008). Data on these issues in Brazil is of questionable quality,[97] but the same sources indicate that the publishing industry grew an unimpressive 5.79 percent between 2005 and 2015, mainly supported by government purchases of books for primary and secondary education. Some of what the industry calls crisis, then, is about slow growth and structural change relative to the otherwise rapid growth of the Brazilian economy in the period.[98] Another part of the story is that Brazil, in general, continues to do poorly in surveys of reading habits,[99] with the result that only a tiny percentage of household expenses is devoted to reading materials. This situation did not change between 2002 and 2009, despite a 4.6 percent increase in income between those years (Beltrão and Duchiade 2014).

In many respects, the perception of decline reflects the failure of the educational publishing ecosystem to effectively respond to the expansion of higher education, which saw the student population increase from approximately 2.7 million in 2000 to 6.6 million in 2015.[100] Although some of this growth was absorbed by the public system, the most significant change was the boom of private institutions after regulations on the sector were relaxed in 1996.[101] Between 1997 and 2006, the number of private institutions skyrocketed from 689 to over 2000. By 2015, private higher education enrolled 4.8 million students, compared to 1.8 million in public institutions.[102]

From the earliest days, the publishers' association ABDR was profoundly concerned with this expansion. While a larger student population meant a larger potential market for educational materials, ABDR feared that that market would be lost to copyright infringement—particularly in the new schools, which generally served low-income students. As ABDR lawyer Dalton Morato observed: "the average profile of a student, today, is that of a person who works during the day so that they can study at night in a private institution and who has no capacity to pay anything else other than tuition." Indeed, comparisons between the growth in student enrollments and alleged declining book sales became a fixture of ABDR discourse. Morato again:

the number of copies of university books in Brazil has fallen, or better yet, free-fallen, from 30,636,000 copies, in 1995, to 16,875,000 in 2004—a decrease of over 44 percent. During this same period (from 1992 to 2003), the average income of the Brazilian worker grew 16.3 percent. If this decline continues, economic activity geared towards the university book sector will become economically impossible and will not take place. [103]

As we have seen, this reasoning oversimplifies a complex scenario. Concerns for affordability drive copying—and not exclusively among low-income students—but it is clear that students also purchase books, and that issues of convenience and accessibility play significant roles. There has never been a serious prospect of recapturing student copying activity under the current publishing model, and trends in higher education enrollment have made that task more difficult, not easier.

Stresses on the ecosystem are, of course, not evenly distributed. Restructuring and consolidation have their winners. When asked about the state of the book industry, Mauro Koogan, the head of a major publishing group, put it differently:

crisis is a word that is perhaps a bit strong … for example, we are debating the matter of bookstores a lot … it is obvious that the more bookstores the better, but it's useless to protect a bookstore that has yearly revenues amounting to 50,000 reais, because it's not sustainable [as a business] … in the same way, if you have a publisher that publishes three books, it won't sustain itself as business, so it's in crisis. But it's in crisis not because the publishing market is in crisis, but because it's not a sustainable business. What I think is happening with books, and what I can say applies to my area, which is university, scientific, and professional books, is a change in paradigm, in how people learn, and what they use to learn and keep up-to-date. And there was a great change there, partly because of technology.[104]

Koogan has a point: the Brazilian publishing sector has a handful of conglomerates at the top and thousands of small publishers at the bottom (Barcellos 2010), producing small print runs of books that are generally cut off from significant distribution. As Milene Duchiade put it earlier in this chapter, Brazil is a country of "first and only editions." But this is largely a legacy of public investment decisions, not inexorable publishing trends.

In Brazil, the state plays the dominant role in educational and scholarly publishing through a number of channels, of which the purchasing of materials for primary and secondary education is only the most visible. This public investment shapes the current system at every level, both directly and indirectly, from research grants to university staff salaries to tax breaks for the publishing sector.[105] It has led to market concentration in primary and secondary education publishing (Cassiano 2013), turned Brazil into the major Latin American subscriber to journal databases through the CAPES portal, and funded much of the output of university presses through public research foundations, much of which remains available only on closed-access terms.

This same public investment creates a powerful lever and, indeed, obligation, to change the ecosystem in ways that advance the public interest. The open models now in circulation, in particular, provide an attractive alternative to public support for an industry that has never cracked the problem of affordability and that—in its ABDR guise—has waged war on the actual practices that enable the expansion of Brazilian higher education. Rethinking public investment as viewed through the lens of access, with different strategies for textbooks, journal articles, and monographs, is a long-overdue task. So is the task of copyright reform: many curricular needs involve materials that can't easily be "opened," such as out-of-print works and books with limited print runs. Broader copyright limitations would facilitate access to such works and, in turn, could coexist with a fair collective-licensing system for uses that go beyond the limitations.

In the end, most Brazilian students can take a basic level of access for granted, whether through book buying or photocopying, via the university library or loaned from a colleague, or downloaded from a shadow library or class Facebook group. Most students will get what they need. Unfortunately, since 1998, most of those strategies have made criminals out of students and faculty, and put universities through contortions as they try to guarantee the basic structure of access to materials for their students. Solving this problem, as we have seen, is not rocket science, but the recent turn in Brazilian politics appears to have put it temporarily out of reach. The question for the future, in Brazil and elsewhere, is not access vs. deprivation, but *how* and *under what terms* students will get the materials they need.

Notes

1. "The reproduction of a single copy, of any work, as long as it is not intended for for-profit use" (Article 46, II, Law 5988/73). This provision was an innovation of the 1973 law; previous versions of this exception in the Medeiros and Albuquerque Law (Law 496/1898) and the Civil Code of 1916 did not permit the full reproduction of copyrighted content for private use. Neither of these laws, however, was drafted in a time when photocopying technology was readily available and deployed in universities.

2. Research for the first two sections of this chapter draws on around twenty in-depth, semi-structured interviews with a variety of actors and stakeholders involved in the production, consumption, and access of the ecosystem, including government representatives, professors, publishers, librarians, bookstores, and entrepreneurs.

3. Focus groups were undertaken with students in the same fields. Clave de Fá Pesquisas and Elizete Ignácio collected data in 2014, under supervision of the authors, and the technical guidance of Kaizô Iwakami Beltrão, who designed the sample and helped with the treatment of the quantitative data we draw from.

4. These generally rent space for third-party copy machine operators. Interview with Gláucio Pereira, *Quartet Editora* and *Livraria República*, April 15, 2015.

5. Felipe Lindoso, "Mais uma entidade?," *PublishNews*, August 25, 2016. www.publishnews.com.br/materias/2016/08/25/mais-uma-entidade.

6. "Juiz proíbe que faculdade venda 'xerox' de livro," *Folha de S. Paulo*, December 16, 1993, 3-2.

7. "UFSCAR assina convênio e vai pagar direitos sobre reprodução de livros," *Folha de S. Paulo*, September 19, 1996.

8. Conversions between Brazilian reais and dollars were made on March 31 and April 1, 2017, using the rates provided by xe.com.

9. Jotabê Medeiros, "TVs devem mais de R$50 milhões de direitos autorais," *O Estado de São Paulo*, July 27, 1998.

10. Jotabê Medeiros, "Lei do Direito Autoral leva o primeiro à cadeia," *O Estado de São Paulo*, March 4, 1999.

11. Fábio Takahashi, "Internet é opção contra cópia ilegal," *Folha de São Paulo*, May 30, 2005, http://www1.folha.uol.com.br/fsp/cotidian/ff3005200521.htm.

12. Felipe Lindoso, "Reprografia, direito autoral e licenciamento—para lembrar da história," *O Xis do Problema* (blog), 2012, http://oxisdoproblema.com.br/?p=867.

13. Lúcia Martins, "Cópia de Livros Didáticos Agora É Caso de Polícia," *O Estado de São Paulo*, November 11, 2002.

14. ABDR, Cartilha, http://www.abdr.org.br/cartilha.pdf.

15. Article 46, II, Law 9610/98.

16. Interview, José Castilho of Editora UNESP (press), April 8, 2015.

17. Marcelo Gutierres and Simone Harnik, "Editoras Dão Descontos para Coibir Xerox," *Folha de São Paulo*, October 27, 2005.

18. Marcelo Godoy, "Deic Apura a Ação de Professores em Xerox," *O Estado de S. Paulo*, March 4, 2005.

19. Fábio Takahashi, "Universidade propõe sistema para evitar Xerox," *Folha de São Paulo*, May 1, 2005.

20. Gutierres and Harnik, "Editoras Dão Descontos para Coibir Xerox."

21. Agnaldo Brito, "Livro sob encomenda vira arma contra fraude," *O Estado de São Paulo*, June 8, 2005.

22. Renata Cafardo, "Contra xerox de livros, cópias legais," *O Estado de São Paulo*, August 25, 2007.

23. Interview with Richardt Rocha Feller, Minha Biblioteca, February 13, 2015.

24. Fábio Takahashi, "PUC libera uso de Xerox de livros por alunos," *Folha de São Paulo*, September 9, 2005.

25. The U.S. copyright industry umbrella group, the IIPA, has always expressed serious concerns about the role of universities in encouraging "book piracy" in Brazil. The following selection from the 2005 submission is representative: "Unauthorized photocopying continues to undermine the legitimate book publishing markets. The publishing industry reports that unauthorized photocopying of entire textbooks as well as study materials, individual lessons and chapters from textbooks continues to be the major form of book piracy in Brazil. AAP [Association of American Publishers] estimates losses to its members of US$18 million in 2004 and those losses multiply sharply for local Brazilian publishers. Many university texts used are apostilas, anthologies made up of chapters from various books copied illegally, both in English and in translation. Some professors make photocopied compilations of materials before the first day of classes, which gives the booksellers no chance to import or sell the books before classes. Some estimate that the annual number of unauthorized photocopies ranges from 3 to 5 billion pages. Universities are tacitly, and sometimes actively, condoning these practices, and are certainly taking no role at present in fighting these illegal activities in and around their campuses. The Ministry of Education has likewise failed to address this issue in any way, and the publishing industry really needs this ministry to step up and engage on this issue. Furthermore, illegal copying flourishes in commercial establishments adjacent to institutions of higher learning. Government action on illegal photocopying of academic materials, which cost[s] both domestic and foreign publishers millions

of dollars and cost[s] the Brazilian government thousands of jobs and millions in tax revenues, is practically nonexistent. IIPA asks the Ministry of Education and the administrative bodies of universities and colleges to work with the enforcement authorities to make sure that a clear message is sent to those engaged in illegal photocopying, both on and off campus, that this activity will not be tolerated. The recently reorganized Associacão Brasileira de Direitos Reprograficos (ABDR) has been working with authorities to conduct enforcement actions and plan for future endeavors" (IIPA 2005, 56).

26. Fábio Takahashi, "Universitários Lançam Frente Pró-Xerox," *Folha de São Paulo*, February 22, 2006, www1.folha.uol.com.br/fsp/cotidian/ff2202200618.htm.

27. *Diário do Congresso Nacional*, October 24, 1973, 1555–1570.

28. Amendment 233. "Art. … It is prohibited for the proprietors, operators and/or lessees of reprographic equipment—photographic, heliographic, photoelectric or photoelectronic—to produce copies of printed works, literary, artistic, didactical, technical, or scientific, in full or in part, in a single or multiple copies, with intent to profit, except under formal authorization of the rightsholder." In *Diário da Câmara dos Deputados,* November 8, 1973, 1817.

29. At the time, the ABDR claimed this change was only intended as a "defensive" measure to incentivize licensing, and even garnered support from the Xerox Corporation, which was worried about the association of its brand with piracy. See Felipe Lindoso, "Reprografia, direito autoral e licenciamento—para lembrar da história," *O Xis do Problema* (blog), 2012, http://oxisdoproblema.com.br/?p=867.

30. *Diário da Câmara dos Deputados*, December 6, 1997, 40420.

31. Other proposals dealt with the issue of university photocopies, both in favor and against the practice: Bill 1197/2007 (Dep. Bilac Pinto, PR-MG): Prohibits the presence of copy machines, or any other devices that allow the reproduction of literary works, in higher education institutions, archived; Bill 5046/2005 (Dep. Antonio Carlos Mendes Thame, PSDB-SP): Allows the reproduction of an entire work, in a single copy, for the exclusive, not-for-profit use of university students, archived; Bill 7458/2010 (Dep. Dr. Talmir, PV-SP): Allows the reproduction of an entire work, in a single copy, for the purposes of research, by graduate students, following a signed declaration of the student's supervisor, filed with the higher learning institution; Bill 131/2006 (Sen. Valdir Raupp, PMDB-RP): Allows the reproduction of 25 percent of work for private, not-for-profit use, archived, resubmitted as Bill 34/2015.

32. ECAD was in a fragile political position following an unfavorable final report from a Senate investigation and a decision by antitrust authority Administrative Council of Economic Defense (CADE, Conselho Administrativo de Defesa Econômica) that established that ECAD was acting as a cartel. On the former, see Cristina Tardáguila, "CPI do Ecad: Relatório Final Sugere 21 Indiciamentos e Propõe Nova Lei," *O Globo*, April 21, 2012, http://oglobo.globo.com/cultura/cpi-do-ecad-relatorio-final-sugere-21-indiciamentos-propoe-nova-lei-4696319. On the latter, see Célia Froufe, "Cade Condena Ecad por Cartel no Mercado Musical," *O Estado de São Paulo*, March 20, 2013, http://www.estadao.com.br/noticias/geral,cade-condena-ecad-por-cartel-no-mercado-musical,1011141.

33. It also took steps to ensure the transparency of collection and distribution of royalties (Francisco and Valente 2016; Wachowicz 2015). The constitutionality of Law 12853/13 was challenged at the Supreme Federal Court by collecting societies, but the law was declared to be constitutional in 2016.

34. Former Minister of Culture Juca Ferreira denounced the actions of his successors in very strong terms: "Sadly, the coup's government perfectly destroyed [the Intellectual Rights Directorship] as quickly as it could. Marcelo Calero, the brief [note: Calero was only in office for a few months], first listened to a lobbyist from the Hollywood movie industry. Then he sat down with the directors of the associations who were defeated in the ADINs [note: the legal procedures that challenged Law 12853/13's constitutionality]. Anxious to gain support to maintain himself in a position for which he was never adequate, he irresponsibly eliminated half of the Ministry of Culture's Intellectual Rights Directorship, handing its control to names appointed by the aforementioned lobbyists. And, in an equally irresponsible manner, he stripped the competences attributed to the Ministry for the enforcement of Law 12.853/13 [...] The Intellectual Rights Directorship stopped monitoring the ECAD and its member associations." See Ferreira 2017.

35. See http://www2.cultura.gov.br/consultadireitoautoral/wp-content/uploads/2010/06/Lei9610 _Consolidada_Consulta_Publica.pdf.

36. ABRELIVROS, contribution to the copyright reform debate, 2010, http://www2.cultura.gov.br/ consultadireitoautoral/wp-content/uploads/2010/09/ABRELIVROS.pdf.

37. SNEL, contribution to the copyright reform debate, 2010, http://www2.cultura.gov.br/ consultadireitoautoral/wp-content/uploads/2010/09/SNEL1.pdf.

38. Leonardo Neto, "Livro Ganha Mais uma Entidade," *Publishnews*, August 24, 2016, http:// www.publishnews.com.br/materias/2016/08/24/livro-ganha-mais-uma-entidade.

39. Writing in 2004, Fisher proposed: "In brief, here's how such a system would work. A creator who wished to collect revenue when his or her song or film was heard or watched would register it with the Copyright Office. With registration would come a unique filename, which would be used to track transmissions of digital copies of the work. The government would raise, through taxes, sufficient money to compensate registrants for making their works available to the public. Using techniques pioneered by American and European performing rights organizations and television rating services, a government agency would estimate the frequency with which each song and film was heard or watched by consumers. Each registrant would then periodically be paid by the agency a share of the tax revenues proportional to the relative popularity of his or her creation" (Fisher 2004, 202). The Brazilian discussion drew more closely on versions of this model formulated by Fred von Lohmann (2004) and Philippe Aigrain (2012).

40. Instrução Normativa n. 2, May 2016.

41. The summary of the document proposes: "1. Analysis and discussion of legal frameworks used to protect works in digital services; 2. Analysis and discussion of the role of companies and corporations that make use of protected works in the digital environment and their way of action, including the verification of the level of transparency on business and the proportions of copy-

right and related rights payment to the multiple rights holders; 3. Building consensus on the management of copyright in the digital environment, in order to deal with the problems associated to this matter, from the low payment of authors and artists to the limitations and exceptions to copyrights in the digital environment." GRULAC, Proposal for Analysis of Copyright Related to the Digital Environment," December 1, 2015. Document presented at WIPO SCCR, session 32, http://www.wipo.int/edocs/mdocs/copyright/en/sccr_31/sccr_31_4.pdf.

42. Brazil, nonetheless, reintroduced the topics of transparency, territoriality, and balance of rights in digital copyright as a discussion on electronic commerce at the WTO TRIPS Council in early 2017. See Jeremy Malcolm, "Brazil Proposes New Digital Copyright Rules for the WTO," Electronic Frontier Foundation, https://www.eff.org/deeplinks/2017/03/brazil-proposes-new -digital-copyright-rules-wto.

43. Interview with Thiago Cândido on *Folha de São Paulo*. See Joselia Aguiar, "Livro Impresso, PDF, Legal Ou Ilegal? Livrosdehumanas.org Se Defende," *Folha de São Paulo*, May 21, 2012, http:// livrosetc.blogfolha.uol.com.br/2012/05/21/livro-impresso-pdf-legal-ou-ilegal-livrosdehumanas -se-defende/.

44. "ABDR promove caça a piratas digitais," *O Estado de São Paulo*, July 12, 2010; Bruno Galo, "Falta de alternativa estimula a pirataria," *O Estado de São Paulo*, November 2, 2009.

45. Mônica Bergamo, "Leitura pirata," *Folha de São Paulo*, September 27, 2014.

46. Tatiana de Mello Dias, "O custo da cópia," *O Estado de São Paulo*, June 18, 2012.

47. Publishers Forense and Contexto, both ABDR affiliates, protested the lawsuit. Raquel Cozer, "Difusão vs. Pirataria," *Folha de São Paulo*, May 19, 2012, http://www1.folha.uol.com.br/fsp/ ilustrada/43655-difusao-vs-pirataria.shtml.

48. A letter signed by seven professors and writers described the case in the following terms: "[...] The new virtual libraries are based in storage and dissemination like the material libraries of old, but they offer a decisive change because storage depends on distribution and not the opposite: it is the diffusion of files that guarantees their decentralized storage. It's a non-profit library, built in this modern and democratic format, that is under threat by the lawsuit brought by the Brazilian Reprographic Rights Association (ABDR), under the pretext of copyright infringement. The high prices of books, and the growing costs for photocopies, led a university student to make available online to his colleagues texts that are out-of-print or difficult to access. The initiative grew, attracted the attention of students and professors from all over the country, and became the most well-known virtual library of academic texts, becoming as prestigious as the comparable 'Derrida en castellano' website, which was the target of a similar lawsuit and was cleared by Argentinian courts, as we expect 'livrosdehumanas.org' will be by the Brazilian Judiciary." See "Em carta aberta, intelectuais apoiam blog Livros de Humanas," *O Globo*, June 2, 2012, http:// blogs.oglobo.globo.com/prosa/post/em-carta-aberta-intelectuais-apoiam-blog-livros-de- humanas-448445.html.

49. In a blog post, Coelho defended Livros de Humanas and Thiago Cândido, arguing that the publishing industry—like the music industry—must adapt to technological change, and that

book piracy does not harm industry profits. The author then asked his readers to send the ABDR copies of the post, or messages written by the readers themselves, with the observation that "trolling, in this case, is allowed." See Coelho's post at http://paulocoelhoblog.com/2012/08/12/ e-permitido-trollar/.

50. See https://twitter.com/neilhimself/status/204657543312707587.

51. Interview with Milena Piraccini Duchiade, Leonardo da Vinci Bookstore, March 25, 2015.

52. Miguel Conde, "Suspensão de Blog Com Livros Piratas Cria Discussão Na Web," *O Globo*, April 29, 2011, http://blogs.oglobo.globo.com/prosa/post/suspensao-de-blog-com-livros-piratas-cria-discussao-na-web-377257.html.

53. Apelação nº0123514–64.2012.8.26.0100, TJ-SP. Decided on June 1, 2016.

54. See https://thepiratebay.org/user/livroslivres/.

55. Lê Livros has switched domain names a few times. As of February 2017, it can be found at https://lelivros.pro/.

56. See https://lelivros.pro/sobre-nos/.

57. After the site was taken offline, a torrent with 1,300 books was released. "Após Fechamento do site iOS Books, Piratas Liberam Lista Completa de 1300 Livros Pirateados," *Tecnoarte News*, March 27, 2012, http://www.tecnoartenews.com/share/apos-fechamento-do-site-ios-books -piratas-liberam-lista-completa-de-1300-livros-pirateados/.

58. "This cyberlocker site is well-known globally and is particularly popular in Brazil. While 4shared provides legitimate file-storage services, the site also facilitates the streaming and down-loading of high volumes of allegedly pirated videos, music, books, and video games. 4shared mobile apps reportedly enable users to stream infringing content to mobile devices, while certain search and music player features may encourage music infringement. Right holders use 4shared's notice-and-takedown mechanism frequently but with little apparent impact on the overall levels of infringing content stored on and accessed through the site. Looking for other ways to steer Internet traffic away from infringing files, right holders have requested more than fifty million removals of 4shared URLs from prominent search engine results since June 2011; more than any other domain. While major U.S. payment providers no longer service 4shared, site operators continue to collect revenue from premium accounts and advertising by using resellers and offshore payment processors. 4Shared is registered to an entity in the British Virgin Islands and hosted by a company in Cyprus" (USTR 2016, 7).

59. The first version of the public consultation text included a takedown system partially inspired by the DMCA, but used it to regulate *all* types of content removal requests, including those based on defamation. This provoked a strong reaction from the National Association of Newspapers (ANJ, Associação Nacional de Jornais), on the grounds that it could lead to censorship. The Ministry of Justice, which was in charge of the consultation, quickly backtracked and established the current system, based on judicial orders, that was eventually approved in the final text of the law, and which does not apply to copyright infringement. See Cruz (2015) and Flávio Ferreira, "Pro-

jeto Pode Ferir Liberdade na Internet, Dizem Entidades," *Folha de São Paulo*, April 29, 2010, http://www1.folha.uol.com.br/fsp/brasil/fc2904201015.htm.

60. The latest draft of the bill, pre-impeachment, contained a novel notice-and-takedown regime that allowed for the forced remuneration of content that was not removed by users, to be requested directly from the platform or service provider. This version of the text was never published, but was leaked to civil society, industry, and academia, and is in file with the authors of the present chapter but not available online.

61. "Taking part in 4shared Partnership Program for copyright holders also presupposes your ability to search for content and mark it as yours, in case you own the copyright on the found files. Moreover, being a 4shared partner you can choose what you want to do with found files: block them or make money. At the same time, you can also opt for publishing the copyrighted materials yourself in the fast and convenient way." 4shared, Partnership Program for Copyright Holders, https://www.4shared.com/copyright-center.jsp.

62. Kyle Orland, "Dropbox Knows When You're Playing Pirate," *Wired*, March 31, 2014, http://www.wired.co.uk/article/dropbox-dmca-position.

63. See https://issuu.com/editora-saraiva.

64. See https://issuu.com/grupogen.

65. See http://www.snel.org.br/acordo-inedito-contra-pirataria-beneficia-associados-do-snel-2/.

66. See http://www.ebah.com.br/copyright.

67. Interview with Beatriz Fazolo, *Passei Direto*, April 16, 2015.

68. São Paulo, 11ª Vara Cível—Foro Central Cível, processo n. 1044001–59.2014.8.26.0100.

69. See https://www.passeidireto.com/blog/passei-direto/uma-nova-forma-de-ver-os-materiais-de-estudo-no-passei-direto/.

70. See http://www.minhabiblioteca.com.br/.

71. See https://pastadoprofessor.com/.

72. See http://www.bvirtual.com.br/sobre

73. Roberta Campassi, "Regra do MEC Pode Estimular Demanda por E-Book nas Universidades," *PublishNews*, May 7, 2012, http://www.publishnews.com.br/materias/2012/05/07/68240-regra-do-mec-pode-estimular-demanda-por-ebook-nas-universidades.

74. Interview with Mauro Koogan of *Grupo Gen*, October 12, 2014.

75. Brazilian Digital Library of Theses and Dissertations (BDTD, Biblioteca Digital Brasileira de Teses e Dissertações), http://Bdtd.Ibict.Br/.

76. Interview with Bianca Amaro of IBICT, December 19, 2014.

77. CAPES, Portaria 13, February 15, 2006 https://www.capes.gov.br/images/stories/download/legislacao/Portaria_013_2006.pdf. The Coordination for the Improvement of Higher Education Personnel (CAPES, Coordenação para o Aperfeiçoamento de Pessoal de Nível Superior) is further discussed in the section on the CAPES Journals Portal.

78. Portaria 329/2014, https://portal.fiocruz.br/sites/portal.fiocruz.br/files/documentos/portaria _-_politica_de_acesso_aberto_ao_conhecimento_na_fiocruz.pdf.

79. Bill 387/2011, Sen. Rodrigo Rollemberg, RJ.

80. SciELO began with support from the São Paulo Research Foundation (FAPESP, Fundação de Apoio a Pesquisa do Estado de São Paulo), the Brazilian National Council for Scientific and Technological Development (CNPq, Conselho Nacional de Desenvolvimento Científico e Tecnológico), and the Latin American and Caribbean Center on Health Sciences Information (BIREME, Centro Latino-Americano e do Caribe de Informação em Ciências da Saúde). Currently, most of the funds come from FAPESP.

81. Interview with Abel Packer, SciELO, April 9, 2015.

82. Ibid.

83. The project started with a group of three university presses (Editora UNESP, EdUFBA, and Editora FIOCruz) and has since expanded to ten.

84. Interview with Abel Packer, SciELO, April 9, 2015.

85. The city of São Paulo approved an executive decree in 2011 that established that educational materials produced by public municipal schools must be published under an open license; a bill proposing similar policy at the state level, however, was vetoed by the governor of São Paulo after being approved by the legislative. As of 2014, the state of Paraná and the Federal District were also debating OER legislation, and a federal bill establishing open licensing for primary and secondary education *and* universities was proposed in 2011. See Rossini and Castro 2016.

86. See http://periodicos.capes.gov.br/.

87. CAPES stands for Coordenação para o Aperfeiçoamento de Pessoal de Nível Superior—roughly, Coordination for the Improvement of Higher Education Personnel. CAPES is a foundation linked to the Ministry of Education and plays a variety of roles in Brazilian academic research, including evaluating graduate programs and promoting international scientific cooperation. From História e Missão, http://www.capes.gov.br/historia-e-missao.

88. The National Textbook Program (PNLD) was created in 1985, succeeding the PLIDEF (Programa do Livro Didático para o Ensino Fundamental), and previous attempts dating back to the National Institute of the Book (INL, Instituto Nacional do Livro), founded in 1937, and National Textbook Commission (CNLD, Comissão Nacional do Livro Didático), established in 1938. The PNLD provides free and universal distribution of textbooks for primary education students enrolled in public schools, and has been managed, since 1997, by the National Fund for the Development of Education (FNDE, Fundo Nacional de Desenvolvimento da Educação), a federal

agency linked to the Ministry of Education. The PNLD was later joined by two other programs, PNLEM and PNLD EJA, targeting secondary education and adult illiteracy, respectively (Cassiano 2013; Soares 2007). The Brazilian government, due to these programs, is one of the main book buyers in the Latin America, to the point where one of the main book market surveys available in Brazil, carried out by Institute of Economic Research Foundation (FIPE, Fundação Instituto de Pesquisas Econômicas) and SNEL, includes government purchases as a separate category in its reports.

89. Two attempts were undertaken during the Lula mandates, first via the Ministry of Education's Book Portal in 2004, and later via the Censo Bibligráfico da Graduação in 2006, a proposed database of titles used by federal university professors intended to provide a basis for book acquisition (Rosa 2007, 106–107). The very nature of higher education courses, which accommodate a much greater diversity in subjects and content, is not compatible with massive book-buying programs such as the PNLD, which demand a great degree of standardization of content in order to allow for gains in scale.

90. CAPES, "Relatório de Gestão," 2014, http://www.capes.gov.br/images/stories/download/Contas_Publicas/2014_Relatorio_de_Gestao_CAPES.pdf.

91. Interview with Sueli Mara Ferreira, University of São Paulo, November 26, 2014.

92. Interview with Bianca Amaro, IBICT, December 19, 2014.

93. Maurício Tuffani, "Capes Anuncia Projeto de Internacionalização de Revistas Científicas Brasileiras," *Folha de São Paulo*, October 31, 2014, www1.folha.uol.com.br/ciencia/2014/10/1541286-capes-anuncia-projeto-de-internacionalizacao-de-revistas-cientificas-brasileiras.shtml.

94. The sample was randomly drawn from institutions chosen from a list of existing schools offering courses in the aforementioned areas in 2014. As a criterion for selection, we randomly selected schools from two distinct categories: those that had more than 200 final-year (senior) students per year, and those that had fewer than 200. This process generated a pool of 2,340 responses, divided into six equal groups. Students in their first year of studies were not included in this survey, so a filter was used by applicants when approaching students on different campuses. The final questionnaire had more than fifty questions and was applied in person by a trained team, between November 2014 and April 2015. We also conducted a focus group in each disciplinary field with the participation of between five and eight students. The questions asked during the focus group reflect the survey questions, and quotes from the participating students are included to illustrate the data presented here. Data collection for the surveys and focus groups was undertaken by Clave de Fá Pesquisas and Elizete Ignácio, under supervision of the authors. Sample design and the treatment of survey data was done with the assistance of Kaizô Iwakami Beltrão.

95. Interview, Alexandre Camargo of Estante Virtual, June 11, 2015.

96. We also asked a series of more directed questions to gauge the popularity of well-established legal sources. Here, Google Scholar and SciELO have received the most mentions, with the CAPES portal trailing well behind. This is likely due to the fact that CAPES portal databases are not made

available to all institutions, and that they mostly cover English-language content that is more useful at a graduate level.

97. The FIPE/SNEL surveys used by Earp and Kornis are based on self-reporting by publishers, which, according to a well-informed source interviewed by Earp and Kornis, tends to paint an overly optimistic picture of their businesses (Earp and Kornis 2005:29). As of 2015, Nielsen extended its BookScan measuring service to Brazil, relying on data provided by bookstores—mainly large retailers. The results for 2016 show a decline of 9.2 percent in sales for the year. See Leonardo Neto, "Faturamento de livrarias cai 9.2 percent em 2016," *PublishNews*, January 16, 2017, http://www.publishnews.com.br/materias/2017/01/16/faturamento-de-livrarias-cai-92-em -2016.

98. Overall GDP grew 39.45 percent for the same period. Carlo Carrenho, "A Década Parada," *PublishNews*, June 9, 2015, http://www.publishnews.com.br/materias/2015/06/09/82226-a-decada -parada.

99. According to Retratos da Leitura, the only major survey of reading habits carried out in Brazil, 44 percent of the population had not read a book from beginning to end in the previous three months (interviewed in 2015). See Instituto Pró-Livro, *Pesquisa Retratos da Leitura,* 2016, http:// prolivro.org.br/home/images/2016/Pesquisa_Retratos_da_Leitura_no_Brasil_-_2015.pdf.

100. Student population data was taken from *Sinopses Estatísticas da Educação Superior—Gradua- ção, INEP,* http://inep.gov.br/web/guest/sinopses-estatisticas-da-educacao-superior.

101. For an overview of the sector, see Schwartzman and Schwartzman 2002; Almeida 2014; Martins 2009; Sécca and Leal 2009; Severino 2008.

102. This growth was facilitated by government programs that expanded student loans to private institutions (FIES, starting in 1999) and scholarships (ProUni, starting in 2005). Cuts in both, as well as the economic and political crises that affected Brazil by 2016, make the future uncertain for much the private education sector. Public universities are also suffering; one of Brazil's most prestigious public universities, the State University of Rio de Janeiro (Universidade Estadual do Rio de Janeiro, UERJ), founded in 1950, was at risk of shutting down in 2017 due to budgetary problems. See André Cabette Fábio, "Como a Uerj chegou à maior crise de sua história. E quem é afetado por isso," *Nexo Jornal*, January 11, 2017. https://www.nexojornal.com.br/expresso/ 2017/01/11/Como-a-Uerj-chegou-à-maior-crise-de-sua-história.-E-quem-é-afetado-por-isso.

103. Dalton Morato, "Mesa 4. Usos educacionais de conteúdos protegidos," *Anais do Seminário de Direitos Autorais e Acesso à Cultura*, August 2008, http://www.cultura.gov.br/documents/10883/ 38605/anais_sem_direitos_autorais_acesso_cultura_sao_paulo.pdf.

104. Interview with Mauro Koogan of Grupo GEN, December 10, 2014.

105. For a breakdown of the public investment that goes into the production of educational materials eventually sold by commercial publishers, see Craveiro, Machado, and Ortellado 2010.

References

ABDR (Associação Brasileira de Direitos Reprográficos [Brazilian Reprographic Rights Association]). n.d. "O Que É Direito Autoral (cartilha)." http://www.abdr.org.br/cartilha.pdf.

Aigrain, Philippe. 2012. *Sharing: Culture and the Economy in the Internet Age*. Amsterdam: Amsterdam University Press. http://oapen.org/search?identifier=409602.

Almeida, Elenara Chaves Edler de, Jorge Almeida Guimarães, and Isabel Teresa Gama Alves. 2010. "Dez anos do Portal de Periódicos da Capes: Histórico, Evolução e Utilização." *Revista Brasileira de Pós-Graduação* 7 (13). doi:10.21713/2358-2332.2010.v7.194.

Almeida, Wilson Mesquita de. 2014. *ProUni e o Ensino Superior Privado Lucrativo em São Paulo: uma Análise Sociológica*. São Paulo: Musa.

Barcellos, Marília de Araújo. 2010. "As Pequenas e Médias Editoras Diante do Processo de Concentração: Oportunidades e Nichos." In *Imprenso no Brasil: Dois Séculos de Livros Brasileiros*, ed. Aníbal Bragança and Márcia Abreu, 317–329. São Paulo: Editora UNESP.

Beltrão, Kaizô Iwakami, and Milena Piraccini Duchiade. 2014. *Nova Renda, Velhos Hábitos: Consumo de Material de Leitura nas Famílias Brasileiras—2002–2009: um Estudo com Base em Pesquisas de Orçamento Familiar do IBGE*. Rio de Janeiro: SCIENCE—Sociedade Científica.

Bragança, Aníbal. 2009. "As Políticas Públicas Para o Livro e a Leitura No Brasil: O Instituto Nacional do Livro (1937–1967)." *Matrizes* 2 (2): 221–246. doi:10.11606/issn.1982-8160.v2i2p221-246.

Câmara dos Deputados. 2004. *CPI da Pirataria (relatório)*. Brasília: Câmara dos Deputados.

Cassiano, Célia Cristina de Figueiredo. 2013. *O Mercado do Livro Didático no Brasil do Século XXI*. São Paulo: UNESP.

Costa, Eliane. 2011. *Jangada Digital*. Rio de Janeiro: Azougue.

Craveiro, Gisele, Jorge Machado, and Pablo Ortellado. 2008. *O Mercado de Livros Técnicos e Científicos no Brasil: Subsídio Público e Acesso ao Conhecimento*. São Paulo: GPOPAI/USP. http://www.forum-global.de/jm/2008-2009/Relatorio%20Livros-portugues.pdf.

Craveiro, Gisele, Jorge Machado, and Pablo Ortellado. 2010. *A Cadeia de Produção de Artigos Científicos no Brasil: Financiamento Público e Acesso ao Conhecimento*. São Paulo: GPOPAI/USP. http://www.forum-global.de/jm/2008-2009/relatorio-artigos-publicado-book_05-cadernosGPOPAI.pdf.

Cruz, Francisco Carvalho de Brito. 2015. "Direito, Democracia e Cultura Cigital: a Experiência de Elaboração Legislativa do Marco Civil da Internet." Master's thesis, Universidade de São Paulo. http://www.teses.usp.br/teses/disponiveis/2/2139/tde-08042016-154010/.

Dibbel, Julian. 2004. "We Pledge Allegiance to the Penguin." *Wired*. November 1. https://www.wired.com/2004/11/linux-6/.

Earp, Fábio Sá, and George Kornis. 2005. *A Economia Da Cadeia Produtiva Do Livro*. Rio de Janeiro: BNDES.

Earp, Fábio Sá, and George Kornis. 2008. "Queda Livre? A Economia do Livro no Brasil (1995–2006)." *In Impresso no Brasil: Dois Séculos de Livros Brasileiros*, ed. Aníbal Bragança and Márcia Abreu, 349–362. São Paulo: Editora UNESP.

Ferreira, Juca. 2017. "Silêncio Ensurdecedor e Boca Aberta." *Revista Fórum*, February 16. http://www.revistaforum.com.br/2017/02/16/silencio-ensurdecedor-e-boca-aberta/.

Filgueiras, Juliana Miranda. 2015. "As Políticas para o Livro Didático durante a Ditadura Militar: A Colted e a Fename." *History of Education* 19 (45): 85–102. doi:10.1590/2236-3459/44800.

Fisher, William W. 2004. *Promises to Keep: Technology, Law, and the Future of Entertainment.* Stanford: Stanford University Press.

Francisco, Pedro Augusto P., and Mariana Giorgetti Valente. 2016. *Da Rádio ao Streaming.* Rio de Janeiro: Azougue.

Hallewell, Laurence. 2005. *O Livro no Brasil: Sua História.* 3rd ed. São Paulo: EDUSP.

IDEC (Instituto Brasileiro de Defesa do Consumidor). 2008. "Copiar É Preciso." *Revista do IDEC* 121:20–23. http://www.idec.org.br/uploads/revistas_materias/pdfs/2008-04-ed120-pesquisa-livros.pdf.

IDEC (Instituto Brasileiro de Defesa do Consumidor). 2012. "Barreiras ao Conhecimento." *Revista do IDEC* 166. http://www.idec.org.br/em-acao/revista/livros-inacessiveis/materia/barreiras-ao-conhecimento/pagina/175.

IIPA (International Intellectual Property Alliance). 2005. *Report: Brazil* (Special 301 Recommendations). Washington, DC: IIPA. *IIPA* 2005.

IIPA (International Intellectual Property Alliance). 2009. *Report: Brazil* (Special 301 Recommendations). Washington, DC: IIPA. *IIPA* 2009.

IIPA (International Intellectual Property Alliance). 2017. *Report: Brazil* (Special 301 Recommendations). Washington, DC: IIPA.

INEP. 2012a. *ENADE 2012. Relatório Síntese: Comunicação Social—Jornalismo.* Brasília: Ministério da Educação.

INEP. 2012b. *ENADE 2012. Relatório Síntese: Direito.* Brasília: Ministério da Educação.

Machado, Jorge. 2015. "O Projeto de Lei do Compartilhamento de Arquivos Digitais: Uma Possível Solução para o Problema?" *Liinc em Revista* 11 (2). doi:10.18617/liinc.v11i2.811.

Maia, Luiz Cláudio Gomes, and Maria De Souza Lima Santos. 2015. "Gestão Da Biblioteca Universitária: Análise Com Base Nos Indicadores de Avaliação Do MEC." *Perspectivas Em Ciência Da Informação* 20 (2): 100–119. doi:10.1590/1981-5344/2079.

Martins, Carlos Benedito. 2009. "A Reforma Universitária de 1968 E a Abertura Para O Ensino Superior Privado No Brasil." *Educação & Sociedade* 30 (106): 15–35. doi:10.1590/S0101-73302009000100002.

Ministry of Culture. n.d., a. Fórum Nacional de Direito Autoral—Direito Autoral. Conheça e Participe desta Discussão sobre a Cultura no Brasil. Brasília: Ministério da Cultura.

Ministry of Culture. n.d., b. Relatório de Análise das Contribuições ao Anteprojeto de Modernização da Lei de Direitos Autorais (Após a Consulta Pública Realizada de 14/06 a 31/08/2010 e após Debate no Grupo Interministerial de Propriedade Intelectual—GIPI). Brasília: Ministério da Cultura.

Mizukami, Pedro N., Oona Castro, Luiz F. Moncau, and Ronaldo Lemos. 2011. "Brazil." In *Media Piracy in Emerging Economies*, ed. Joe Karaganis, 219–304. New York: Social Science Research Council.

Packer, Abel L., Nicholas Cop, Adriana Luccisano, Amanda Ramalho, and Ernesto Spinak, eds. 2014. *SciELO—15 Anos de Acesso Aberto: Um Estudo Analítico sobre Acesso Aberto e Comunicação Científica*. Paris and São Paulo: UNESCO. 10.7476/9789237012376.

Peres, Eliane, and Mônica Maciel Vahl. 2014. "Programa do livro didático para o ensino fundamental do instituto nacional do livro (PLIDEF/INL, 1971–1976): contribuições à história e às políticas do livro didático no Brasil." *Revista Educação e Políticas em Debate* 3 (1). http://www.seer.ufu.br/index.php/revistaeducaopoliticas/article/view/27682.

Rosa, Flavia Goulart Garcia. 2007. *Pasta Do Professor—O Uso de Cópias nas Universidades*. Edição 1. Maceió-AL: EDUFAL.

Rossini, Carolina, and Oona Castro. 2016. "The State of Open Educational Resources in Brazil: Policies and Realities." In *Open Educational Resources: Policy, Costs and Transformation*, ed. Fengchun Miao, Sanjaya Mishra and Rory McGreal. Paris: UNESCO/Commonwealth of Learning.

Santana, Bianca, Carolina Rossini, and Pretto Nelson de Luca, eds. 2012. *Recursos Educacionais Abertos: Práticas Colaborativas E Políticas Públicas*. Salvador, São Paulo: EDUFBA, Casa da Cultura Digital.

Schwartzman, Jacques, and Simon Schwartzman. 2002. "O Ensino Superior Privado como Setor Econômico." *Ensaio: Avaliação e Políticas Públicas em Educação* 10 (37): 411–440.

Sécca, Rodrigo Ximenes, and Rodrigo Mendes Leal. 2009. "Análise do Setor de Ensino Superior Privado no Brasil." *BNDES Setorial* 30:103–156.

Severino, Antônio Joaquim. 2008. "O Ensino Superior Brasileiro: Novas Configurações e Velhos Desafios." *Educar em Revista* 31:73–89.

Silveira, Sergio Amadeu da, Murilo Bansi Machado, and Rodrigo Tarchiani Savazoni. 2013. "Backward March: The Turnaround in Public Cultural Policy in Brazil." *Media, Culture & Society* 35 (5): 549–564. doi:10.1177/0163443713485491.

Silveiras, Raphael, and Gilda Portugal Gouvêa. 2016. "A presença do Estado na Rede: Marco Civil da Internet e Reforma da Lei de Direito Autoral." *Liinc em Revista* 12 (1). doi:10.18617/liinc.v12i1.856.

Soares, Ricardo Pereira. 2007. "Compras Governamentais para o Programa Nacional do Livro Didático: uma Discussão sobre a Eficiência do Governo." *Texto para Discussão IPEA*, n. 1307. http://repositorio.ipea.gov.br/handle/11058/1414.

Souza, Allan Rocha de, and Luca Schirru. 2016. "Os Direitos Autorais no Marco Civil da Internet." *Liinc em Revista* 12 (1). doi:10.18617/liinc.v12i1.891.

Tavares, Mariana Rodrigues. 2014. "Editando a Nação e Escrevendo sua História: o Instituto Nacional do Livro e as Disputas Editoriais entre 1937–1991." *AEDOS* 6 (15). http://seer.ufrgs.br/index.php/aedos/article/view/45083.

USTR (United States Trade Representative). 2016. 2016 *Special 301 Report*. Washington, DC: USTR. https://ustr.gov/sites/default/files/USTR-2016-Special-301-Report.pdf.

Vahl, Monica Maciel, and Eliane Peres. 2016. "As Disputas Editoriais no Campo do Programa do Livro Didático para o Ensino Fundamental do Instituto Nacional do Livro—Plidef/INL (1971–1976)." *History of Education* 20 (50): 219–41.

Venturini, Jamila. 2014. *Recursos educacionais abertos no Brasil: O Campo, os Recursos e sua Apropriação em Sala de Aula*. São Paulo: Ação Educativa.

von Lohmann, Fred. 2004. "Voluntary Collective Licensing for Music File Sharing." *Communications of the ACM* 47 (10). doi:10.1145/1022594.1022613.

Wachowicz, Marcos. 2015. "A Revisão da Lei Autoral, Principais Alterações: Debates E Motivações." *Revista de Propriedade Intelectual—Direito Contemporâneo E Constituição* 4 (8): 542–562.

9 Coda: Uruguay

Jorge Gemetto and Mariana Fossatti

We end with a familiar scene. On an October morning in 2013, students arrived at the University of the Republic in Montevideo to find a major police operation underway. In collaboration with Interpol, the organized crime unit had raided fifteen copy shops in the area surrounding the law school and detained thirty-two people (El País 2013a). The timing was provocative. The law school—the largest unit at the university with more than fourteen thousand enrolled students (Udelar 2013)—was in the middle of exams. News of the raid spread quickly. The arrests and confiscated photocopy machines were televised and the topic trended on social networks, where it met an avalanche of criticism.

In Uruguay, as in the other countries explored in this book, unauthorized photocopies are still the principal means of access to course materials (Rodés and Pérez Casas 2013)—generalized throughout the academic community and facilitated by faculty. Student centers at nearly all schools have photocopying services, with which they make compendia of materials and CD archives for student use. As materials gradually shift to digital formats, university learning management systems have become distribution and storage platforms, with little attention paid to licensing.[1]

As in many other Latin American countries, all of these forms of access to materials—paper and digital—are illegal under Uruguayan copyright law and subject to punishments ranging from fines to jail terms.[2] Uruguayan law has no exceptions for copying in educational contexts. The law, in effect, makes criminals of most of the students and faculty.

A 2012 survey of students at the University of the Republic by Rodés and Pérez Casas revealed a wide array of material obstacles to education. More than 66 percent said that they used photocopies of portions of books; 58 percent acknowledged copying whole books. Fifty-seven percent of the students indicated that buying books represented a significant portion of their total budgets.[3] Here, the library represented an important source of access for 49 percent of students. Unauthorized downloading trailed slightly at 43 percent.

As elsewhere, students consistently indicated a preference for print over digital materials—including those who downloaded materials. Some 56 percent of the students in the latter group print the materials they download. Such numbers are reflective of the (still) low rate of adoption of e-readers and tablets (Rodés and Pérez Casas 2013).

Perhaps predictably, then, the academic community reacted strongly to the copy shop closures and arrests. Shortly after the raid, the Federation of University Students (FEUU) published a declaration calling for "free and democratic access" to the full corpus of human knowledge (Montevideo Portal 2013). A few days later, students held a demonstration in front of the law school to protest the closures (El Observador 2013). The Student Center at the law school, in turn, launched a petition to demand better access to course materials and reform of the copyright law, including the creation of educational exceptions and the decriminalization of nonprofit infringement. The campaign collected 10,000 signatures and resulted in the presentation of a draft reform bill to Danilo Astori, then vice president of Uruguay (El País 2013b).

Like in Argentina, where cheap-books pioneer Eudeba began to sue students in the 1990s, the raids marked the breakdown of an earlier generation of access strategies. The raids were initiated by a complaint from the Foundation of University Culture (or FCU), which was the main editor, distributor, and vendor of course materials at the Law School. The FCU, in turn, was the descendent of the Office of Course Materials, which was founded by law students at the University of the Republic in the 1940s to make educational materials more available and affordable. Officially, the FCU retains its original goals and even today has formal links to the Student Center. Over time, however, the FCU became a more conventional commercial publisher, offering discounts to students but no longer pushing seriously against the problem of affordability. As in Argentina, the academic publishers ceased to be the main advocates of cheap access. Increasingly, this problem was left to the students.

The FCU enjoys a privileged position at the Law School because the students are essentially a captive audience. In this context, and like most other commercial publishers, it produces small print runs at high prices, deliberately undershooting student enrollment. The cause of this distortion was widely debated in the months following the raids. The Uruguayan Book Association blamed widespread photocopying for the high-price, low-print-run model (180.com.uy 2013a). The students, in turn, blamed high prices for widespread photocopying (180.com.uy 2013b).[4]

Whatever the case, the discussions between the Book Association and the students strongly suggested that the legal market, in its current form, could not readily meet educational needs. A compromise position had been possible as long as there was no active repression of the informal market. When the police began raiding copy shops at the behest of the FCU, that equilibrium was disturbed.

Soon, the various parties to the dispute turned to the state for relief. The draft bill presented by the Student Center was one of these demands. For its part, the Book Association saw an opportunity to increase public purchasing for libraries and licensing of e-books (Espectador 2013). Still other parties to the debate proposed the reinstatement of a private collecting system that could compensate authors for photocopies. This strategy had been tried in the mid-2000s via a collecting society called A.U.T.O.R. Unfortunately, A.U.T.O.R. had difficulty developing a constituency among authors, in part because of lack of transparency regarding royalties. It ceased operations in 2007, without returning any revenues to authors.

In practice, each group tried to capitalize on the crisis. In March 2014, following an agreement with the FCU, the government printing office (the IMPO) launched a digital library focused on educational materials (El Observador 2014). The new service lowered the price of some materials, but also used digital rights management tools that monitored user behavior and prevented copying and printing. Inside the university, opinion split in two directions: one favoring closer relations with the presses and the other supporting open-access policies for scientific and educational materials. Advocates of the latter approach had their own strategy built around support for open access textbooks and an institutional repository for open access materials (called Colibrí, the Conocimiento Libre Repositorio Institucional).

The debate launched by the 2013 raids continues to play out across the university system, the publishing sector, and the state. The number of proposed solutions has grown, but—as we have seen elsewhere in this book—the shape of a durable, legal, and more inclusive approach remains unclear.

The student-led reform effort sought to expand educational exceptions to copyright enough to legalize most educational photocopying. Prospects for such reform dimmed in 2016, however, in the face of publisher opposition. The publishers succeeded in killing key provisions such as personal copy exceptions (which allow a limited number of copies for personal use) and the decriminalization of non-for-profit infringement. The watered-down bill that survived this process remains stalled.

State efforts (such as IMPO's digital library) focus on obtaining more favorable terms for digital licensing from publishers. The IMPO model promises lower prices than the paper equivalents but, as in other digital library efforts, depends on publisher support for affordable licensing and easy access. How these concepts translate into actual pricing and terms of use, however, remains unsettled and history suggests that publishers will eventually charge whatever they believe the market can bear. The large multinational publishers, for their part, have their own online distribution channels and have resisted pressure to make side agreements with IMPO. Students, in turn, have generally balked at the restrictions on copying and printing imposed by the publishers (El País 2014). As we have seen in Uruguay and elsewhere, student preferences tilt sharply toward paper on the one hand, and free digital copies on the other.

The third source of pressure comes from the university sector, which is trying to expand the production of open textbooks and the use of open repositories for research. As we have seen, the main challenge is that these initiatives internalize costs that the university has always treated as externalized in the publisher and student communities. These efforts leave open the question of how the university will finance these projects over the long term and whether an open textbook ecosystem, in particular, can grow and effectively compete with the commercial sector without those financial assurances.

As elsewhere in this book, the main obstacle to change is the complexity and resilience of the status quo. For students, ad hoc combinations of buying, borrowing, and copying get most of them through most of their classes. For researchers, they provide access to most of the work they need most of the time. For publishers, informal copying erodes the commercial market but also reduces pressure for noncommercial solutions such as open models and more flexible copyright rules. For universities, the mixed ecosystem saves them from taking on new expenses, responsibilities, and forms of liability for their students. This is a moment of oddly balanced forces, with evolving commercial strategies, open models, and unauthorized copying all exerting forms of pressure and constraint. There is no reason to assume that this balance is stable but, as with most complex systems, the effects of any significant change are hard to predict. In practice, organizational conservativism and inaction tend to win out. In Montevideo, the political cost of a real crisis over access to materials was too high. The copy shop networks reopened soon after the raids and students returned to their usual patterns of activity. In Delhi, publishers and universities are fighting over whether the university will incorporate some portion of the copying that everyone knows will happen anyway. In either case, the growing abundance of research and instructional materials and the diversity of ways to copy and distribute them favor the students. It's up to everyone else to make their access easier and legal.

Notes

1. In the case of the University of the Republic, this "virtual learning environment" (Entornos Virtuales de Aprendizaje, or EVA) was introduced in 2008 and uses Moodle software.

2. Uruguayan copyright law (9.739) dates to 1937 and has been modified several times. The most important of these modifications came in 2003 with the passage of Law 17.616, which brought Uruguay into compliance with the TRIPS agreement. Although TRIPS says little about enforcement, the law responded to rights holder anxiety about the rise of CD and DVD piracy—adding restrictions and increasing penalties to a maximum of three years in prison for infringement with a commercial motive. The text of the law is available at: http://www.wipo.int/wipolex/es/text.jsp?file_id=196344 (accessed March 2, 2017).

3. The survey was taken by 771 students at the University of the Republic. The data is presented in Rodés et al. 2012 as part of a larger comparative inquiry into student practices and attitudes around books, digitization, and open access materials.

4. In the course of this debate, the then president of the Book Association, Alicia Guglielmo, sought to reframe the issue in economic terms, arguing that photocopying threatened 1,200 jobs in the editorial sector (180.com.uy 2013a). But this claim met with some skepticism. Photocopying had been ubiquitous in the university community for decades, with no clear evidence of growth or decline over the period. According to publishing representatives, the piracy of books in other sectors is low (DICREA 2009:37), suggesting a problem mostly limited to course materials.

References

180.com.uy. 2013a. "Las fotocopias hacen inviable el trabajo editorial." October 22. http://www.180.com.uy/articulo/36340 (accessed March 2, 2017).

180.com.uy. 2013b. "Entre derechos y bibliotecas llenas de fotocopias." October 22. http://www.180.com.uy/articulo/36345_Entre-derechos-y-bibliotecas-hechas-de-fotocopias (accessed March 2, 2017).

DICREA. 2009. "Conglomerado Editorial. Plan de refuerzo de la competitividad." http://www.cultura.mec.gub.uy/innovaportal/file/5535/1/conglomerado_editorial_plan_refuerzo_de_la_competitividad.pdf (accessed March 2, 2017).

El Observador. 2013. "Estudiantes protestaron contra ilegalidad de fotocopias: 'La solución es socializar, no privatizar.'" October 24. http://www.elobservador.com.uy/noticia/263511/estudiantes-protestaron-contra-ilegalidad-de-fotocopias-la-solucion-es-socializar-no-privatizar/ (accessed March 2, 2017).

El Observador. 2014. "El lunes se estrena el primer servicio de libros digitales para estudiantes en Uruguay." March 5. http://www.elobservador.com.uy/noticia/273224/el-lunes-se-estrena-el-primer-servicio-de-libros-digitales-para-estudiantes-en-uruguay/ (accessed March 2, 2017).

El País. 2013a. "Allanan locales y estudiantes no saben qué hacer." October. http://www
.elpais.com.uy/informacion/allanan-locales-fotocopias-estudiantes-no.html (accessed March 2,
2017).

El País. 2013b. "Estudiantes juntaron 10 mil firmas a favor de su campaña por fotocopias."
November (accessed March 2, 2017).

El País. 2014. "Fotocopias ilegales de libros no cesaron y habrá más denuncias." November
30. http://www.elpais.com.uy/informacion/fotocopias-ilegales-libros-no-cesaron.html (accessed
March 2, 2017).

Espectador. 2013. "Cámara Uruguaya del Libro: 'no se puede seguir estudiando en fotocopias (...)
le está haciendo mucho daño a la sociedad.'" October 28. http://www.espectador.com/cultura/
277054/camara-uruguaya-del-libro-no-se-puede-seguir-estudiando-en-fotocopias-le-esta-haciendo
-mucho-dano-a-la-sociedad (accessed March 2, 2017).

Montevideo Portal. 2013. "FEUU preocupada por caso fotocopias. Pasado de toner." October 24.
http://www.montevideo.com.uy/auc.aspx?217094 (accessed March 2, 2017).

Rodés, V., and A. Pérez Casas. 2013. "Percepciones, actitudes y prácticas respecto a los libros de
texto y al uso de libros digitales en formatos abiertos por parte de estudiantes de la Universidad de
la República." Programa de Entornos Virtuales de Aprendizaje, Departamento de Apoyo Técnico
Académico, Comisión Sectorial de Enseñanza (Udelar), Informe Técnico. http://proeva.edu.uy/
files/2016/04/Percepciones-actitudes-y-pra%CC%81cticas-respecto-a-los-libros-de-texto-y-al-uso
-de-libros-digitales-en-formatos-abiertos-por-parte-de-estudiantes-de-la-Universidad-de-la
-Repu%CC%81blica.pdf (accessed March 2, 2017).

Rodés, V., A. Pérez Casas, X. Ochoa, and I. Frango. 2012. "Percepciones, actitudes y prácticas
respecto a los libros de texto, digitales y en formatos abiertos por parte de estudiantes de universidades de América Latina." http://www.proyectolatin.org/pdfs/need_analysis/1893-3020-1-SM.pdf
(accessed March 2, 2017).

Udelar. 2013. "Censo de estudiantes universitarios de grado Udelar—2012." http://www.snep
.edu.uy/files/2013/12/vii_censo_de_estudiantes_de_grado_2012.pdf (accessed March 2, 2017).

Contributors

Balázs Bodó, is a socio-legal research scientist at the Institute for Information Law (IViR) at the University of Amsterdam. He is a two-time Fulbright Scholar (Stanford University's Center for Internet and Society in 2006–2007 and Harvard University's Berkman Center for Internet and Society in 2012). In 2013–2015, he was a Marie Curie Fellow at the IViR. Balázs is an internationally renowned expert in cultural black markets, piracy, informal media economies, and the digital underground. He is conducting normative research on a number of rapidly emerging technologies, including algorithmic news recommenders, blockchains, and smart contracts.

Laura Czerniewicz is the director of the Centre for Innovation in Learning and Teaching (CILT) at the University of Cape Town in South Africa. She is an associate professor in the Centre for Higher Education Development, committed to equity of access and success in higher education. Her research interests include the technologically mediated practices of students and academics and the nature of the changing higher education environment and the geopolitics of knowledge, underpinned by a commitment to surfacing the expressions of inequality within and across contexts. She is leading a project on the Unbundled University: researching emerging models in an unequal landscape (http://unbundleduni.com/) with colleagues at Leeds University. Czerniewicz is involved with policy work, contributes to national and global conversations in varied formats, and serves on the advisory boards of education and technology publications in international higher education. Much of her work is available online at https://uct.academia.edu/LauraCzerniewicz. She blogs intermittently and can be followed on Twitter as @czernie.

Mirosław Filiciak is the director of Institute of Cultural Studies, SWPS University of Social Sciences and Humanities, Warsaw, and the editor of *Kultura popularna* (Popular Culture), the open-access quarterly on Polish cultural studies. Filiciak is interested in the theory of media studies, archeology of media, and the relations between media technologies and cultural practices. He has led many research projects, including The Circulations of Culture (2012) and Youth and Media (2013). He also works on strategies of collecting, restoring, and simulating old technical media, using the case of the pinball community.

Mariana Fossatti is a sociologist, MSSc on Society and Development, and graduate of the University of the Republic, Uruguay. She is the director of the online cultural center Ártica and a member of the Uruguayan chapter of Creative Commons. Fossatti focuses on the study and application of ICT and e-learning in culture, education, and social organizations. As a consultant, she has worked with the Ministry of Education and Culture of Uruguay. As a teacher, she has taught on society, new technologies, and e-learning in the Centro Latinoamericano de Economía Humana (CLAEH), the University of Salamanca, and the Plan Ceibal, among others.

Jorge Gemetto is coordinator of the online cultural center Ártica and is a member of the Uruguayan chapter of Creative Commons. He coauthored the e-books *Young Art and Digital Culture* and *Arts and Culture in Circulation: Introduction to Copyright and Free Licenses*. A member of the research group Access to Knowledge and Culture in the XXI Century at CSIC, University of the Republic, Uruguay, Gemetto's degree is in psychology. In 2014, he contributed to FLOK Society, a collaborative research project about free knowledge and public policies in Ecuador. He is also a contributor to the free culture magazine *Pillku*.

Eve Gray is a senior research associate in the IP Law and Policy Unit at the University of Cape Town, South Africa, working at the juncture of publishing practice, digital media, and changing copyright models. Since the early 1990s, Gray has been interested in the disruptive potential of digital publishing, working as a university press director, academic textbook publishing director, and publishing consultant. For the last decade, as a researcher, she has dealt with university publishing in Africa, open copyright, and access to knowledge. She is an internationally recognized specialist on open access and the geopolitics of university publishing, an issue of new urgency in the wake of the 2015 Rhodes Must Fall student protest movement and growing demand for the decolonization of the university in South Africa.

Evelin Heidel is an independent researcher and member of Creative Commons. She works with the DIY Book Scanner Project and other groups working on the field of digitization, copyright, and access to knowledge.

Joe Karaganis, editor, is vice president at the American Assembly at Columbia University. His work focuses on the regulation of the knowledge economy, and has recently included research on intermediary liability, broadband adoption, and media piracy. He also directs the Open Syllabus Project.

Lawrence Liang is a lawyer and writer based in New Delhi. A cofounder of the Alternative Law Forum, he is a professor of law at the School of Law, Governance and Citizenship, Ambedkar University. Liang has worked on issues of access to knowledge and the politics of copyright for over a decade. In particular, he focuses on the creative potential of piracy in the Global South and is the author of *Invisible Libraries*, a book of speculative fiction about the future of libraries.

Pedro Mizukami is a researcher at the Center for Technology and Society at FGV Law School. His research interests cover a wide range of topics related to access to knowledge, piracy, open licensing, and Internet regulation. He is a PhD candidate in public policy at the Federal University of Rio de Janeiro's Institute of Economics, and holds a master's degree in constitutional law from the Pontifical Catholic University of São Paulo.

Jhessica Reia is a project manager and researcher at the Center for Technology and Society at FGV Law School. She holds a PhD and a master's degree in communication and culture at the Federal University of Rio de Janeiro, as well as earning her BA in public policy at the University of São Paulo. Reia was as a visiting researcher at the McGill Institute for the Study of Canada and graduate research trainee from 2015 to 2016. Her research interests include free culture, piracy, copyright, Internet regulation, and urban communication.

Alek Tarkowski is a sociologist and the director and founder of Centrum Cyfrowe, a Polish digital think tank. He is also cofounder and public lead of Creative Commons Poland and a European policy fellow at Creative Commons. He is a member of Communia, the international association on the public domain, and founding member of the Polish Coalition for Open Education (KOED). Tarkowski is active in advocacy work on copyright reform and open licensing policies in Poland and in Europe, particularly advocacy for strong education exceptions to copyright. His research activities focus on digital education and skills, as well as social and cultural aspects of the intellectual property system.

Index

Note: t after a page number indicates a table; f after a page number indicates a figure.

Ministry of Culture and, 230–234, 241, 262n34

music industry and, 229–231, 233–234, 237, 263n49, 264n58

National Antipiracy Plan and, 226

National Textbook Program (PNLD) and, 242, 266n88, 267n89

online services and, 236–238

open access and, 6, 223–224, 239–241, 243, 246

photocopying and, 18, 223–235, 244–248, 251, 254–255, 258, 259n1, 260n25, 261n31, 263n48

piracy and, 226, 228, 235, 237, 255, 260n25, 261n29, 263n49

publishers and, 223–229, 232, 235, 237–246, 255–258, 259n2, 260n25, 268nn97,105

reading habits in, 268n99

reform and, 37, 223–224, 229–232, 237, 258, 262n36

Rousseff and, 231, 234

scanning and, 235, 238, 268n97

SciELO and, 6, 27, 128, 150n26, 239–241, 243, 246, 266n80, 267n96

shadow libraries and, 18, 223–224, 234–236, 254, 258

sharing and, 18, 234–238, 242, 247, 249–254

students and, 7, 223–224, 226–228, 234–259, 261n31, 263n48, 266n88, 267n94, 268n102

subscriptions and, 239, 242–243, 258

subsidies and, 8

takedown requests and, 59, 233–238, 264n58, 265n60

textbooks and, 238–242, 246, 258, 260n25, 266n88, 267n89

United States and, 229

University of São Paulo and, 227, 233, 235, 255

Wiley and, 241, 243

Xerox and, 224, 229, 261n29

Brazilian Association for the Protection of Editorial and Authors' Rights (ABPDEA), 225–226

Brazilian Association of Scientific Editors (ABEC), 243

Brazilian Collective Licensing Association (ABRALC), 232

Brazilian Consumer Defense Institute, 255

Brazilian Reprographic Rights Association (ABDR), 49, 225–229, 235–238, 257–258, 260n25, 261n29, 263n48

British Copyright Act of 1916, 130

Brotchie, Eric Antony, 201

Brown, D. J., 9

Budapest Declaration, 6, 19n1

Budylin, S., 42

Bulletin board systems (BBSs), 34, 42

Bunting, Ian, 114

Bursary system, 114, 135–138, 140, 145, 147, 153n50

Bush, V., 25

Business models

Argentina and, 93

Brazil and, 223

Library Genesis and, 39

licenses and, 4

Russia and, 39

South Africa and, 128, 144

Butterworths, 119

CADRA, 92, 96–97, 102n23

Caesar, 189

Calero, Marcelo, 262n34

Camargo, Alexandre, 245

Cambridge University Press, 10, 20n10, 58t, 200, 208, 241

Canada, 20n9, 234

Cândido, Thiago, 235–236

CAPES Journals Portal, 241–244, 266n7

Cassiano, Célia Cristina de Figueiredo, 258

Castilho, José, 226–227

Castro, Oona, 241

CDs, 3–4, 35, 42–43, 88, 94, 219n52, 226, 273, 277n2

CEDRO, 93